O
B

Au
Spo...g
Anecdotes

Edited by
Richard Cashman
David Headon
Graeme Kinross-Smith

Melbourne

OXFORD UNIVERSITY PRESS

Oxford Auckland New York

OXFORD UNIVERSITY PRESS AUSTRALIA

Oxford   New York
Athens   Auckland   Bangkok   Bombay
Calcutta   Cape Town   Dar es Salaam   Delhi
Florence   Hong Kong   Istanbul   Karachi
Kuala Lumpur   Madras   Madrid   Melbourne
Mexico City   Nairobi   Paris   Singapore
Taipei   Tokyo   Toronto

and associated companies in
Berlin   Ibadan

OXFORD is a trade mark of Oxford University Press

National Library of Australia
Cataloguing-in-Publication data:

The Oxford book of Australian sporting anecdotes.

   Bibliography.
   Includes index.
   ISBN 0 19 553698 3.

   1. Sports—Australia—Anecdotes. 2. Athletes—Australia—
   Anecdotes. I. Cashman, Richard, 1940–   . II. Headon, David
   John, 1950–   . III. Kinross-Smith, Graeme, 1936–   . IV. Title:
   Book of Australian sporting anecdotes.

796.0994

Typeset by Solo Typesetting, South Australia
Printed by McPherson's Printing Group
Published by Oxford University Press,
253 Normanby Road, South Melbourne, Australia

CONTENTS

INTRODUCTION

Australian sport has produced many classic stories of success and failure. Some have assumed legendary proportions and have become part of the fabric of our culture. The astonishing feats of the 'Flying Pieman' last century, Keith Miller's nonchalance on the cricket field, John Landy's sportsmanship, Dawn Fraser's nocturnal adventures in Tokyo, Adam Lindsay Gordon's almost suicidal horsemanship . . . These are at least as well-known and representative as any political anecdotes.

But what exactly is an anecdote? How to define these fragments, these snapshots, these asides that somehow lodge in the popular memory—at once absurd and profound, ironic and philosophical. Most anecdotes start out as simple stories or yarns, often with a humorous twist. Their subjects range from the extraordinary to the bizarre to the melancholy. Slowly, with frequent retelling and embellishment, they begin to encompass what is best and most memorable in a particular area of human endeavour. Australian sport has its own unique tradition. In a curious way, our sporting anecdotes tell us something about the forever changing nature of Australian identity and the national temperament. Sometimes, these kernels of sport become myth.

The Oxford Book of Australian Sporting Anecdotes contains 255 such snapshots, drawing on our extensive sporting literature. As such, it offers a kind of kaleidoscopic history of Australian sport, capturing its essential humour, eccentricity, larrikinism, poignancy and heroism. While many of these anecdotes celebrate sport, others record its less positive moments. There are accounts of notorious failures, debilitating injury, crass officialdom, and racist taunts.

This anthology attempts to provide a well-balanced perspective on Australian sport and differs in this respect from many previous ones, which are rather more celebratory. It also diverges from previous collections in that it covers all the major sports played in this country—not just one highly publicised code. There are anecdotes about tennis, cricket, soccer, basketball, yachting, athletics, billiards, surfing, Australian Rules, Rugby Union and League, as well as wood-chopping, skiing and pistol-shooting. Every attempt has been made to do justice to all the popular sports, but in some cases the paucity of available literature has reduced the editors' choices.

We have arranged the anecdotes chronologically, thus enabling readers to observe changes in the language, humour and values of the Australian sporting story over almost two centuries. Contemporary readers will gain insight into the transience of social mores and values. Some we now find distressing, even repellent. As Australian sport developed in a male context, it is hardly surprising that some stories strike us as sexist. However, to exclude those anecdotes which do not conform to modern sensibilities would result in an unrepresentative and distorted collection. The inclusion of items recounting sexist, violent and racist events helps us to understand how sport—and, indeed, Australian society—has been constructed.

We have presented Australian sport as it has presented itself—in a book which brings together many legendary stories. Some will undoubtedly prompt readers to dig more deeply and to explore the political, social and even moral contexts in which these anecdotes emerged. Others may be read as sheer entertainment. Humour, that gadfly on the body of Australian sport, is always ready to prick a reputation or deflate pomposity. As this collection demonstrates, our sporting humour has evolved along quite idiosyncratic lines: earthy, ironic, disrespectful and very dry.

The rich variety of sports that demand years, decades, even lifetimes of dedication, has produced an abundance of stories. Each sport has its own rules, conventions and physical silhouette, each has its own ballet of movement. And each has a plethora of utterly distinctive participants, with appropriate (or inappropriate) idiosyncrasies: Betty Cuthbert defying the stopwatches of the world with her trade-mark 'open mouth' style; Bobby McDonald squatting down on a bitter night to avoid the wind and discovering the crouch start; the effervescence of Socceroo coach Frank Arok; Aboriginal cricketer Eddie Gilbert, and his thunderbolt bowling, banned either because he was a 'chucker', or because he was too quick and too good; Olga Masters, renowned Australian writer, but also footy mum of her boy Roy; and Lou Richards, clown prince and fine footballer, a man just as entertaining to the public after his career with the Magpies ended. The legend of 'Louie the Lip' was born when Lou Richards hung up his boots.

Some of the smallest anecdotes can represent the largest of stories. Epic tales of pathos shade into tragedy. Recall the story of boxer Les Darcy, his life in Australia, along with his misrepresented and fatal sojourn in America during Australia's First World War conscription debates. Darcy had a passion for clean living, as exemplified in the haltingly expressed letter in this volume in which he assures his mentor, Father Coady, that in his Tennessee training camps he is in no danger of succumbing to the sins of the flesh. It was grimly ironic that he would die of blood poisoning shortly after, in the prime of his life. Then there is Walter Lindrum, aghast at the memory of how, attempting a fancy shot, he tore up the cloth of a billiard table during a clandestine practice session as a boy. Not too many years later, championship billiard rules had to be changed. Lindrum had turned a sport into an art form, which he had mastered completely.

There are also many touching folk stories in Australian sport: the second floor factory window smashed by Victor Trumper's towering hit in a Sydney club game in 1903, preserved in its broken state for sixty years as 'a memorial to the mighty stroke'; or the cold Australian outfielder in a cricket match against a north country side in Britain who collected a pile of sticks and grass, lit it with a spectator's match and warmed his hands over the fire. Beside these curios range some stories that intrigue with their cross-sporting flavour. In the book we recall H. C. A. Harrison, the founder of Australian Rules football and also a keen cyclist, who rode a bike from Melbourne to Sydney in the January heat of 1896 to indulge his third passion, cricket. For the record, he arrived in comfortable time for the final Test match between Australia and the visiting English XI.

There are byways in Australian sport that, via the anecdote, yield answers to a most fascinating set of questions. Why, for example, was Hubert Opperman ('Oppy') voted the 1928 most popular sportsman in France? (Some claim it was because of his novel method of emptying his bladder during marathon cycling events in Europe. Read on!). How far back was Walla Walla? Why did Kenneth Slessor suggest that Australian Rugby League players should wear six-inch spikes and chromium-plated spurs? What about the story of Bob Chitty's severed finger? How do you go about killing a mosquito with a number one wood? When were one hundred bronzed lifesavers seen to walk on water and why? Who was the tragic stunt swimmer 'Tums' Cavill, how many times did he manage to elude death, and how did death finally catch up with him? Read on indeed!

List of Symbols

The following symbols are used to indicate the sport covered in each anecdote.

 athletics (includes skiing)

 aviation

 basketball

 billiards

 boxing

 car and motorcycle racing

 cricket

 cycling

 football (including Australian Rules, Rugby Union and Rugby League)

 golf

horse-racing, pacing and jumping

 rowing, sculling and kayaking

 shooting (including hunting and pistol shooting)

 soccer

 surfing and surf lifesaving

 swimming and body surfing

 tennis and squash

 woodchopping

 yachting

CAPTAIN COOK DISCOVERS SURFING

Australia's surfing connection goes back to 1778.

Right from the start there has been a link between surfing and Australia, for the first white man to see surfboard riding was Captain Cook [who discovered Eastern Australia for the British in 1770]. Sailing into Kealakekua Bay, Hawaii [in 1778], he recorded his astonishment at seeing the natives swimming happily in the surf and even catching the waves on boards:

> The surf, which breaks on the coast around the bay, extends to the distance of about 150 yards from the shore, within which space the surges of the sea, accumulating from the shallowness of the water, are dashed against the beach with prodigious violence. Whenever, from stormy weather or any extraordinary swell at sea, the impetuosity of the surf is increased to its utmost height, they choose that time for this amusement ...
>
> Twenty or thirty of the natives, taking each a long narrow board, rounded at the ends, set out together from the shore. The first wave they meet they plunge under, and suffering it to roll over them, rise again beyond it, and make the best of their way by swimming out into sea. The second wave is encountered in the same manner as the first; the great difficulty consisting in seizing the proper moment of diving under it which, if missed, the person is caught by the surf and driven back again with great violence, and all his dexterity is then required to prevent himself from being dashed against the rocks.
>
> As soon as they have gained, by these repeated efforts, the smooth water beyond the surf they lay themselves at length on their boards and prepare for their return. As the surf consists of a number of waves, of which every third is remarked to be always much larger than the others and to flow higher on the shore ... their first object is to place themselves on the summit of the largest surge, by which they are driven along with amazing rapidity toward the shore. If by mistake they should place themselves on one of the smaller waves which break before they reach the land, or should not be able to keep their plank in a proper direction on the top of the swell, they are left exposed to the fury of the next; and to avoid it are obliged again to dive or regain the place from which they have set out.

Those who succeed in their object of reaching the shore have still the greatest danger to encounter. The coast being guarded by a chain of rocks with, here and there, a small opening between them, they are obliged to steer their board through one of these or, in case of failure, to quit it before they reach the rocks and, plunging under the wave, make the best of their way back again. This is reckoned very disgraceful and is also attended with a loss of board, which I have often seen, with great terror, dashed to pieces at the very moment the islander quitted it.

The boldness and address with which we saw them perform these difficult and dangerous manoeuvres was altogether astonishing and is scarce to be credited.

Farrelly, *This Surfing Life* (1965), p. 107.

BEARDS XI VERSUS CLEAN-SHAVEN XI

In its early years Melbourne boasted only two cricket clubs, the Melbourne and the Union. Eventually they tired of playing against each other and decided to organise more varied contests.

The Melbourne Cricket Club did not have all the good cricketers. There were the retailers, the tradesmen and the artisans. They banded together to form 'The Melbourne Union Cricket Club'. So on January 12, 1839, the gentlemen of the MCC played the tradesmen. The tradesmen beat the gentlemen so mercilessly that as a point of honour it was necessary to have a return match on January 19. This time the gentlemen won comfortably. The MCC president, Gentleman Powlett, scored 120 runs, the first century to be scored in the colony. The star of the tradesmen was Mr Thomas Halfpenny, a strapping mountain of a man. He did well both at batting and wicketkeeping.

The greatest problem of all was to organise suitable matches. There were only two cricket clubs. They couldn't continue interminably playing each other Saturday after Saturday. So the committee members had to think of matches that were a trifle different. They played the Benedicts v. Bachelors. The husbands won, and Husband Powlett scored a total of 101 out of 180. There were more matches between the military and the civilians, alphabetical games—the first half of the alphabet against the second half—and a match which caused great interest was the Whiskers v. Clean Shaven contest. It took the Gold Rush of 1851 to bring the beard to its full glory of goatee, mutton chop, squatter's gap, Lord Dundreary, or the unlimited growth as exhibited by Dr Grace. Before then the majority of the men in the colony were clean-shaven. The beards won by seven wickets. As for Mr Powlett, history does not record how many runs Bearded Powlett made.

Dunstan, *The Paddock that Grew* (1962), p. 8.

HUNTING IN AUSTRALIA

Hunting in Australia in the early nineteenth century was totally different from that in Britain, and alternatives to the fox and stag were eagerly pursued.

Shooting, hunting and fishing in the English tradition seem to have constituted John Hood's principal conception of sport. He said in 1842:

There is but little sport in Australia ... some time ago, when times were good, there existed what was called the Cumberland hunt: they pursued the native dog, which always made a capital run; and the kangaroo. But that meritorious fraternity has been broken up; and horse-racing seems to be almost the only bond of union among sportsmen. The hunting of the roo was generally a quick affair: he made a tremendous burst, leaping, not running, with incredible speed; but it was soon over. The native dog afforded another description of chase, giving a long run, and occasionally, very nervous work. Galloping in the forest required the most constant exercise of eye and hand imaginable; and the poor wight was truly to be pitied, whose nag was not fine in the mouth;—the pace was tremendous and he was a fortunate, as well as a skilful man, that descended from his saddle unscathed. The bushman's pursuit of his wild and wandering bullocks is now the nearest approach in New South Wales to Melton, and a most perilous affair it is.

Cumes, *Their Chastity was not too Rigid* (1979), p. 252.

King Of The Ultramarathon

William Francis King, who became known as the 'Flying Pieman',
performed countless bizarre and eccentric feats in public in the 1840s,
including a walk of 1634 miles.

During this period of many, varied and extraordinary pedestrian
feats, one performer who stood out was a quite remarkable man
called William Francis King, later known exquisitely as the
Flying Pieman, who came to Sydney from England in 1829 at the
age of 22, became a clerk and a schoolmaster near Bong Bong and
then served as tutor to the children of William Kern near
Campbelltown. In a fit of irritation he left his post, intending to
return to England, but instead became a barman at the Hope and
Anchor [in] Sydney. He enjoyed performing feats of pedestrianism
as a pastime. On one occasion, he walked 1634 miles (2614 km)
in thirty-nine days only nine of which were reported to have
offered fair weather. He carried a 70 lb (32 kg) dog in walking
from Campbelltown to Sydney in just over 8½ hours and a 92 lb
(41.7 kg) live goat, plus a dead weight of 12 lbs (5.4 kg) in
walking from Brickfield Hill, Sydney, to Parramatta in 6 hours
48 minutes. He beat the coach from Windsor to Sydney by seven
minutes and walked from Sydney to Parramatta and back twice a
day for six consecutive days.

Sometimes King's efforts caused his friends understandable
concern. For £30 a side, he undertook to walk 360 miles (579
km) in seventy-two hours, starting on 15 November 1844. To
sustain him on his arduous journey, he drank a small tumbler of
brandy and ate a biscuit every two hours. Quite a crowd accompanied him to and from Black Watch Swamp, most of them in
gigs or on horseback. In the end, he accomplished his feat within
two minutes of the time allowed, but many of his friends and
backers became alarmed that he would kill himself. On the last
day, his strength began to fail and he showed symptoms of
extreme exhaustion. The Pieman assured his friends that he knew
his own constitution, he had trained well and 'there was not the
slightest cause for any apprehension on his account'. He proved
that he was right.

... In October 1847, now called 'the Ladies' Flying Pieman', he was reported to have performed 'the unparallel Feat, of Walking 192 miles in 46 hours'. This feat, performed at the 'Maitland Race Course' with '3 minutes to spare', was in fact much less unparallelled than the 1844 feat. He was then 'rusticating' on the Hunter River and seems to have regarded his 192 mile (308 km) effort as something of a warm-up for a walk, between 8 and 18 November, of 'a thousand quarter-miles in a thousand quarter-hours' and, three months later, '500 half-miles in 500 half-hours'. While these two efforts were less demanding than some of his earlier feats, the punters bet against him because he had become so 'corpulent'. However, King won. Then he went to Moreton Bay where, carrying a heavy pole, he beat the coach from Brisbane to Ipswich by about an hour and still had enough wind left to deliver a long speech to his open-mouthed admirers.

Cumes, Their Chastity was not too Rigid (1979), pp. 286–8.

EMU HUNTER TO RACEHORSE

The racehorse Petrel defied the critics to win some major events at Flemington in the 1840s.

The principal event at the annual Flemington meeting was the Town Plate, two miles and a distance, weight for age, and Petrel won it in 1845, '46, and '48. Three races each day over a distance were thought nothing of in those times, but probably they were not run from end to end, as are most of our races of the present day.

There was no celebrity, biped or quadruped, in the province half such a favourite as Petrel. The name was a household word, and nothing else was talked about for months before and after the meetings.

Little was known of Petrel's breeding. The Sydney horse, Steeltrap, was supposed to be his sire, and there was a strong resemblance between the two. All that was known of Petrel's dam was that, in 1841, a man journeying overland from Sydney to Adelaide stayed for a short time at the Grampians. He had in his possession two fine mares, supposed to have been stolen, and both in foal. The stranger found employment on the station of a Mr Riley, where the mares foaled, and one of the youngsters was Petrel. They remained there a couple of years, and in 1843, when horseflesh was beginning to command something like a price, John Giveng, an overseer of Dr Martin's, bought both colts for £36. Petrel was then turned into a stock horse, and, possessing much speed, was often exhibited as a sort of show animal before strangers.

One day, as several stockmen were out riding, an emu was sighted, a hunt extemporised, and Petrel not only distanced all the others, but actually ran the emu down. Petrel at this time was rising four years old, a dark chestnut, 16.1 [hands] high, the head beautifully formed, but the build of the animal, though symmetrical, was considered by some of the critics as too powerful and clumsy for a racer. They were mistaken, it turned out, for distance, whether long or short, or weight, light or heavy, were matters of small moment to him.

Griffiths, *Turf and Heath* (1906), pp. 21–2.

A GRINNING MATCH

Racegoers in the 1840s were entertained by some of the ugliest men in the crowd, who performed with aids such as horse collars.

In those far-off days, side shows of various kinds were occasionally provided for the delectation of racegoers who were not devoted heart and soul to the racing, just as the flatites are catered for on Cup Day at the present time. But no modern racegoer ever beheld a show half so queer as that to which the visitors to a Melbourne meeting in the 'forties' were treated.

Included in the day's programme was 'a grinning match', an amusement—if such it can be termed—happily long since obsolete. Each competitor was supplied with a horse collar, through which he was to perform, and four or five of the ugliest fellows of the crowd duly entered. The conditions were that each was to give a five minutes' facial distortion, and then all were to join in a grinning chorus, the owner of the most hideous face to take the prize, which was a handful of silver subscribed by the onlookers.

A burly ticket-of-leave man, named 'Big Mick', a well-known character of the period, acted as master of the ceremonies. When the competing team appeared, the favourite was found in the person of a carpenter named Thomas Curnew, a red-headed fellow, with a huge mouth, set off by an enormous set of tusky teeth. With his head through the horse collar, this competitor gave such a display of physiognomical posturing that he was accorded a walkover, and it is recorded that 'his antics evoked thunders of acclamation, in the midst of which he left the platform, secured the proceeds of the hat-shaking, and betook himself to the booth, where the stakes were speedily melted down through the agency of "fire-water".' This, the first 'grinning contest', was probably the last held in Victoria—or in any other part of Australia, for that matter.

Griffiths, *Turf and Heath* (1906), pp. 17–18.

Too Much 'Quaffing' At The Petersham Races

One of the participants at the Petersham Racecourse found it heavy going in the 1840s.

In addition to major carnivals there were also more informal race meetings-cum-sports days. *Bell's Life* reported on 25 January 1846 that there had been a variety of events at the Petersham course on Friday, 17 January.

... After Mr Aiton's pony Tommy raced George Evans' Skewbald for £20, Mr King's Rob Roy raced J. Little's Alderman for £3.

Next there was a foot race for a small stake between N. Dillon and an unnamed 'native boy' over one mile (1.6 km) with the latter receiving a start of twenty yards (18.3 m).

They went off at a good pace, the style of running being excellent. Dillon, however, who had been rather deeply quaffing 'the flowing bowl' during the morning, soon became overpowered, and after rolling to and fro for several yards, fell severely into the small drain which marks the boundary. The native, who had still kept his head, finished the race at almost the same pace he took up at starting.

Cashman, *Rise of Organized Sport in Australia* (in press).

WHEN MELBOURNE GRAMMAR FAILED TO SHOW

The celebrated 1858 match between forty of Melbourne Grammar and forty of the Scotch College ended in a draw, even though the students played over three Saturdays.

As a spectacle the game was hardly a success. As a test of footballing ability it was a dismal failure, but the players seem to have had a lot of fun, even if the onlookers had been rather nonplussed.

The playing space extended from the Jolimont end of the ground where Cliveden Mansions now stand to Punt Road, Richmond, which meant that the goal posts were more than a quarter of a mile apart, so scoring was rather difficult. It was decided that the side that first scored two goals would be the winner of the match. The game started off rather brightly. However, three hours had elapsed before the Scotch boys notched a goal. After a lot more skirmishings, darkness set in with no further score, so it was agreed to resume the match on the next Saturday. But someone bungled the arrangements—and next Saturday—Melbourne Grammar failed to appear. The secretary of Grammar then wrote to the *Argus*, offering to continue the match on the following Saturday. Scotch agreed to this, and so once more the eighty stalwarts took up their positions on the Jolimont Parkland to settle this footballing issue once and for all. They ran, they kicked, they jostled, they tucked the ball under their arms, and generally expended a great deal of energy, all to no avail, for when darkness once more fell upon the animated scene the result still stood—one goal to Scotch.

On September 4, one week later, the two teams tried for a third time to bring the game to a conclusion. When the sides lined up to continue the battle, the fierce light of resolution shone from their eyes, the whole eighty of them. This was going to be 'it'. But though they strove and strained even more desperately than before neither team could add another goal to the score. The game had to be abandoned, and it was officially registered as a draw.

Throughout most of this herculean but somewhat futile contest the ball was bottled up in the north-west corner of the park, which meant that those barrackers who had taken up their positions in the north-east corner saw very little of the game. In fact, were it not for occasional 'runners' dashing up with latest news of the state of the game the Nor-Easters would not have known there was a match on at all. Tiring of all this frustration, a Grammar player took the ball behind his own goal and ran with it right round the other side of the cricket boundary, but the Scotch boys contended that this was carrying a good thing too far.

Taylor, *100 Years of Football* (1957), p. 18.

EASY COME, EASY GO

Joe Thompson, a bookmaker in the 1860s, had a colourful career.

In the year 1861 we enter upon the most eventful era, and at the same time, turning point of Joe Thompson's career. It was at this date that he, heartily tired of the gold fields and the accompanying monotonous existence, made his way to Beechworth in time for the races held in that place, and which in those days were regarded as the inauguration of the series of meetings held in the Ovens district. Well, at Beechworth, Joe proved successful, for though only making a ten pound book, he had such a happy knack of working doubles, (an old cunning not altogether extinct now,) that he astonished himself by being a winner of some £50 or £60. Chiltern, Yackandandah, Wahgunyah, Wangaratta, Rutherglen, and the meetings of all the towns in the Ovens then followed; these were, as a matter of course visited by our then juvenile Joe, who, with the old boy's luck, carried all before him, and three or four hundred pounds in his kick beside. This was the start. The seed of the leviathan had been set, fertile was the soil, and the only succour required to mature the grain into a plant of gigantic proportions, was a little of the filthy lucre within reach of the bursting tendrils. Joe never knew what it was to have so much money before, and without any delay, came out a regular toff in a flash crimean, white moleskins, knee boots, spanking new cabbage-tree, and last, which it would be death to forget a crimson sash round the waist, with tassels hanging on each side. Thus attired Joe appeared on the Lachlan, and there he first met Billy Yeomans, then a jockey, who rode a horse for the local maiden plate, called Counsellor, which was a rank outsider, but, nevertheless, proved to be the winner of the race. On this little dark event Joe managed to land a pot, having made a plunge on the unknown. Luck was in, and Joe, well seasoned in the ready, determined to go to Sydney once again. He now thought himself somebody, and walked about Sydney with his nose cocked so high, that people wondered if he had something with an unpleasant odour for a breast pin. Such is the vanity of nature and mad folly of youth, always to be dispelled, but never more promptly than in Joe's case, for he decided to try conclusions with old Nash at a taking little innocent pastime, called hazard. Two or three hours—sweet and fleeting hours—sufficed to transfer the sum total of Joe's capital to Nash, and that compassionate old gentleman offered this piece of advice to Joe as consolation,

'You are a fine strong young man, and you had better get back to work again.'

Tip and Tony, The Life, Adventures and Sporting
Career of Joe Thompson (1877), p. 12.

SALT JUNK AND DAMPER

'Sailor Bill' rolled out the red carpet for visitors to the Victorian Alpine country in the nineteenth century.

The first building ever at St Bernard was built by 'Mother' Morrell in 1863. 'Mother' also had another accommodation 'house' where, in the old days, the Dargo River track joined the Dargo High Plains track in a wistful, windswept void. Towards the end of 'Mother's' tenure, a wonderful character appeared on the St Bernard scene. This was one, Boustead, known to one and all as 'Sailor Bill'. 'Sailor Bill' had joined the dirty rush of gold-crazed sailors whose precipitate exit to the new gold fields had left ship after ship completely deserted at Port Melbourne. 'Sailor Bill' landed up eventually at the gold diggings of the Crooked River and from there, gloriously broke, landed up at 'Mother's', where he was taken on as general handyman. What his relationships with 'Mother' actually were are unstated, but whatever they were he certainly did all right for himself because in 1870 when 'Mother' died she left him the 'Hospice' as it had begun to be called.

Old Sailor then proceeded to do something he had never done before in his life and that was to get married and settle down. He and his wife, a local girl then proceeded, by their cheerfulness and kindness to people crossing the Alps, to build up a very happy phase of Victorian Alpine history. Their trade was further helped ten years or so later, in 1880, when the present road was put in to replace the old track, that tiny almost invisible bond holding Omeo to Harrietville. This not only made things considerably easier for Sailor getting supplies in from Harrietville, but also brought a number of distinguished visitors including Lady Bowen, after whom the Diamentina Springs were named, Lord Brassey, and our old friend Baron Sir Ferdinand von Mueller.

While the personal welcome was all you could want, the fare, even if plentiful, was pretty rough and ready, but who would argue with a meal that only cost 2/6? The principal item was strong salt junk which Sailor hauled out for you from a formidable array of large wooden barrels where it had reposed since it was killed months beforehand. There was also damper and, of course, tea; strong, black and hairy. The latter you could break down with goat's milk from Sailor's herd that grazed around the nearby slopes.

Stephenson, *Skiing in the High Plains* (1982), pp. xiii–xiv.

ALF'S MUG

Colonial boxers in the 1860s fought bareknuckle and contests sometimes went for more than 100 rounds. The damage to the face (and body) of contestants was considerable.

... *Bell's Life* did pass a few comments about the fight between Mat Hardy and Alf McLaren, fought near Lal Lal in July 1863. It lasted for four hours fifty-five minutes and both fighters failed to come up for the eighty-second round. In the twenty-fifth round Mat had his lip split halfway to the nostril. By the twenty-ninth 'his face was literally chiselled all over; there was not a square inch that was not cut up and carved'. Alf had a dislocated knee-cap and fought for four hours on one leg. In the thirty-third round, 'Alf's mug began to swell. In the thirty-fifth round from blows on the nose Alf was bleeding like a pig. Then from the fifty-fourth to the eighty-first Alf continued to bleed getting weaker and weaker ...'

Bell's reported, 'Mat's face next day looked a very pretty picture, highly coloured like a coconut, beautifully carved. Constant fomentations had got Alf's head back into shape.'

Dunstan, *Sports* (1973), p. 182.

'Specs'

Playing sport in glasses has its disadvantages, as Australian Rules footballer Jack Bennie well realised in the 1860s.

Jack Bennie was known to the public as 'specs'. He always played in glasses, and used to bring half a dozen pairs to the ground every Saturday, and leave them in the care of the umpire, who would hand them out in turn to him as each was broken. They would all be repaired by the next Saturday, only to meet with their inevitable fate again!

Mancini and Hibbins, *Running with the Ball* (1987), p. 122.

Stocking Our Barren Bush

The lack of game in the Australian bush was a situation gentlemen in the 1860s attempted to remedy with introduced species.

Bell's Life ... produced a very interesting leading article [on 3 June 1865]; interesting for two reasons—it explained the need for gentlemen to have something to shoot at, and it explained the contempt for Australian wild life.

> Mr Austin and those like him who have endeavoured to stock our barren bush with animals that shall administer to our pleasure and serve for food, deserve the gratitude of all classes. Probably there is no country on the face of the globe so sparsely supplied with animals that come under the definition of game as Australia. The kangaroo is almost worthless, except as regards its tail for soup, and skin for leather, and when we enumerate the bustard, the duck tribe, quail and snipe, we have exhausted the catalogue of birds which the sportsmen will care to fire at. The magnificent game which abounds in the forests of Asia is unknown to us ... We need to create in the southern hemisphere an exact counterpart of that country which is so dear to most of us.

Dunstan, *Sports* (1973), pp. 324–5.

CHALLENGING THE RULES

Melbourne footballer J.E. Clarke deliberately challenged the running rule in Australian Rules football last century.

Although the 1865 meeting of the Melbourne Football Club did not address itself to the problem, this year saw the resolution of the conflict. In a match between the MFC and Royal Park, a goal was 'run'—clearly a breach of the rules but allowed by the umpire. Theodore Marshall later explained how the situation arose:

> At this time Royal Park played Melbourne. I was captain of the Royal Park [side], and in the team was J.E. Clarke, second only in fleetness on the football field at that time to Harrison. Before the game was commenced, I determined to test the running with the ball question, and it was arranged that if Clarke got the ball, he was to tuck it under his arm and run as far as possible without bouncing it. Clarke, seizing a favourable opportunity, bolted with the ball along the wing, dodging several Melbourne players on the way and, without once bouncing it, flew towards the goal and kicked it. When Clarke had overrun the orthodox 40 or 50 yards, the Melbourne men stood wondering at his audacity, and ceased to interfere with him. Harrison who was nearly a 40 yard man himself, asked me what it meant! I answered that I simply wanted to settle once and for all how far a man should be allowed to run with the ball without bouncing it. After consultation it was agreed that the ball should be bounced at least once in every ten yards, and so this important point in our game was brought about.

Mancini and Hibbins, *Running with the Ball* (1987), p. 45.

THE SHAPE OF THE BALL

The Carlton team had some excuse for fumbling the ball in the 1865 Australian Rules season.

Some teams preferred the oval ball and some the round ball. As a football was expensive—and some matches were abandoned when the football burst—a match possibly could begin with an oval ball and conclude with a round ball. When Carlton in 1865 played one of its first matches, its players were clearly accustomed to a round ball. It so happened that an oval ball, rather small in size, was used that afternoon, and Carlton could not cope with its erratic bounce. That match was long remembered for Carlton's confusion and for an astonishing kick made by one of Carlton's opponents, Henry H. Budd, a young solicitor. His kick was inconceivable a decade earlier when footballs were made more roughly. Budd had decided, far from goal, to try a place kick. He sent the ball through the goals with probably the longest kick seen in Australia up to that time. A decade later it was excitedly recalled as '70 yards if it was an inch'.

Blainey, *A Game of Our Own* (1990), p. 43.

THE KANGAROO BATTUE

Killing kangaroos was a popular pastime in Victoria in the 1860s and 1870s.

The slaughter of the kangaroo around Melbourne was a particularly popular pastime in the 1860s and 1870s, though not so much later on because there weren't any left. Hunt clubs, beautifully dressed in the proper English regalia, would run them down with dogs. But the sport written about in the most enthusiastic terms was the kangaroo battue.

The best place for doing this was around Dromana and Arthur's Seat and in the wild country through to Cape Schanck. The well-to-do people would set out from Melbourne by steamer at night, have themselves landed at Dromana just before dawn, and there would be met by stockmen and horses.

An *Illustrated Australian News* of 1865 printed 'a letter from a shooter back home' which told how they had seventeen guns, arranged in a semi-circle, each man a hundred and fifty yards apart. Then they had two stockmen, Billy and George, both six foot four inches in their socks. They carried immense fifteen foot stockwhips which they cracked over their heads, with reports louder than gun shots. Cracking their whips, shouting and yelling 'like Maoris' they drove hundreds of kangaroos towards the guns. The shooter proudly tells in his letter how they bagged two hundred kangaroos in a day, and when this was done they went off shooting possums.

Dunstan, Sports (1973), pp. 325–6.

FOOTBALL VERSUS CRICKET

The committee members of the Melbourne Cricket Club were reluctant to allow footballers to play on their beloved turf in the 1860s, as H.C.A. Harrison, one of the early exponents of Australian Rules football, recounts.

For years the Melbourne Football Club played in the Richmond paddock, outside the MCC ground. We had no enclosure, and the boundaries were roughly marked by gum trees, from whose boughs the game was often watched by enthusiastic onlookers. Many leading citizens have since told me that they, as boys, spent many happy hours thus perched on high watching the play. But an occasional goal was lost through the ball's colliding with a tree on its way! In time we were allowed to put up a movable boundary fence. Until that was done the game has always been interfered with by the encroachment of the public.

It took me some years to persuade the MCC to allow us to play on their ground, their objection being that the turf would be spoilt for cricket. But in the end, the committee consented to let us have some trial matches, and found that, instead of ruining the ground, the case was quite the reverse.

The first game on the MCC ground was that played in 1869 against the Victorian Police Force, captained by Superintendent T. O'Callaghan. They played a good, hard game, but we managed to beat them. The proceeds (about £50) were given to the Children's Hospital ...

With reference to this match, I went down to inspect the ground next day, and found two or three members of the committee, all with very gloomy faces, who met me with the words, 'Harrison! You have ruined our ground!' Of course I laughed at the idea, but we were not allowed to play on the ground again for some time. But at last, after a Carlton v. Melbourne match, which we were allowed to play as a great favour, it was found that the gate money was so much that the committee began to think the risk to the ground was worthwhile! Then we were permitted to play for half the season, namely, to within six weeks of the cricket season. Now-a-days, a football match may be played with impunity, a few days before the cricket season opens!

Harrison, *The Story of an Athlete* (1923), pp. 94–5.

THE DUKE'S FORTY-THREE POSSUMS

Prince Alfred, the second son of Queen Victoria, spread his carnage across the colonies when he visited Australia.

In October 1867, HRH Prince Alfred, Duke of Edinburgh, the 23-year-old second son of Queen Victoria, arrived aboard HMS *Galatea* and he spread his carnage across five colonies. In South Australia the Governor took him to the Government Farm in the Adelaide Hills. The ideal situation for possum shooting was a moonlight night. One looked up through the trees, silhouetted the possum against the moon and fired. It was difficult to miss.

The *Advertiser* in Adelaide reported that the Duke was a very good sportsman. He shot fifty-two possums, forty-three of which he brought home, leaving the rest in the trees. He went on numerous kangaroo shoots, but one of his more spectacular expeditions was to Mr Thomas Austin's property at Barwon Park. Mr Austin won eternal fame by introducing the rabbit to Victoria. The rabbits, which were bred in cages, were carefully led to the slaughter.

The Duke killed eighty-six on the first day and he found it such good fun he asked for a second shoot the following morning, thereby upsetting his entire schedule through the Western District. The *Illustrated Australian News* reported that a dozen guns went out that morning and together they 'dealt to death 1000 innocents'. The Duke used two Wesley Richards' breech loaders and he killed four hundred and sixteen of the thousand. In one place where the rabbits were trapped in a corner he shot sixty-eight in ten minutes. He had a man standing behind him, who loaded while he shot, but even so the guns became so hot they blistered the hand. Finally he could hold them only by the stock.

Dunstan, *Sports* (1973), pp. 321–2.

CRICKET FASHION — 1868

Kerry Packer did not invent coloured clothing for cricketers. In fact, the World Series Cricket uniforms were rather staid compared with the costume designed by Manager Charles Lawrence for the Aboriginal cricketers who toured England in 1868.

Lawrence must have drawn upon his experience of the All-England XI tours, with their standardized shirts, sashes and hat bands. His cricketers may not have looked modish, but they were colourful. They took to the cricket field decked in white flannel trousers, military red shirts (a shirt-like blouse called a Garibaldi), with diagonal blue flannel sashes, blue elastic belts and neckties, white linen collars and beneath this finery were 'French merino undershirts'. The ensemble was completed with individually coloured peaked caps. For athletics, there were individually coloured caps and trunks, with long white tights worn beneath (described in one of the English papers as 'Oh-no-we-never-mention-'ems').

The coloured caps had been decided upon before the team left Edenhope, and not after the team's arrival in England as some writers have suggested. As befitted a European, Lawrence wore a white cap; why Red Cap was cast as the villain in a black cap is beyond explanation. Mullagh donned the red; Cuzens wore purple; Dick-a-dick, yellow; Mosquito, dark blue; Peter, green; Jim Crow (Neddy), pink; Bullocky, chocolate; King Cole, magenta; Sundown, check; H. Rose, Victoria plaid; and Twopenny, McGregor plaid. However, by the time the team played in England some caps had changed heads and each cap bore an emblem of a silver boomerang and a bat, and players also wore a sash of their own colour to facilitate identification.

Mulvaney and Harcourt, Cricket Walkabout (1988), pp. 70–1.

'A POSITIVE RAIN OF CRICKET BALLS'

The Aboriginal cricketers who toured England in 1868 entertained the crowds in many unusual ways.

Dick-a-Dick ... was adept at running backwards and he invariably won or came second in that curious 100-yard event. He also participated in normal flat races and demonstrated his stamina at Nottingham when he won the 100-yard race, followed by a win in the 150-yard hurdle, even though he fell at the second hurdle. At Eastbourne, his natural action in the high jump was commented on because it contrasted with the 'rather clumsy manner' of the other Aborigines. (However, Mullagh, the best at high jumping, did not compete.) But his reputation chiefly rested upon his remarkable adaptation of a native practice to a European application. His crowd-pleasing act began when he stood in the arena grasping a narrow wooden parrying shield in his left hand. This was the standard Victorian defensive weapon. It averaged a metre in length, nine centimetres in width and was triangular in cross section, with a hand-grip carved out of the solid wood. A parrying shield weighed about one and a half kilograms and was decorated with deeply incised lines and other geometric designs. Dick-a-Dick protected the region of the hand-grip with a pad of possum skin. He held a curved wooden club, a single-combat weapon termed a 'leowell' or 'langeel', in his right hand. Dick-a-Dick challenged all-comers to stand 15 or 20 metres distant and pelt him with cricket balls. He protected his body and head with the shield and his legs with the club, used baseball-bat fashion to deflect the missiles. Pitt-Rivers saw him ward off balls thrown simultaneously and forcefully by three men, and Wood described 'a positive rain of cricket balls'. On one occasion in Australia 60 balls had been aimed at him. Wood felt astonished at the 'almost intuitive knowledge that he seemed to possess'.

Mulvaney and Harcourt, *Cricket Walkabout* (1988), pp. 125–6.

GORDON'S LEAP

While the colonial poet Adam Lindsay Gordon was a skilled rider, his fearlessness led him to perform many extraordinary feats.

It was while Gordon was living in the Mount Gambier district that he made his famous leap over a fence on the edge of a precipice, though the exact place and the exact date seem to be in dispute. Mr Howlett Ross quotes 'Bruni' of the *Australasian* with reference to the fact. 'Following the metalled road about a quarter of a mile further, I reach the path trending to the right which leads to the summit of the Mount. It was near this spot that the late A.L. Gordon is said to have jumped his horse in and out of the fence that runs round the Blue Lake. The fence, though of a good height and strongly made, is one that any ordinary hunter could clear with ease, but the feat is rendered extremely dangerous owing to the small space on the lake side of the fence for a horse to land and take off again. The slightest mistake would have hurled horse and rider into the lake two hundred feet below. It is just such a thing as Gordon would have done in those days.' The poet and some sporting friends from Victoria were riding in the neighbourhood, and the conversation turned on feats of horsemanship witnessed in the vicinity. Gordon was immediately inflamed with a desire to perform a feat that he felt sure none of his friends would dare emulate. He carried Red Lancer over the fence, and, by leaping from rock to rock, cleared a chasm more than forty feet wide, the noble horse seeming to be inspired with the fearless courage of its rider. Among the friends who were present was Mr W. Trainor of Coleraine.

Sladen, *Adam Lindsay Gordon* (1934), p. 90.

HORSEMAN *PAR EXCELLENCE*

Adam Lindsay Gordon's passion for horse-racing bordered on the obsessive.

The gifted, but unfortunate poet registered a performance one October afternoon in 1868 that has seldom—if ever—been equalled by any other cross-country rider, amateur or professional. On Babbler, who carried 13 st 4 lb, he won the Melbourne Hunt Club Cup; then, with his own horse, Viking, landed first money in the Metropolitan Steeplechase; and, to wind up with, took the Selling Steeplechase with Cadger. Each race was run over three miles of the Flemington country, which was just as formidable then as it is now. A jockey that could make three long trips over it, within a couple of hours, must be a veritable glutton, and there can be no two opinions regarding Gordon's love of the sport.

Griffiths, *Turf and Heath* (1906), 50-1.

THIS TIME HE WAS 'DONE FOR'

In 1870, Adam Lindsay Gordon, needing money to clear his debts, accepted an offer to ride Major Baker's horse, Prince Rupert, in a steeplechase at Flemington.

There were eleven starters, among them being Babbler, whom Gordon had previously steered to victory. The others got away before him, but at the sheds Gordon caught them. At the first jump all five horses rose almost together. At the second Prince Rupert and Reindeer had the lead, and at the log fence immediately ahead, Prince Rupert led the field, but he took the leap too eagerly, and struck. Gordon was thrown over the horse's head and fell in a dangerous fashion. He jumped to his feet again and was at once in the saddle. The blow, however, had been a serious one, and he was seen to reel in his seat. He said afterwards that he was 'quite dazed and hardly knew where he was or what he was doing'. Yet he recovered his lost ground and led all the way past the Abattoirs. Then his skill seemed to leave him: he swayed heavily and his hand lost its steadiness. At the third and last fence, Prince Rupert fell, and again Gordon was thrown heavily. This time his horse got away; the race became a struggle between Reindeer and Dutchman, and at the winning post Dutchman by a strenuous effort secured the victory. Among those present was Mr Blackmore, Parliamentary Librarian at Adelaide, who was in Melbourne on a holiday. He took the injured man to Brighton, and on the Monday following Major Baker drove him into town to see a doctor. The verdict was ominous; there were internal injuries which could be mended, but the already much-battered head was not likely to stand this fresh mishap. He lay in bed five days, but as he could neither sleep nor rest he rose and went about his business. His letters written at that time expressed the belief that this time he was 'done for'.

Robb, *Poems of Adam Lindsay Gordon* (1913), pp. lxxi–lxxii.

'HUGGING AND HITTING'

Football matches against Garrison teams in Melbourne in the 1860s were rough affairs.

Games against a red-coat regiment provided a unique brand of football. On 17 July 1869, Albert Park played the 14th Regiment in a ground at the end of Clarendon Street, obviously the later South Melbourne ground, and about a thousand people arrived to receive 'an infinity of amusement' from the rough and tumble play of both teams. It seems that several of the soldiers favoured more a soccer-type game and they secured the winning goal first by dribbling the ball into the forward line where at last a strong kick guided the ball through the posts. Curiously the Albert Park goal keeper was no more familiar than the soldiers with the rules and tactics, and instead of stopping the ball in front of the goal posts he marked the ball after it had passed through. This match suddenly came to an end in the second half after a field umpire's decision had been fiercely disputed.

Harrison, captaining Melbourne in its first match against the Garrison, wisely allowed the soldiers some latitude. (They probably thought they gave him the same privilege). In later matches Harrison called for stricter adherence to the rules agreed upon, and The Garrison probably said yes, but what the 'yes' meant was open to doubt. Their mode of play was described as 'hugging and hitting'. With their sturdy physique, a willingness to use heavy soldiers' boots to kick an opponent in the shins, and coloured handkerchiefs tied around their brow in the manner of modern Aboriginal nationalists, they appeared 'pretty awe-inspiring', noted Harrison. He especially relished the soldiers' way of forming a bodyguard to protect their captain when he fell panting to the ground, the ball beneath him.

As many of the soldiers were Irish they possibly liked to play a version of what they saw as Gaelic football. Theoretically this was one way in which Irish football could have influenced the game played in Victoria; but such an influence, if it existed, probably promoted a Victorian distaste for Irish football rather than admiration for it.

Blainey, A Game of Our Own (1990), p. 52.

A MOST ASTUTE AND MEMORABLE CHARACTER

Unable to secure work as a music teacher or a concert artist, a better-than-average pianist made his mark on horse-racing.

In the [late 1800s], there was no great scope in Victoria for a better than average pianist either as concert artist or music teacher. A pity, of course, but this unhappy chance gave to the Australian turf one of its most astute and memorable characters in the person of Mr Austin Saqui. Mr Saqui, a young man, caught the attention of a Mr E.N. Abrahams, one of Victoria's earliest bookmakers, whose impeccable English, courtesy and fastidious dress brought him the nickname 'The Count'. Mr Abrahams, a music lover, became friendly with Mr Saqui through a shared interest, of all things, in 'two-up', and soon advised him that he was more likely to earn a living as a bookmaker than as a pianist because he thought that Saqui had 'a skill in handling figures unmatched in Melbourne'.

That testimony could explain a claim that Mr Saqui, turned bookmaker, was the first of his calling in Melbourne to 'bet over and round'. That is, his speed of accurate calculation enabled him to bet his clients such prices, and to such amounts, that he was often able to pay winners from other punters' wagers without risking his own money. In short he aimed at and often succeeded in holding at least £100 of punters' money (and more to cover every £100 that he would have to pay out). The effect was that it was comparatively unimportant to Mr Saqui which horse won. In addition to mathematical skill, he had an ability to judge the fitness of horses and to assess their race prospects.

Saqui demonstrated that skill when he fielded at the 1869 AJC Epsom-Metropolitan meeting at Randwick. He had backed Circassian well to win the Epsom and, when he reached Sydney, took an option at £400 on the horse, 'operable if he wins the Epsom'. Circassian not only won the Epsom but the Metropolitan as well. He was weighted at 7.8 for the two miles Metropolitan actually as a non-stayer.

As Circassian would have to carry only 6 lb more in the Melbourne Cup Victorian enthusiasts generally anticipated that Mr Saqui would exercise his option even though the horse was promptly established hot favourite for the Melbourne Cup. Mr Saqui very civilly advised Circassian's owner, Mr E. Winch, that he wished him luck with the horse in Melbourne, but he had decided not to exercise his option.

Mr Winch, for his part, thanked Mr Saqui and told him that he thought that the 5/2 on offer Circassian for the Melbourne Cup was a false price and not good value. He would be prepared to accept a bet from Saqui of £400 to £100 against the horse. Mr Saqui obliged, and advised Mr Winch to have a 'saver' on Warrior at 20/1 . . .

Instead of buying Circassian, the formerly popular concert artist turned fielder bought Warrior, a six-year-old gelding by New Warrior (imp.), who had run third to Circassian in the Metropolitan. The bookmaker not only thought that Warrior had been unlucky at Randwick, but that he had pulled up as would a horse badly needing the run. In addition, Warrior was handicapped in the Cup at 3 lb less than he had carried in the Metropolitan. Mr Saqui gave Warrior to then up-and-coming trainer, Robert Standish Sevior, to be prepared for racing. Sevior, a handsome, well-educated and fearless punter, later a successful bookmaker and, later still, a memorable figure on the English racing scene, tested Warrior on the track to be a 'Cup certainty'. It was at his insistence, that Mr Saqui took a bet of £8000 to £500 from a consortium of bookmakers—Joseph and Bernard Thompson (brothers) and Phil Glenister—and, when the horse came into 10/1 on the track, a further £2000 to £200. In addition, Mr Saqui laid Circassian heavily, believing, as did the horse's owner, that the price available on the day (2/1) was not value.

When Warrior, ridden by Joe Morrison, beat 200/1 chance The Monk by two lengths, with Phoebe (20/1) a length farther back third, Mr Saqui was credited with winning nearly £20000, including the £1190 first prize. The day after Mr Saqui accepted the £8000 to £500 bet, he went to Flemington to see the horse work. Warrior, ridden by then 17-year-old Andrew Mitchelson, worked poorly and the owner was far from satisfied with both horse and rider. He said so, and Mitchelson told him what he could do with his horse—a comment that earned Mitchelson a kick on the seat of the pants from Sevior. Warrior won the Cup comfortably in the hands of Joe Morrison and it was a most welcome change of luck for the jockey. Morrison had broken an arm when Despatch fell in the first Cup, was third on Camden in the next, and second on Panic in Toryboy's Cup (1865). This was his seventh ride in the race. According to Mr Mitchelson, Mr Saqui gave him £100 from his winnings, for his help in riding work, and, to quote Mitchelson, 'another kick on the backside, for answering back'. Mitchelson gave Sevior £50 from the gift—an act that staggered Sevior, who never forgot it. Even when in England, Sevior sent Mitchelson a 'tenner' each Cup time for more than 20 years to put on his Cup pick.

For the record, Circassian, starting 2/1 favourite for the 1869 Melbourne Cup, finished eighth.

Ahern, A Century of Winners (1982), pp. 21–2.

CARRIED OFF ON A DOOR

Football matches in Tasmania in the 1860s and 1870s were sometimes abandoned for reasons that would be found strange in later times.

The football was as unpredictable as the hunt. In the winter of 1868, two matches in Hobart were abandoned because the football burst, and several matches were postponed because of wet weather or abandoned when rain poured down. Furthermore, a match could be abandoned for reasons which twenty years later would not have been accepted. On Saturday, 12 August 1871, at the New Town ground, Myles Coverdale kicked at the ball at the same time as a Break O'Day player. Their legs collided, and Coverdale fractured the tibia of his right leg. The match was abandoned after Coverdale was placed on a door and carried to his home at the Queen's Asylum.

Blainey, A Game of Our Own (1990), p. 80.

NOT A WINNING DREAM

There are many stories of punters who dream of winners of horse races. Few are as sombre as this.

Legend has it that Craig, builder of the imposing 'Craig's Hotel' in Ballarat, which still stands, dreamed that his horse, Nimblefoot, won the 1870 Cup—but that its jockey wore black armbands.

Nimblefoot won the 1870 Melbourne Cup, all right, but Craig, the owner, didn't see the race. He had died the previous week.

Higgins and Prior, The Jockey Who Laughed (1982), p. 42.

ORANGEMAN VERSUS CATHOLIC

The famous Sydney bareknuckle boxer Larry Foley was involved in a strange bout in 1871, where the venue was a paddock and there was no purse.

A prize fight took place at George's River yesterday between two natives of the colony, one named Ross (a cabman) and the other Foley. The combatants and their friends and backers started as early as half-past 2 a.m. for the scene of the encounter; and although the police got scent of the occurrence during the morning, it is said that the affair was decided before their arrival.

The fight is represented as having been a desperate encounter, lasting over two hours and a half, and resulting in a drawn battle, although victory was claimed in favour of Foley, who represented the green, while his opponent wore the orange colours. The brutal affair seems to have excited a good deal of interest in certain quarters, as the combatants, although natives, were regarded as representing the two antagonistic sections into which Irish nationality is unfortunately divided. It is much to be regretted that some of those in a higher station who have done, and are still doing their worst to stir up and intensify the diabolical feeling of party strife in this community, could not be got to hammer each other a little, in proof of the goodness of their cause, as these stupid young men Ross and Foley have done. Both of the pugilists are said to be severely injured. Ross having his wrist sprained or dislocated, and his adversary suffering from severe bruises about the breast and sides.

The Empire, 29 March 1871.

'MUFF MATCH'

During the 1873–74 cricket season a match was played between two local sides to select the South Australian team to play England. Afterwards there was a 'muff match' for duffers.

After the match, a scratch game took place for the enjoyment of the spectators. These 'Muff Matches' as they were called were played by enthusiastic men who were poor cricketers but just enjoyed a game. Following that, the celebrations carried on into the evening, with *The Register* reporting on the Monday:

> Those in attendance appeared to enjoy the junketing much more than they had the unevenness of the Adelaide ground. The grape [wine] and the juniper [gin] were thirstily sought after by the parched participants, several of whom slept the night on the ground. One over-indulged gentleman fell out of his gig in the early hours of the morning and crushed his top hat. Another cooled himself off by accepting a bet to swim the river.

Harte, *SACA: A History of the South Australian Cricket Association* (1990), p. 42.

TACKLED BY A SHARK

Star Victorian footballer George Coulthard gave up his mission to promote Australian football in Sydney in the 1870s after he received a low blow.

It is not generally known that George Coulthard ... was invited by Phil Sheridan, a trustee of the Sydney Cricket Ground, to pay him a visit with an idea of discussing possibilities of establishing the Victorian game in Sydney.

Coulthard accepted the invitation willingly. But he had an unfortunate experience. He was invited by his Sydney host to join in a fishing expedition in Sydney harbour. While sitting on the side of the boat with his coat-tail trailing in the water he was tackled by a shark, which nearly pulled him in. Fortunately all that the shark relieved him of was his coat. The shock so upset Coulthard that he immediately returned to Melbourne without carrying out his mission. And so the Rugby game still flourishes in New South Wales—thanks to the shark.

Taylor, *100 Years of Football* (1957), p. 27.

VICTORIANS? 'LET THEM DROWN!'

Rivalry between New South Wales and Victorian sportsmen was a very serious matter in the 1870s. It was not forgotten even when they were touring together as part of the Australian cricket team.

I doubt if Englishmen will ever understand the spirit of rivalry that runs high between the colonies of Victoria and New South Wales. The spirit is not limited to the field: it extends to politics, to society, to every side of life, indeed, in which the two are brought into contact one with another. Often enough this rivalry went too far; and in the matter of the selection of the first team, the Press and public were widely at variance. One felt Victoria had been slighted, another New South Wales; and even on the tour itself the players might be seen separating themselves as far as possible from their compatriots of the other colony. Let me give one example. While we were coasting along New Zealand we were caught by a terrible storm; and, being in a very small steamer, we were in considerable danger. Charles Bannerman, who was an expert swimmer, was very frightened. He refused to go into his cabin, and said if he ever got on dry land again he would never leave it as long as he lived.

'Well,' I said, 'suppose we *are* wrecked. What will you do?'

'First,' he said, 'I'll save Alick [his brother], then Murdoch, then yourself.'

'Well, but what about the Victorians?' I asked.

'Let them drown,' he replied, 'Let them drown. D'you think I'm going to risk my life for them?'

Spofforth, 'Australian Cricket and Cricketers: A Retrospect' (1894), p. 515.

THESE DIRECTIONS SHALL BE OBEYED

The rules of the Melbourne Bicycle Club, founded in 1878, were particularly comprehensive.

Annual subscription twelve shillings and sixpence.

That the club uniform consist of myrtle green coat, knicker bockers, stockings and cap, and silver badge. Members are requested to wear the same at Club meetings and when touring. White straw hats with club ribbon (green and gold) to be worn in summer. Club costumiers Alston & Brown Collins Street West. That the uniform and badge be not worn on Sundays, except on runs extending over several days.

Regulations.

1   The captain, or in his absence the vice-captain, or any member of the committee shall act as leader in every excursion, and his directions shall be obeyed.

2   That the vice-captain in all runs shall keep the rear, and signal (one whistle) to the leader whenever the tail of the company is getting out-distanced. On hearing the signal the leader shall

slacken till he receives a second whistle (two whistles), indicating that they have closed up.

3 That the strictest order be maintained during all runs.

4 That when riding in single file, an interval of two yards shall be kept between each rider, and when in double file, three yards. In hilly country these distances should be doubled.

5 That each member is requested to carry a bell or whistle and to use a lamp when riding at night.

BUGLE CALLS

Attention.

The Assembly or Prepare to Mount.

Mount.

Dismount.

Form Single File.

Form Twos.

Dinner Call.

Attention should be sounded before the Assembly or Dinner Calls, to indicate to riders that they are official.

Dunstan, Sports (1973), p. 251.

A Surging Mob

English cricket captain Lord Harris was struck when some 2000 larrikins invaded the pitch at the Sydney Cricket Ground in 1879—the most celebrated sports riot in Australian history.

By far the most celebrated and infamous incident of this era, a cricket riot, occurred on 8 February 1879 on the second day of the England v. New South Wales match at the SCG with the Governor and his wife as 'pained witnesses'. After England had totalled 267 the home side managed only 177, despite an excellent innings of 82 not out by the popular idol, Murdoch, and was forced to follow on. In front of a Saturday crowd of around 10 000 Murdoch and Bannerman took the score to 18 before Murdoch was given run out by the Victorian professional, Coulthard, who had been engaged as an umpire by the English team on the recommendation of the Melbourne Cricket Club.

Such an unpopular decision brought an immediate chorus of 'groaning and hooting' and cries of 'Not out', 'Go back, Murdoch!' and 'Another umpire' by a batch of 'adult larrikins'. They were led, according to the *Australasian* of 15 February 1879 by a 'well-known and ill-favoured bookmaker' who had backed the local side to the extent of nearly £1000.

Gregory, the home captain, instead of sending in another man, hesitated, and Lord Harris, the English captain, possibly headed towards the pavilion to discuss the situation with Gregory at about the same time. Then a large number of 'larrikins', sitting at the bottom of the terrace and within the boundary fence, 'made a rush for the centre of the ground' noted the *Sydney Morning Herald* of 10 February 1879 and were quickly followed by 'hundreds of roughs who took possession of the wickets'. Subsequent disclosures in the Press and at court make it clear that the protests emanated both from the pavilion and the Outer. In fact Mr Driver stated that it was the 'inmates of the pavilion', spurred on by a bookmaker, who had 'initiated the disturbance' though it is not entirely clear whether the juvenile element which rushed the ground included members. Presumably it did because not only was the bookmaker ejected but a number of members had their fees returned and were banned.

The English team soon found itself in the centre of a 'surging, gesticulating, and shouting mob' continued the *Sydney Morning Herald* in its account of the riot; it was later estimated that some 2000 spectators poured on to the ground. One person tried to strike Coulthard but was floored. Harris was struck across the body with a whip or a stick, by a 'rough'. Another English player, Hornby, promptly tackled his captain's assailant and with the assistance of some gentlemen and members dragged the person to the pavilion. This was no easy task as some of the 'roughs' made unsuccessful attempts to snatch their cohort from the clutches of Hornby. No serious injuries resulted from the fracas. Hornby had his clothes torn, and was struck on the face, and a few others had scratches. Harris had even landed a few blows himself, in self defence, or so the *Australasian* thought. The mêlée lasted 30 minutes and throughout it the pavilion bell was rung, rather optimistically it seems, with 'the vigour of a fire alarm' to encourage spectators to clear the ground.

Meanwhile Gregory seemed to be doing his best to aggravate the situation. He had come to the conclusion, possibly based on Murdoch's version of the run out, that Coulthard was incompetent and should be replaced. Harris refused whereupon Gregory told him that the game was over. (Harris had kept his team on the field throughout the riot fearing that Gregory might claim the match through forfeit.) Gregory later relented and decided to let the match continue, with Coulthard officiating, but the crowd would not accept this and twice more invaded the pitch so that the match was called off for the day. It was completed on Monday without further incident.

It is worth exploring some of the ingredients of this riot to establish its links with previous unrest. One continuing factor was the strong crowd identification with the home team which represented a form of nationalism or perhaps chauvinism. It was possibly fuelled by the reported comments of two English professionals, Emmett and Ulyett, who referred to the crowd as 'sons of convicts' and supposedly about the time Harris was struck. Emmett and Ulyett later denied making the remarks and were supported in their stand by the other umpire, a future Prime Minister, Edmund Barton. In the face of these denials the *Sydney Morning Herald* reporter stuck to his guns and published a letter on 13 February from a 'well-known citizen' who wrote, 'I can only tell you that I heard the remark, and that it spread like wild fire round the ground'.

The controversy over an umpire represented another link with the past and it was the opinion of the *Australasian* of 15 February 1879 that it would be a happy day when the 'present loose system of appointing umpires is done away with'. The problem with this system was that a particular umpire was identified with a team and was regarded as something less than an impartial arbiter of the law. The system also encouraged captains to question the authority of umpires from time to time and assume some of the decision-making powers themselves. Regarding the 1879 incident, Harris later admitted that he may have made a mistake selecting a professional umpire on the recommendation of the Melbourne Cricket Club, as he had no idea of the depth of inter-city rivalry.

Cashman, *'Ave a Go, Yer Mug!* (1984), pp. 30–2.

CHAMPIONSHIP BOUT AMONG THE RED GUMS

When Abe Hickin challenged Larry Foley to the boxing championship of Australia in 1879, the promoters devised elaborate plans to outwit the police.

The *Riverine Herald* noted their arrival and observed coldly that the bout had created immense interest in both colonies 'with a certain type of person' and warned that boxers had entered into recognizances for £500 each.

There were careful plans to outwit the police. Word went around that there were two possible sites for the battle. It could take place up the river beyond the Goulburn. Fighters would rendezvous on the other side of the Murray and go there by means of the Barmah Punt. Alternatively it could be on the Perricoota Run, ten miles down the river from Echuca.

The rumour was pushed from pub to pub with such finesse that not only did police head for the Goulburn but a large section of the crowd as well. The *Argus* suggested later, with some wisdom, that if the police had really wanted to stop the fight then they were not over-diligent about it.

The greatest migration out of Echuca started at 1 a.m. There was a long cavalcade of every conceivable type of horse-drawn vehicle, plus a crowd on foot. There were two bridges across the Campaspe River. The upper bridge meant an extra walk of two miles, but the crowd decided to take that one because it led them away from the Police Barracks. In the early hours of the morning they rested at Timothy O'Sullivan's Hotel at Wharparilla for drinks, then moved on.

Finally, they came to a great camp fire where they sat around, sang, and made merry until the dawn. Now the big problem was to get across the Murray River. The reporter from the *Riverine Herald* was appalled. He said they had only three small boats 'of hasty amateur construction—surely the crankiest and most perilous craft ever set eyes on'. Slowly in ones, twos and threes the big crowd had to be ferried over. The *Herald* man was horrified at the danger, horrified at the price, half a crown each, and horrified at the disastrous damage to clothes. Not only did everyone have their trousers ruined, their clothes were thoroughly soaked as well.

But the site was good. A narrow glade in the midst of heavy belts of red gum timber, situated on one of a labyrinth of points along the river, just below Dead Horse Point. It was beautifully secluded, a perfect natural stadium. The organizers brought out ropes, stakes and constructed a ring, thirty feet by thirty feet.

Dunstan, *Sports* (1973), pp. 189–90.

TRICKETT TRICKED

Edward Trickett, world champion sculler in 1876, was humiliated by a brash newcomer from Canada in 1880.

The race took place on 15 November 1880. For a short time Trickett held his own, but he drifted further and further behind. For Hanlan it was all too easy. He was so far ahead he started playing pranks. First he rowed with one hand, then with the other. He took his cap off and waved to friends on the bank. Once he stopped altogether and washed his face in the water. One newspaper described his pranks as risky and in bad taste. He won by three lengths, but if he wished he could have won by half a mile.

The Australian's humiliation was terrible. Trickett's life as a hotel-keeper had been too much. He was out of training and he had gone through an agonizing weight-reduction programme to meet Hanlan. There was a letter to the *Sydney Morning Herald* which accused Australians of being bad losers. 'The infatuated Trickett admirers are now heaping coals of fire on his head, charging him with turpitude of the basest kind.'

Dunstan, *Sports* (1973), pp. 164–5.

Sculling Race Adjourns Parliament

Sydney politicians took more than a passing interesting when a big bushman, Elias Laycock, challenged the Canadian world champion sculler Edward Hanlan in the 1880s.

The race was on 22 May 1884. Late on 21 May, Mr F.B. Suttor, MLA, moved in the Assembly that the House should adjourn until 7 p.m. the following day. Seeing that the Hanlan-Laycock race was tomorrow there would be no hope of getting a quorum anyway. Mr Stuart, MLA, was shocked:

> I trust the House will not accede to the suggestion? With the enormous amount of highly important work which we have before us it would not be creditable to us as a legislative body to adjourn for the purpose of attending a boat-race. I feel sure there will be no lack of members to form a quorum.

Mr Stuart was so wrong. He was beaten twenty-one votes to sixteen and they all went to the boat-race. The Legislative Council also adjourned because it could not get a quorum.

Dunstan, *Sports* (1973), pp. 165–6.

'I'll Make You Take Off Your Shirt'

Bill Beach lived up to his boast when he defeated Canadian world champion sculler, Edward Hanlan, in the 1880s.

The race took place on 16 August 1884. Hanlan, the little man, announced that they would row on the ebb tide. Big Bill Beach was too smart for that one. 'We'll row on the making tide,' said he. Even so Hanlan had no self-doubts, and he announced: 'I can beat that big blacksmith. He don't know how to row.'

At the start of the three and a quarter mile course on the Parramatta River, Beach took off his shirt, threw it into the river and set himself for the start. 'Why take off your shirt?', said Hanlan, 'you'll need it soon.' Beach replied: 'I'll make you take off your shirt Hanlan, you won't have time for monkey tricks today.'

Hanlan had a good start and built up an early lead, and at the half way mark he was four lengths in front. The *Sydney Echo* reported that amongst the crowd of a hundred thousand people along the bank there was deep despondency. The comments were: 'It's the old story.' 'He plays with him.' 'Only a procession' and the odds increased to ten to one to Hanlan. But then Beach began to close the gap and steadily he gained, and gained.

When they drew alongside each other Hanlan made a frantic effort to clash oars and foul Beach. The Sydney newspapers devoted page after page to this race. The *Sydney Echo* reporter was aboard the vessel *Tomki* and had he been describing the final stages of the Battle of Waterloo he could not have been more triumphant.

Dunstan, *Sports* (1973), pp. 167–9.

'DEERFOOT OF AUSTRALIA'

Aboriginal Charles Samuels was considered by many to be the world sprint champion in the 1880s and early 1890s.

The 'deerfoot of Australia', Samuels was regarded as the fastest man in the world in his prime. Born on a cattle station on Queensland's Darling Downs, he was almost invincible at distances from 50 to 130 yards. Samuels defeated Australian champion Jim McGarrigal over 130 yards in Dalby in 1885 after giving his opponent a four-yard start. Two years later Samuels beat English champion Harry Hutchens in Sydney over 150 yards, clocking up 14.9 seconds. A month later he beat Hutchens again in 15.1 seconds. But Hutchens, regarded as the premier sprinter of the nineteenth century, out-paced Samuels in two later events.

Apart from his celebrated victories over Hutchens, Samuels' most notable triumphs were his wins against the Irish champion Tom Malone and Ted Lazarus. There were claims that he ran 100 yards in a phenomenal 9.1 seconds in a heat at Botany in 1888, but this time may well be inaccurate. Samuels' wonderful achievements were grudgingly recognised by the *Referee* in 1894.

> Thus it is that I am about to claim for an Aboriginal runner what an overwhelming majority of foot-racing critics will concede is his due—the Championship of Australia. It might be [a] more pleasant reflection to Australians, perhaps, if a white man could be quoted as champion; but as we are sizing up the runners on the 'all-in' principle, a black Aboriginal has to be accorded the laurel crown. Samuels has, in a long course of consistent and brilliant running, established his claim, not only to be the Australian champion, but also to have been one of the best exponents of sprint running the world has ever seen.

Harris, The Proud Champions (1989), p. 25.

THE DAY THE UMPIRE'S TONGUE SLIPPED

The clash between two strong personalities, the 'Demon' Spofforth and Umpire Jim Phillips, led to a celebrated exchange at the Sydney Cricket Ground in the 1880s, as recounted by former Test cricketer John Worrall.

Spofforth, like another heady bowler of a previous era, T.W. Wills, was keen to establish psychological dominance of everyone on the field and this included the umpires. In the days before the crease was widened, Spofforth, who was then representing Victoria, went outside the crease and bowled several no-balls when striving for extra variation. He was called by the umpire, whereupon Spofforth 'became nettled':

> Going outside deliberately he was in the act of delivering the ball when Phillips 'called'. But the cunning old fox held tight to the ball, and Phillips had of necessity to reverse his decision. Things went on quietly for a while until Spofforth failed in another attempt at

trapping the umpire, covering up his intention by remarking, 'Oh, Phillips, my foot slipped this time'. Big, burly, red-headed Jim of Dimboola, with brown eyes, made no remark and as he had the face of a sphinx the game proceeded. But he was only biding his time, and at last, when the bowler had delivered the ball with his foot fairly planted behind and within the crease, Phillips yelled out in stentorian tones, 'No-ball': 'Oh, Phillips,' said Spofforth, 'I have never bowled a fairer ball in my life.' 'I know that,' said the umpire, 'but my tongue slipped that time.' That incident ended the feud, and all the rest was peace.

Cashman, The 'Demon' Spofforth (1990), p. 178.

THE DERIVATION OF 'DALLY'

'Dally' Messenger, Rugby League's first star, earned his nickname because of his youthful paunch.

One day in late 1885, when Herbert Henry was a little over two years old, his mother caught the four-horse bus to town and he was left in the care of his father. Herbert, a fat little fellow in shorts and a jersey over his bulging stomach, was playing in the shavings of the boat-building corner of the boatshed when the distinguished visitor arrived.

W.B. Dalley was then a QC and Attorney-General in the New South Wales ministry. He was a portly gentleman, so Charlie Messenger, pointing to his son's paunch, said jokingly, 'I have another little Dalley here'. From then on, he was called 'Dalley'. In time, the 'e' was dropped and the name 'Dally' was passed on to his only son, his grandson and great-grandson. His mother and sisters, however, always called him 'Bert' or 'Bertie'.

Messenger, The Master (1982), p. 13.

THE 'SEAWEEDS' VERSUS THE 'COWDUNGS'

Pick-up games between neighbourhood teams on rough ground, with no shoes, have traditionally been tough affairs. It was no different for 'Dally' Messenger and his brothers in the 1890s.

Dally and his brothers went to Double Bay Primary School where they learned the rudiments of Rugby Union football. When Dally was nine he played scrum-half for the school, Bill Lees, thirteen, was full-back, and Charlie Messenger, the same age, played in the forwards. Dally was the youngest member of the team. The primary school at Double Bay was never beaten in a school competition. They had an excellent Master and coach, a weedy little man called Moclair, who taught them all the basic points of the game. Led by Moclair, they often had to walk long distances to play matches, sometimes as far afield as Centennial Park and Moore Park in Sydney. The winners of the primary school competition regularly played the winners of the senior one. When the Messengers and Lees were in the team, the Double Bay primary school team defeated Fort Street school who in those same years were winners of the high school rugby union competition.

They were demons of sport, these young men of the Bay, and some of Australia's greatest champions have come from this area. Outside school hours, the boys of the neighbourhood played down near the beach. It was tough football for there were no shoes and the ground was rough. Attendance on, or comfort to, the injured player was unheard of. On Saturday mornings there was always a 'friendly' match between the boys who lived and played around the Messenger boatshed, and the boys from the local dairy and its surroundings—the 'Seaweeds' and 'Cowdungs' respectively. Bill Lees recalled that there was never a winner because, though a 'friendly' match, it always ended in a fight. The Seaweeds boasted such players as Sid and Harry Pearce, the Messenger brothers, Bill and Charlie Lees, 'Squirrel' Oates and 'Ugly' Burns. They must have been gluttons for punishment because after the Saturday morning skirmish, they regularly trooped off on the long walk of several miles to the Sydney Showground to watch the match of the day.

The 'Seaweed' and 'Cowdung' rivalry was a tradition which carried on for many years. The boundary was William Street, Double Bay, and the followers were coded according to the side of the street on which they lived. The border was an invisible line which ran down the middle of the street and the names originated from the traditional fight which took place over this line. Each side, heavily armed, would assemble on their respective side of the 'line', one throwing seaweed and the other throwing cowdung. After this combat, according to an agreed truce, they would all head down to the beach for a swim, as they did after the football.

Messenger, The Master (1982), p. 13.

THE THRILL OF BODY SURFING

When body surfing first became popular in Australia in the 1880s, it was regarded as a unique pleasure.

When I first went into the surf regularly, at the age of seven years, and though I felt it strongly attracting me towards something I could not define, it appeared to belong to some past life. At first I was content to play about amongst the rolling surf, and get the warmth that their friction and tumbling about activity would engender. But as the days went on I wasn't satisfied. There was still something missing, a missing link, as it were, between this and another life. Then, unconsciously, I found myself plunging with the wave as it rolled to the shore. And then swimming with the wave that broke within my own depth. And struggling to stay on it. Some of the other surfers, particularly the Plumb boys and girls, watched me with much interest, and tried to divine what I was trying to achieve in this year of our Lord, 1886. At the time when I started it, I did not know myself. I was but following a certain course set for me, stage by stage, to recover in another life man's greatest, most thrilling, and cheapest sport ever. Requiring no clubs, bats nor balls, next to no garments. Just one's body and health and strength. Then came the day when, just before I reached the eighth year of my life, when I went for a wave just beyond my own depth, caught it, and shot with my head and shoulders well out in front, steered through my fellow-bathers successfully, and grounded my chin on the shoreline, i.e., the beach. I rolled over and sat up, looking back, and calculating how far was the quite considerable distance I had travelled. Without any other form of propulsion but that of the wave itself. I saw the hands of Charlie Plumb and his sister waving to me, and smiling and shouting their congratulations. And as I rose to my feet, as it was time, viz., 7 a.m., to leave the surf, and the Plumbs had reached me, I knew that the link with the past had finished its work. And I felt very grateful to it. Though years after, when the South Hebridean Islander, Tommy Tanne, came from the Island of Tanna, southern island of the new Hebrides Group, and taught me to go far out and into the shark area, and for which I have been ever grateful, and take the big waves from there, I look back on that wave in 1886 as the greatest and most important one in my life.

Lowe, *Surfing, Surf-shooting, and Surf Life Saving Pioneering* (1958), p. 24.

DRUG ASSISTED

Sportspeople endorsing products is not a new phenomenon. Bill Beach, world champion sculler, did it as early as 1886.

THE INVINCIBLE

Gentlemen—Feeling unwell during my training for the second contest with Edward Hanlan of Toronto, for the championship of the world, my trainer purchased for me Warner's Safe Cure and Safe Pills, and I was agreeably astonished at the great benefit which followed their use.

—William Beach.
Champion Sculler of the World.

Dunstan, *Sports* (1973), pp. 169–70.

DISCOVERY OF THE CROUCH START

In 1887 Aboriginal athlete Bobby McDonald discovered the crouch start for sprinting by accident. He first used it simply to avoid cold winds at night while training, before he discovered that it was a beneficial starting technique.

In 1887, on a bitterly cold night at the Carrington ground, Bobby McDonald surprised officials and fellow competitors by crouching in a squatting position on his mark. As the gun fired, McDonald was off like a bullet and won the race. He used the squatting style in the semifinals and won easily. Officials barred him from using the crouch start in the final, as he seemed to gain an unfair advantage. It was more by accident than design that McDonald had discovered the crouch start. To avoid the cold winds at night while training, he would squat on his haunches. From this sitting position he bounded up and found he was faster away and balanced much quicker than under the old erect style of starting. Realising he had made a useful discovery, he perfected it and adopted an all-fours style that got the best results. Harry Bushell took it a step further and dug two holes for his kick-off. Putting his hands over the mark, he found he could leave the mark with greater acceleration. The crouch method caught on and was universally adopted. Today it is the recognised means of starting.

Mason, *Professional Athletics in Australia* (1985), p. 77.

Englishmen Try Australian Rules Football

An English football team in 1888 played Rugby in New South Wales but attempted to play Australian Rules football in the southern states.

The history of Australian football in international matches is brief, although in 1888 the visit of an English football team gave the game a huge boost. The team, led by England's Test cricketing entrepreneurs J.J. Lillywhite and A. Shrewsbury, played Rugby in New Zealand and New South Wales while learning Australian football in order to play leading Victorian and South Australian clubs.

The Englishmen, though a stone heavier than the Australians, were equal in speed and understood the theory of the game but did not have sufficient knowledge to put practice into effect. Few could mark or kick, the feature of their game being a continued charge which none of the local players could withstand. Some of them, however, played a fine, dashing game especially Stoddart, another Test cricketer who kicked more than half their goals. In all the team played twenty-five matches, winning fourteen and losing eleven. In Adelaide the Englishmen recorded one win and three losses; defeating Port Adelaide and losing to South Adelaide, Adelaide, and Norwood.

At the end of the tour it was decided to send a team to England for return matches; however the Victorian Football Association, as the major administrative body in the country, thought that the move was too big for confirmation and postponed final arrangements. Unfortunately they were never finalised and football lost its best chance to go international.

Whimpress, *The South Australian Football Story* (1983), pp. 97–8.

THE DEATH OF A YOUNG CHAMPION

The crowd at the funeral of champion sculler Henry Searle, who died in 1889, was as large as the one which farewelled the Soudan contingent in 1885.

Despite the warmth of the day most wore heavy black, and conditions must have been trying in the struggling mass that assembled in the streets. The crowd was enormous with the *Sydney Morning Herald* describing the sight of so many people as 'one of the most imposing and remarkable events ever witnessed in New South Wales or, indeed, Australia'. Traffic along the entire length of the procession's route was suspended; one estimate of the numbers at the junction of Harris and George Streets, alone, put the figure at 'fully' 20 000. Estimates of crowd size are notoriously inaccurate, but even if grossly overstated, the very fact of the overstatement is often sufficient to convey the impression of immensity felt by the observer. One hundred thousand in the streets was the estimate of the *Tamworth News* correspondent, 170 000 was guessed by another, 175 000 and 200 000 were also mentioned. The correspondent for the *Brisbane Courier* hedged his bets with a figure of 150 000–200 000. All agreed that the crowd was huge, and it reminded many of the great farewell given the Soudan contingent in 1885.

Bennett, *Clarence Comet* (1973), p. 87.

CARBINE, THE CALM CHAMPION

Carbine was such a popular champion that admirers pulled hair from his tail and mane, and even stole one of his racing shoes, when he won the Melbourne Cup in 1890.

A roar of applause, such as never before was heard at the famous Flemington course, greeted the appearance of 'Old Jack'. A stable boy led him past the stand. Ramage, his jockey, sat jauntily atop the favourite (4/1). Carbine's ears pricked, as the immensity of the cheering was flung across the racing track, from the stand, the Hill and the Flat. His fine head was held high; he lifted his heels to the feel of the springy turf, as he moved towards the starting point. Five horses from the inside rail, he was. He stood steady, waiting for the drop of the flag. The heavy burden he carried seemed as nothing to him. Yet he seemed keyed up for the coming struggle. The huge crowd was hushed. All eyes were centred on the 39 horses, as they shifted into line. Most eyes were riveted on the black and white jacket, and scarlet cap, of Carbine . . .

The flag dropped, the black and white jacket flashed into the lead . . . a deafening filter of noise smashed over the course. But Carbine did not lead for long. Soon he was lost in the ruck of galloping horses. His young jockey was not going to waste the topweight thus early in the race. Let the lightweights make the pace and wear themselves out first. Seventh or eighth would do for the first mile or so. And so it was . . . with the people who had come to Flemington just to see Carbine win the Cup, asking, with bated breath, 'Where is he?' Half a mile from the winning post Enuc was leading, but struggling. Soon Melos, highly fancied, was in the van. Highborn was close behind and, on the outside, Carbine just beginning to show his true pace. They turned into the straight, Carbine lying fourth. Ramage shook his whip vigorously, and 'Old Jack' flashed to the front. Melos tackled him and capitulated, Highborn reached his girth then dropped back. And so to the post, still hard ridden, although the race was all over. Carbine galloped to pass it, a winner by two and a half lengths.

The crowd at Flemington went mad . . . all Melbourne went mad. His owner, Mr D.S. Wallace, was mobbed; the horse and jockey were mobbed. Carbine seemed to be the calmest of all in that great excitement-mad assemblage. It was with difficulty that the champion was got to his stall. On the way, admirers pulled hairs from his tail and from his mane. People crowded his stall so much, his trainer had to take him home from the course before he could give the horse a rub down. When they got 'Old Jack' home, it was found someone had stolen one of his racing shoes.

Ahern, A *Century of Winners* (1982), pp. 87–8.

LEFT IN CENTRE FIELD NAKED

Finding himself in an embarrassing state of near-nudity inspired a New South Wales player to score a fine individual try in 1892.

The initial interstate match was not without its amusing moments, not the least being 'Son' Fry's embarrassing run to the Queensland tryline. One of the prime movers of the new game at South Sydney, Fry, an outstanding, dropkicking centre who had played rugby union since 1892, was determined to impress his mother and his fiancee. During the match, Fry made a break that took him to the Queensland halfway mark where a maroon defender only succeeded in ripping off his shorts. Fry had forgotten to put on underpants and was left in centre field naked except for his jersey, and under the gaze of his mother and the woman he loved.

Fry saw that the least number of spectators were congregated near the Queensland end of the field and his efforts in reaching the tryline suggested the utmost urgency—and embarrassment. He threw himself at the line and stayed there until another pair of shorts were found. It was one of the finest individual tries of the period.

Lester, The Story of Australian Rugby League (1988), p. 43.

AUSSIE RULES IN NEW ZEALAND

Surprisingly, Australian football was popular in New Zealand in the 1880s and 1890s.

Australian football was played in New Zealand from the 1880s and in 1893 there were forty-four clubs in the Dominion centred in the chief cities of Auckland, Wellington, Christchurch, and Dunedin. The game began to wane in the first decade of this century but New Zealand was invited to compete in the Melbourne Carnival and won two of its four matches, defeating New

South Wales and Queensland. They did not play South Australia in that series but shortly afterwards came here, meeting the State team on the Adelaide Oval on August 30, 1908.

Unfortunately the game was played in appalling conditions, the rain beat down heavily and there was a biting wind to accompany it. South Australia's handball was superior in the first quarter but after that all men, soaked to the skin, ran on the ball in an endeavour to keep warm and in the last three quarters the New Zealanders tripled our score. Nevertheless the margin at the finish was ten points in South Australia's favour:

Teams	first	second	third	final	points
South Australia	4.5	4.6	5.8	5.8	38
New Zealand	0.1	1.7	1.7	3.10	28

Whimpress, *The South Australian Football Story* (1983), pp. 99–100.

HOT POTATOES IN HIS POCKET

Cricketers have done some very strange things to keep warm on bitter English summer days.

In 1893, when the Australians were playing against eighteen of Blackpool, an amusing incident occurred during the local men's innings. Arthur Coningham was fielding in the 'country.' It was a cold, raw day, and the Australians were playing in their sweaters. The batting not being too brilliant or lively, the outfields had little to do, and the idea evidently struck Coningham that he would like to get warm, so he gathered some bits of sticks and grass, piled them up, and then asked one of the spectators for a match. Having obtained this, he set fire to the little pile of grass and commenced to warm his hands. It amused a section of the spectators, who applauded him, and one wag suggested he should go inside and get a couple of hot potatoes to put in his pocket.

Turner in Mullins and Derriman, *Bat and Pad* (1984), p. 32.

Pursued By A Pack Of Dingoes

In 1894 cyclist J.H.C. Bamblett literally raced for his life between Dundas and Coolgardie.

The only recorded instance in which a cyclist was attacked by animals took place in the latter part of '94, between Dundas and Coolgardie. Probably few men on the field were better known than J.H.C. Bamblett, who was special cyclist, and carried the special mails to Dundas. When nearing the 'Forty-Mile Rocks' on one of his trips he thought he heard a peculiar noise behind him. At last he stopped his bicycle to find out what this noise was, and, to his intense astonishment and horror, discovered that he was being followed by a pack of dingoes, which were close to his heels by the time he had mounted his bike. He was quite taken aback, and could scarcely believe that he saw aright, as such an experience was entirely new on the fields; but the snarling of the brutes soon roused him to a sense of the danger of his position. Mr. Bamblett was an expert rider, with an extraordinary development of 'calf', and he soon got going in good style. The road was smooth, and the dingoes did their best also, as the cyclist often had them close to his pedals. The race went on between cyclist and dingoes for several miles, and it seemed to the former that the latter would have a decent meal out of his lunch-bag, if not off himself. At last that part of the track was reached which crosses the end of Lake Cowan—a great saltwater lake when rain falls, but which, at this time, was perfectly dry, with a smooth, hard surface admirably adapted for cycling, and Bamblett went on at a rate he had never previously attained. The going appeared to be equally good for the dingoes, as they kept up the pace, although it was a regular cracker. For a few miles this terrific speed was kept up, until one by one the dingoes got tired out and had to retire baffled and beaten.

During the whole of the race the cyclist knew that, barring accidents—such as his tyres getting punctured, or a stick getting into his wheel, or losing his pedals or his balance—he could easily win the race for life in which he was engaged. When he was well away from the brutes Bamblett got off his bike, nearly done up with his tremendous exertions. By this time night was rapidly approaching, but there was a good full moon, and he did the last twenty miles of his journey by moonlight, reaching his rendezvous for the night after a most exciting and trying day's work, the like of which had never been previously experienced on the Coolgardie goldfields.

Fitzpatrick, The Bicycle and the Bush (1980), p. 117.

AUSTRALIA'S SUPREME DAY

American writer Mark Twain had no doubt that Melbourne Cup Day was Australia's supreme national event when he visited the country in 1895.

[Melbourne] is the mitred Metropolitan of the Horse-Racing Cult. Its raceground is the Mecca of Australasia. On the great annual day of sacrifice—the 5th of November, Guy Fawkes's Day—business is suspended over a stretch of land and sea as wide as from New York to San Francisco, and deeper than from the northern lakes to the Gulf of Mexico; and every man and woman, of high degree or low, who can afford the expense, put away their other duties and come. They begin to swarm in by ship and rail a fortnight before the day, and they swarm thicker and thicker day after day, until all the vehicles of transportation are taxed to their uttermost to meet the demands of the occasion, and all hotels and lodgings are bulging outward because of the pressure from within. They come a hundred thousand strong, as all the best authorities say, and they pack the spacious grounds and grandstands and make a spectacle such as is never to be seen in Australasia elsewhere.

It is the 'Melbourne Cup' that brings this multitude together. Their clothes have been ordered long ago, at unlimited cost, and without bounds as to beauty and magnificence, and have been kept in concealment until now, for unto this day are they consecrate. I am speaking of the *ladies'* clothes; but one might know that.

And so the grandstands make a brilliant and wonderful spectacle, a delirium of color, a vision of beauty. The champagne flows, everybody is vivacious, excited, happy; everybody bets, and gloves and fortunes change hands right along, all the time. Day after day the races go on, and the fun and the excitement are kept at white heat; and when each day is done, the people dance all night so as to be fresh for the race in the morning. And at the end of the great week the swarms secure lodgings and transportation for next year, then flock away to their remote homes and count their gains and losses, and order next year's Cup-clothes, and then lie down and sleep two weeks, and get up sorry to reflect that a whole year must be put in somehow or other before they can be wholly happy again.

The Melbourne Cup is the Australasian National Day. It would be difficult to overstate its importance. It overshadows all other holidays and specialized days of whatever sort in that congeries of colonies. Overshadows them? I might almost say it blots them out. Each of them gets attention, but not everybody's; each of them evokes interest, but not everybody's; each of them rouses enthusiasm, but not everybody's; in each case a part of the attention, interest, and enthusiasm is a matter of habit and custom, and another part of it is official and perfunctory. Cup Day, and Cup Day only, commands an attention, an interest, and an enthusiasm which are universal—and spontaneous, not perfunctory. Cup Day is supreme—it has no rival. I can call to mind no specialized annual day, in any country, which can be named by that large name—Supreme. I can call to mind no specialized annual day, in any country, whose approach fires the whole land with a conflagration of conversation and preparation and anticipation and jubilation. No day save this one; but this one does it.

Twain, *Following the Equator* (1897), pp. 161–3.

'KILL HIM'

Hostility towards the umpire has a long history in Australia. Women, as well as men, have been keen to 'kill the ref', as the aftermath of a close match between Collingwood and North Melbourne, played at North Melbourne in 1896, indicates.

Owing to a disturbance which took place on the Collingwood ground when these two teams met there last year, there was probably some ill-feeling between their partisans at starting, and this was raised to fever heat by the exciting events of one of the hardest games played this season. In the early stages of the match, J. Roberts, formerly a well-known Carlton player, who acted as umpire, was severe on the players for passing the ball for little marks, instead of kicking it, and the local twenty were the chief sufferers by it. There was some hooting at that stage, but later on, when North Melbourne, by a fine effort, had made the game almost even again, this was forgotten. Had they won, all would have been well, but unfortunately for the umpire, they were beaten by a goal, and someone had to suffer. The moment that the final bell rang, there was a rush of people in the reserve to the pavilion gate, and as it was evident that some of them meant mischief, several of the Collingwood players and a few North Melbourne quietly got round the umpire, who had to run the gauntlet of this ruffianism to reach the dressing-room. It was well that they did so, or Roberts would either have been killed or seriously injured, for the moment he stepped through the gate scores of men rushed at him like wolves, and a scene of indescribable tumult followed. Fists and sticks were going, and one man in the thick of the crowd with some implement wrapped in paper was making desperate efforts to fracture someone's skull. In the first rush Roberts was seized by the hair and dragged down, and but for the splendid help given him just then, notably by Proudfoot, of Collingwood, who, holding one arm over his head to shield himself against a rain of blows and with the other round the umpire, literally carried him through the pack with one of his football rushes. Strickland, who at one time got separated from his men, had to fight hard for his own safety, and many of the Collingwood men were mauled before they reached the pavilion. M'Dougall, one of the North Melbourne players, was apparently the worst sufferer by the mêlée, as he received a very nasty blow on the head which left him almost insensible.

Even when the players and umpire had reached the pavilion their troubles were not over, for they had still to get to their cabs, and the crowd were waiting for a chance to renew the attack, but fresh police were brought and the ground cleared. A 'lady' had the enviable honour of starting this disturbance. As the players were coming in at half-time she waited near the gate and struck Roberts in the face. Afterwards her shrill voice as she leaned over the fence added a high treble to the torrent of abuse rained on the unfortunate umpire whenever he approached the pavilion, which, strangely enough, seemed to be the mustering-point for the roughs. The woman 'barracker', indeed, has become one of the most objectionable of football surroundings. On some grounds they actually spit in the faces of players as they come to the dressing-rooms, or wreak their spite much more maliciously with long hat pins. In the heights of this mêlée some of the women screamed with fear. Others screamed 'Kill him.' One of these gentle maidens at the close of the struggle remarked regretfully that it was a pity they 'let off' the umpire in the Geelong match, as they should have killed him. Yet these women consider themselves respectable, and they 'support' football, which is consequently in a serious decline.

Argus, 27 July 1896.

BILL AND JIM NEARLY GET TAKEN DOWN

A.B. 'Banjo' Paterson wrote many wonderful racing stories. Here is one.

'You see, it was this way,' said Bill reflectively, as we sat on the rails of the horse yard, 'me and Jim was down at Buckatowndown show with that jumpin' pony Jim has, and in the high jump our pony jumped seven foot, and they gave the prize to Spondulix that only jumped six foot ten. *You* know what these country shows are; a man can't get no sort of fair play at all. We asked the stooards why the prize was give to Spondulix, and they said because he jumped better style than the pony. So Jim he ups and whips the saddle and bridle off the pony, and he says to the cove at the jump, "Put the bar up to seven foot six," he says, and he rides the pony at it without saddle or bridle, and over he goes, never lays a toe on it, and Spondulix was frighted to come at it. And we offered to jump Spondulix for a hundred quid any time. And I went to the stooards and I offered to back the pony to run any horse on the ground two miles over as many fences as they could put up in the distance, and the bigger the better; and Jim, he offered to fight as many of the stooards as could get into a room with him. And even then they wouldn't give us the prize — a man can't even get fair play at a country show. But what I wanted to tell you about was the way we almost got took down afterwards. By gum, it was a near thing!

'We went down from the show to the pub, and there was a lot o' toffs at the pub was bettin' Jim a pound here and a pound there that he wouldn't ride the pony at this fence and at that fence, and Jim picked up a few quid jumpin' 'em easy, for most of the fences weren't no more than six foot six high and, of course, that was like drinkin' tea to the pony. And at last one cove he points to a big palin' fence, and he says; "I'll bet you a fiver your horse won't get over that one safely." Well, of course, it was a fair-sized fence, being seven feet solid palin's, but we knew the pony could do it all right, and Jim wheels round to go at it. And just as he sails at it, I runs up to the fence and pulls myself up with my hands and looks over, and there was a great gully the other side a hundred feet deep and all rocks and stones. So I yelled out at Jim to stop, but it was too late, for he had set the pony going, and once that pony went at a fence you couldn't stop him with a block and tackle. And the pony rose over the fence, and when Jim saw what was the other side, what do you think he did! Why, he turned the pony round in the air, and came back again to the same side he started from! My oath, it astonished those toffs. You see, they thought they would take us down about getting over safely, but they had to pay up because he went over the fence and back again as safe as a church. Did you say Jim must have been a good rider—well, not too bad, but that was nothin' to—hello, here comes the boss; I must be off. So long!'

Bulletin, 3 April 1897.

CYCLING 600 MILES TO ATTEND A TEST

H.C.A. Harrison, one of the early exponents of Australian Rules football, liked to set himself a challenge. In 1896, at the age of sixty-two, he rode from Melbourne to Sydney in the hottest part of the year to attend a Test match.

Two years after my retirement, I decided to work off my superfluous energy by riding to Sydney on my bicycle. The last Test match between the Australians and the English Eleven, captained by Stoddart, was to take place there in February, 1896, and I timed myself to arrive for it, thus travelling in the very hottest season of the year. The journey took me nine and a half days, travelling on an average of sixty-three miles a day. I followed the old Sydney Road, which I had not travelled over since my babyhood, and then under very different circumstances. Instead of a rough track through the bush, there was a hard metalled road a good part of the way, and instead of camping in tents or waggons on the way-side every night, I was able to put up at some quite comfortable inns. Instead of being on my guard against attacks by blacks, all I saw of them were two poor old fellows from a neighbouring mission station, whom I met while sitting on the verandah of a hotel, where I happened to be lunching, about a hundred miles from Sydney, and with whom I had a long and friendly 'yabber'.

I shouted them drinks in memory of old times, and, before I left, they presented me with a dirty scrap of paper, requesting me to write something down at their dictation, in their own language. This I did phonetically, much to their apparent satisfaction. I then, naturally, asked for a translation, which they frankly and gleefully gave: 'Landlord, give Jackie and Tommy another drink!'

I passed through Albury, calling on a few relatives and old friends there, and then on through Germanton, Goulburn, Moss Vale, and Picton. It was the first time I had revisited the place of my birth, and I received the kindest of welcomes from John Antill, (eldest son of the late Major) and all at Jarvisfield. I did not stay longer than a few hours, as I had to hurry on to be in time for the match. Picton is about sixty miles from Sydney, and I felt, on leaving there, that my effort was practically over. But, strange to say, I had my first accident after negotiating the (then) difficult road over Razorback. I ran into a stump and twisted the pedal just before reaching Minto. Fortunately an obliging blacksmith was able to straighten it out for me. The bicycle, by the way, was an Elswick, very strongly and solidly built, with rubber tyres, but had no free wheel at that time. I afterwards had one put on.

I stayed the night at Minto, with my sister, Mrs Ohlfsen Bagge, who was living there at the time.

On arriving at Strathfield I left the bicycle to be repaired. At about 8 o'clock in the evening, I took a tram into Sydney, and put up at the Hotel Australia, where the cricketers were. I was greeted with surprise by them all, as they had predicted that I should break down before getting half-way, and be obliged to finish the journey by train. Prince Ranjitsinhji added his congratulations to the others and said, 'I should think, Mr Harrison, that this ride, for a man of your age, must be a world's record'. I have no idea as to that, but I appreciated such praise from so famous an athlete and sportsman.

I think I lost about eight pounds weight on the journey, which was not so much considering the continuous exertion in great heat. But I never felt fitter, and could have continued the ride indefinitely.

Mancini and Hibbins, *Running with the Ball* (1987), pp. 154–5.

'GRACE BEFORE MEAT'

Women's cricket has often been treated as a joke but the Bulletin *had the last laugh at the expense of the men in 1897.*

The Forget-me-nots, lady-cricketers, of Warrnambool played a local team of fat old men the other day. The male eleven did not contain a man under 50 or less than 15 st[one]. The girls won. Grace before meat.

Bulletin, 10 April 1897.

'AS A CHILD I WAS A WEAKLING'

Annette Kellermann began swimming when a child in the 1890s as therapy for her ill health. Overcoming this childhood adversity inspired her to become a champion swimmer.

As a child I was a weakling—in fact an actual cripple—and had to wear painful steel braces on my legs. Such miserable devices only defeat their own ends because they prevent the exercise by which alone strength can be achieved. I could walk only with the greatest difficulty and pain, and for me childish sports were quite impossible. Had it not been for my father's common sense and unusual foresight I should today have been an ill formed cripple. My father, realising that all true development must come from activity, decided that I should learn to swim; for in swimming alone he saw an opportunity for me to gain all-round exercise without bearing my weight on my weakened limbs.

With my shyness and fear born of my weakness, learning to swim was for me a terrible ordeal; but my father persisted and I was taught to swim. No part of the body is wholly independent of the rest. The splendid exercise of swimming built up my vitality and the unused muscles of my weakened limbs partook of the general benefit, so that the horrible steel braces were soon discarded. The early love for the water thus cultivated was never to be lost.

After its original purpose had been achieved I continued through girlhood to be an enthusiastic amateur swimmer. At the age of fifteen I surprised my father by asking his permission to enter a swimming contest, and to his great astonishment I won the race and began my career as a swimmer.

Kellermann, *Physical Beauty* (1918), pp. 83–5.

' 'Ere, Catch Hold Of These, Will Yer?'

The Governor of Victoria, Lord Hopetoun, was both astonished and amused by some of the social customs on Australian race tracks in the 1890s.

The Marquis of Linlithgow, after whom Joe Griffin's colt was named, was a frequent visitor to the Caulfield training tracks— especially at the commencement of the hunting season—while he was Governor of Victoria. During one of these visits Lord Hopetoun (we know him better under that title) had occasion to use an outhouse in the scraping sheds, and had scarcely emerged before a rude little stable-boy made a rough sketch with a piece of chalk of the royal coat-of-arms, and underneath scrawled— 'Patronised by His Excellency the Governor.'

On another occasion Lord Hopetoun wished to school a green hunter, and on inquiring whether he could obtain the services of a professional rider, was referred to a then celebrated cross-country jockey, who was more noted for his horsemanship than for his deportment or neatness of attire. The jockey was seated on a fence, smoking a well-seasoned pipe, when his Lordship rode up and asked him whether he would pop the hunter over a few fences.

'Right oh!' was the off-handed reply, and, shedding his disreputable coat and neckerchief, he thrust them, together with the foul-smelling pipe, into the hands of the astonished Earl (who had by this time dismounted), with, ''Ere, catch hold of these, will yer?'

I shall never forget the look of mingled astonishment and amusement that passed over Lord Hopetoun's gentle face when the garments were thus unceremoniously thrust into his hands. The jockey, quite unconscious of any offence, was quickly in the saddle and away, leaving his Excellency to walk about with the coat over his arm while the jumping was going on.

Griffiths, *Turf and Heath* (1906), pp. 186–7.

THE SHORTEST CRICKET MATCH

When Narbethong played Marysville at Marysville at the turn of the century, the match didn't last long.

On another occasion I took part in that district in what must surely be the shortest cricket match on record. On that occasion Narbethong was to play Marysville at Marysville. The teams were ready to start and the captains had tossed when it was discovered that the only ball had split into two parts. There was no other ball, but a local teacher had an idea that he had seen one of his boys with a ball at the school, so a lad was hoisted up and pushed through the schoolhouse window to search the desks. A small-sized hard rubber ball was found and it was decided to start the game with it, so the match began. The very first ball bowled was slogged by the opening batsman into Stevenson's Creek, beside which a patch of ground had been cleared for the match. The ball sank like a stone and could not be found, and as no other ball could be produced the game ended in a draw.

Mickle, *After the Ball* (1959), p. 27.

JUST ONE BATTING SOCK

H.V. Hordern packed only one cricket sock when he played for a Sydney team against XXII of Eden and Bega at the turn of the century. The locals marvelled.

Sydney Walford organized and captained a fairly strong side to visit Eden and Bega, dairying centres of the far South Coast. A visit by 'The Sydney Cricketers' was quite an event in their lives and we did our best to make it so, both on and off the field.

The good people turned out in their hundreds, some of them riding or driving for miles just to have a look at the invaders of their peace and quiet. They did us well, those dear folks — dreary dinners with long-winded speeches; dances and smoke-concerts, where nearly all the artists insisted on singing 'A Hundred Fathoms Deep', whether they were tenors or basses. They became so fond of us in the end that, unable to bear us out of their sight, *twenty-two* men insisted on playing against us, and *they all fielded*. In the Bega match I made my first hundred, which, with twenty-two stalwarts sprinkled about on every vacant blade of grass, was equivalent, at a conservative estimate, to about five hundred runs.

A rather amusing incident happened in this connection. When packing my clothes I had only put in one cricket sock, and so, perforce, wore a black and a white one. Sitting on the grass with my trousers rolled up, this fact was noticed by one of a dozen small boys who had singled me out for their particular attention — each of our players, by the way, was surrounded by a dozen embryonic dairymen who gazed unblinkingly at their respective hero, as if he were some exhibit in the Milking Shorthorn class. To the small lad's enquiry as to why I wore one black sock and one white, I told him that the black was my batting sock and the white for bowling. This was before I went in to bat and I promptly forgot all about it. On my return, after making my hundred, my twelve admirers had increased to about sixty. If I turned, the sixty turned with me, if I sat down they did the same, *en masse*; and it was in this position that I overheard the following:

'That's the bloke what made a 'undred.'

'Is it?'

'Yairs, an' 'e ony 'ad one bloomin' battin' sock on. Wonder what 'e'd a made if 'e'd 'ad 'em both?' And the delightful part was, it was said in all seriousness.

Hordern, *Googlies* (1932), pp. 27–8.

THE BIGGEST HIT I HAVE EVER SEEN

A giant of a batsman from Manilla, New South Wales, was not content with a huge hit and went off the field to get his heavy bat.

Not a hundred miles from Manilla, New South Wales, an amusing incident happened, and also the biggest hit I have ever seen. I opened the bowling in this particular match. The batsman was a giant of a fellow with a fierce black beard which looked for all the world like a bunch of horsehair, and somewhat resembled the pictures of Ned Kelly, our famous bushranger of bygone days. He had a stance at the wicket like some champion axe-man just about to lower the record. The first ball I sent down was a slow leg-break of quite respectable length and what my horse-haired friend did to it was a shame! He made one terrific lunge and with a sweeping sickle-like movement hit the ball, not only out of the ground, but it went on and on until it looked like a small pea in the ethereal blue. I don't know how far it went, but it took *two men and a boy* to retrieve it. While the ball was doing its comet-like journey to a neighbouring district, Ned Kelly sauntered up the pitch. I managed to gasp out a husky—'Well hit, sir.'

He took not the slightest notice of me, but said to his batting partner:

'I'm going in to get my heavy bat, the bowling's easy.' And off he went—he had plenty of time as the ball was still on its flight.

Hordern, *Googlies* (1932), pp. 19–20.

THE FIRST SURF LIFESAVING
RESUSCITATION

Arthur Lowe recalls his rescue of a fortunate body surfer at Freshwater beach in the early years of body surfing.

Up till the time I had turned 18 years of age we were not troubled very much by other surfers at Freshwater, which was our main Sunday bathing beach. But the day came along during the Xmas period when, having shot a big wave which the others missed, and travelled a long way in to finish up in a big hole between the sandbank and the beach, I had started to swim out again when I heard a voice calling, 'Help! Help!' I stopped swimming to try and find out where it came from. Yes, there it was again. A big man's voice, calling 'Help! Help!' I could not see him, but from the point it seemed to come from he was evidently in the current or channel, as we termed the Rip in those days. And fast going out, as the cry got fainter and fainter. I was hoping some of my mates would turn up, and was beginning to feel a bit dubious about tackling a big surf life saving job alone. And while my bad self was trying to make excuses, my other kept on nagging, 'Coward, coward, go and get him,' and I found myself soon in the channel, and travelling at my top, after him. He was water-logged, and apparently drowned, when I dragged him to the surface, as he was unconscious, and of that blueish appearance the really drowned have. I must get him to the shore, though, I vowed to myself. I trod water for an instant, while I held him up to think how. And the answer came in an instant. Cross the channel with him, as you would a river. For it is a sea river itself, and you will get assistance from the waves, to get him to the shore. I seized him under the armpits, and with both of us on our backs I kicked as both across the channel. Once in the path of the waves, however, I found that to stay in that position all the time was too slow, as the big rushing waves passed over us without taking us any appreciable distance. So I turned us both, before each wave reached us, and reached across his back and seized him under the armpit with my right hand, and jammed his left side against my right, as much as possible, and kicked and stroked with my left arm, so as to get some way on before the wave reached us. I was very exhausted as, simultaneously with reaching the shallows, my mates arrived and took him from me. I said to them, 'I think he's gone, fellows; he has been under a lot before I got to him!' They carried him up the beach to where the sand was dry and warm. And then commenced the oddest, and probably the longest and most successful carrying out of [the] most difficult resuscitation that I have ever witnessed throughout my long association with the Surf Life Saving Movement. It will always rank in my mind as the greatest, also. And we all believed it was the first, as no record is known of any surf life saving resuscitation before then.

Lowe, *Surfing, Surf-shooting, and Surf Life Saving Pioneering* (1958), p. 36.

WHEN THE RED-HOT FAVOURITE WENT 'LAME'

There were many ways that a horse could go lame before a big race; some were not due to natural causes.

Many of the old-time trainers were as full of 'points' as a packet of needles—sharp points, too. Carter once 'looked after' the winner of an important Victorian race, of whom he tells an instructive story. Horse and trainer shall be nameless. After scoring at Melbourne, the animal in question was taken over to Sydney for one of the leading events at Randwick. Carter's charge was a red-hot favorite, and all went well until the night before the race. Just before evening stable-time, the trainer approached Carter and said, 'Here's a sovereign, Joe, you and the other lad can go to the theatre this evening; I'll "do up" the horses.'

Early next morning the trainer was first into the favorite's box, but out he came apparently greatly perturbed. 'Joe,' he exclaimed, '—is lame; he will not be able to run to-day.'

Several prominent racing men who were staying at the same place saw the lame favourite, and all agreed that the case was hopeless, for the near fore leg had filled to the knee. The animal was duly scratched, and even punters who had lost their money, commiserated with owner and trainer. Little these sympathetic people knew that the whole thing was a plant, and that 'the milking process' had been in operation.

Joe Carter was a jockey—a *rara avis*—who would never 'catch hold'; he always rode to win. Knowing the futility of asking Joe to apply the brake, which would, in this particular case, have been a difficult task, so fit was the favourite, other means had to be requisitioned. When the boys had been sent off to the theatre, a silk ligature had been tightly placed on the favourite's leg. This stopped the circulation, and caused the leg to swell. When the crafty trainer removed the ligature in the morning, the cramped condition of the leg caused the animal to walk lame. Of course, the swelling and lameness gradually disappeared, but not before the deception had served its purpose.

Griffiths, *Turf and Heath* (1906), pp. 37–8.

'KEN YER BOWL? . . . THEN 'AVE A OOZLE'

When Crow Flats were at home to the Wattle Wonders a 'frowsy little man' went through the home side in more ways than one.

[An] historic match occurred out at Crow Flat, up north, when the Crow Flats were at home to the Wattle Wonders from a neighbouring shire. When the Wattle Wonders arrived on the ground they were a man short. The Crow Flats couldn't lend them a player because their emergency man was away burying his grandmother. However, a frowsy-looking little man, a stranger, who had wandered across from the local hotel, offered to make up the team. He didn't look much of a cricketer, but he certainly did appear a dangerous man to leave in the vicinity of a barrel of ale. His offer was reluctantly accepted. The match was started.

The Wattle Wonders batted first, and went down like chaff before a drayhorse to the wiles of the Crow Flats' googly bowler. Nine wickets were down for 71, and the Wattle Wonders' stonewaller had increased his score in half an hour from 0 to 1. Then the frowsy-looking little man went in to bat . . . The first ball shaved his off stump, the second sniffed the varnish on his leg stump, the third breathed on the bails, the fourth hit the bat, the fifth went for a fourer, and the sixth for a fiver. After that the frowsy man never looked back. He batted for an hour, and ran up 85 before he got out. The stonewaller had increased his total to 4. The excitement was terrific. The spectator (a stout lady, the publican's wife) fainted. The frowsy-looking little man was hero. The Wattle Wonders were jubilant. The Crow Flats were savage. Then the Crow Flats batted. They got going, and put together 130 for 3 wickets, and every stock bowler was tried. 'Ken yer bowl?' asked the captain desperately of the frowsy-looking little man. 'Some' was the reply. 'Then 'ave a oozle,' said the captain. The first ball from the stranger was a wide, the second a grubber, the third a full toss, the fourth a yorker, the fifth a decent length, and the sixth took a wicket. Then the little man found his length. He went through the Crow Flats like a fire-reel through a poultry farm. He took 7 for 10, and the Wattle Wonders were victorious. There was a sensation. The spectator fainted again. The Crow Flats raised the question whether it could be counted a win, as the stranger wasn't a Wattle Wonder anyway. They accused the Wattle Wonders of importing the stranger from Adelaide, and he might be Clem Hill or Crawford in disguise. A free fight ensued, and three bats were broken through coming into violent contact with heads which no bats were made to withstand. In the confusion the frowsy little man entered the dressing shed, and after taking on a heavy cargo of watches and small change sailed for port unknown without troubling about a bill of lading. It was a historic day at Crow Flat.

Mills, *Square Dinkum* (1917).

A BOWLING ARM IN SPLINTS

Aboriginal fast bowler Jack Marsh went to extraordinary lengths to prove that he was not a 'chucker' in 1900.

Marsh was made a ground bowler at Rushcutter's Bay, and after a period of bowling to the Sydney club's best batsmen at practice was chosen in the club's first grade side. There was something in the flexibility of his bowling arm that enabled him to bowl very easily at exceptional speed. Sydney grade batsmen stamped him as a potential champion. In a trial match between the powerful New South Wales team and a State trial XI at Sydney Cricket Ground in November, 1900, Marsh clean bowled Victor Trumper. This success should have vindicated those who claimed Marsh was a world-beater, but instead it led to trouble. For the umpire at square leg who witnessed Trumper's dismissal, W. Curran, labelled Marsh a chucker and openly said he would no-ball Marsh for it when play resumed next day.

The secretary of the Sydney Club took Marsh to a doctor early the following morning and had Marsh's bowling arm encased in splints and bandages. Marsh arrived at the ground brandishing a medical certificate which said he could not throw the ball with his arm bound up in this way. Curran was at square-leg again when play continued, but despite the bandages and splints Marsh bowled just as fast and still with that easy, fluid hostility. Curran came off at the luncheon interval claiming he had been humiliated and all at the ground agreed that the chucking stigma had been quashed for good by Marsh and his advisers.

Pollard, *Australian Cricket* (1988), p. 724.

Golf's First Published Air Swing

An 'air shot' of Sir John Madden, Lieutenant-Governor of Victoria, achieved considerable publicity in 1901. Madden's miss occurred at the opening of the Royal Melbourne course at Sandringham.

The first 'air shot' recorded by a photographer in Australia and possibly the world was of the Lieutenant-Governor and Chief Justice of Victoria Sir John Madden in 1901 when he attempted to open Royal Melbourne's new course at Sandringham (Vic). His swing was not quite what it should have been and the ball stayed put. The picture was published in the first edition of *The Australian Golfer's Handbook*.

Maclaren, ANZ Golfer's Handbook (1975), p. 147.

Liberating Manly Beach

Archaic laws forbidding daylight surfing existed until 1902, when they were challenged by the editor of the Manly and North Sydney News.

The relaxed atmosphere of the beach and the exhilaration of the surf was something which people in the more tropical climates readily accepted as a wonderful pastime. However, due to the code of ethics and religious attitudes of the Victorian and Edwardian eras, the exposure of any part of the body to the opposite sex, in public, was regarded as something of an offence against decency.

There were scores of bathers who were waiting for something to be done to liberate them from this strange law which allowed them to bathe in the dangerous darkness of morning and night but left them sitting on the beach, fully clothed, just looking at the surf in the blazing heat of day.

The leader of this crusade was a Manly resident William Gocher, editor of a local newspaper the *Manly and North Sydney*

News. On three successive Sundays, in September 1902, he bathed publicly at noon, after having advertised his intention of doing so, with a challenge that he should be arrested and prosecuted as a law breaker. The law, as it was, prevented public bathing between the daylight hours of 6 a.m. and 8 p.m.

By the time the third Sunday arrived public enthusiasm had grown and thousands came to Manly beach to witness his defiance of the regulations. On this third occasion he was arrested and bailed out by a friend Mr Frank Donovan.

Next day Gocher, by request, appeared before Mr Forsby, the Inspector General of Police. Giving an editorial comment in his newspaper afterwards, Gocher said, 'Mr Forsby received me very kindly, with an expression of merriment. I feel sure he had been well posted regarding all happenings at Manly.

'He stated that no magistrate would convict me but men would have to wear neck-to-knee costumes and that the ladies would have to take care not to expose their breasts.

'I thanked him after we had had a long conversation, for granting us the privilege of bathing after the forbidden time, and upon this gentleman the thanks of the community should be bestowed.'

And so the long awaited liberation took place and brought an end to the ridiculous law which prevented bathing during the sunny daylight hours. Manly Council rescinded its by-laws on 2 November 1903.

In an era when train travel was the most efficient and comfortable means of transport, and it was a sheer delight to cross Sydney Harbour in the elegance of the Manly ferries, people from near and far made Manly their weekend rendezvous to enjoy their new found pastime of open surf bathing.

Following the widespread news of Gocher's exploits, people throughout Australia began flocking to their favourite beaches, and surfing, in the general sense of the word, became a national pastime.

Wilson, *Australian Surfing and Surf Life Saving* (1979), pp. 22–3.

TRUMPER'S UNIQUE MEMORIAL

Victor Trumper's big hitting at Redfern Oval, in the 1902–3 season, caused havoc outside the ground.

Back in Australia in 1902–3 in a club game for Paddington at Redfern Oval he played the most phenomenal of all his innings by hitting 22 fives and 39 fours, 266 of a score of 335 compiled in 165 minutes. What today would have been sixes counted five at Redfern then and the hitter of them lost the strike. Trumper hit them from the last balls of overs so he could retain it. While he was batting bowlers on nearby bowling rinks abandoned their play for fear of being maimed and the Chinese proprietors of coster carts sought refuge in safer suburbs. One of Trumper's on-drives broke a window on the second floor of a shoe factory 150 yards from the batting crease. The window was retained in its broken condition for 60 years as a memorial to this mighty stroke.

Whitington, *An Illustrated History of Cricket* (1987), p. 64.

WHEN TRUMPER WENT TO BILLABONG

The match between the Billabong Cricket Club and the Victor Trumper International XI did not follow the anticipated script, at least not according to fiction writer Dal Stivens.

At five minutes to twelve that Wednesday morning Tom Jones the postmaster, the president of the Billabong Cricket Club and the umpire of the big match, was the happiest man in Billabong. By noon he was the saddest.

At five minutes to twelve, too, on that same day, Mallee Mick Sloan was the most popular man in Billabong—as well he might be, our star bat and a good bloke. By noon he was an outcast with all us Billabongites.

What a difference that five minutes made to all of us!

This is how it happened.

When the Billabong Cricket Club arranged for Victor Trumper to bring a team of internationals to Billabong, we Billabongites could talk of nothing else for the six weeks before the big day.

So did our neighbours in Drought Creek, though their talk was different. They said the match should have been on their oval as it was better and that anyway there was sure to be a dust storm. They said we hadn't had a Show that hadn't been ruined by a dust storm for ten years. We had lovely weather for the Show four years ago.

They said, too, we might have a billabong but there hadn't been any water in it since the Lachlan went dry forty years ago. However, we could afford to ignore Drought Creek.

The match took charge of our lives for the next six weeks.

Metho Bill, the town's full-time drunk, swore off the drink and went on the wagon to make sure he would be sober for the match.

Mayor Pook called five special meetings of the Council in three days. The Council decided on a civic reception for the visiting team and declared the big day a universal holiday.

The three bank managers wrote solemn letters to their head offices to seek permission to close under Section 41 of some obscure Act. Permission was granted.

The eight pubkeepers sent off wires to Sydney breweries for extra supplies.

The Billabong Cricket Club committee met every night. For two years we had been asking Lord Mayor Pook to grade the oval and to repair the pavilion. Now suddenly everything was granted.

We couldn't get an insurance policy against a dust storm but to be on the safe side we insured against rain. Our yearly rainfall was ten inches.

Jack Turner, the schoolteacher, who was on the cricket committee said we couldn't expect internationals to field on our oval in its present state—with all respect to the Lord Mayor and the efforts of the Council's grader.

'It's full of gibbers', he pointed out. 'Balls hop up erratically and we must take a national view. What a tragedy—and a rebuke to Billabong—it would be if Victor Trumper was injured and missed the Tests against the Englishmen next year. All Australia would point a finger of scorn at Billabong.'

Jack said he had a remedy, however. He would organise working-bees of school children every afternoon to pick out all the stones.

'It won't do them any harm to miss a few history periods', he said. 'After all, history will be made in Billabong.'

The cricket committee applauded the suggestion. So did everyone else except Bill Reed, the barber, who people said read too many heavy books and had been called 'an agitator' by Mayor Pook.

His kids were sent to school to be educated, he said. They didn't go to pick up stones. And he added that in his opinion it was no wonder Australia was culturally backward because of her people's infantile interest in sport.

However there was a nark even in Eden.

As for the rest of us, we talked and dreamed cricket.

The local team practised nearly every afternoon. Bosses gave them time off.

Out in the bush the interest was just as strong. Swampy Joe Patterson, who hadn't been to town for six years, started breaking in two young horses for the eighty-mile buggy ride.

The eight pubkeepers now began doubling, then trebling, then quadrupling their orders to the breweries in the big smoke, and the breweries wired back: 'Make up your mind. Have you a drought up there?'

All the publicans wired back, it was said, 'We have. Double up again.'

Letters and then wires to Victor Trumper crossed between Sydney and Billabong as the time got near. Tom Jones rubbed his hands as his figures rose and hoped they'd continue so he could ask for two more assistants at the post office and a rise.

The arguments we had picking the final eleven as the big day drew near!

Snowy West, the captain, to our surprise pressed the claims of Alf Tonks. Alf bowled donkey drops. But we saw the light when Snowy said:

'You know what Victor Trumper will do to donkey drops.'

It seemed that every one of us was in the joke except Alf, who turned up at sunrise every morning to bowl to his kids before going off to work in Pook's Emporium.

Other internationals and grade players were in Trumper's team but we didn't take much notice and few of us could remember their names from one cricket committee meeting to another until Tibby Cotter's name was received.

Mallee Mick was seen to go a little pale when Tom Jones, who was president, read out Cotter's name. Not that I blamed Mallee Mick. We had matting wickets and Cotter was the fastest bowler in the world, and I wasn't looking forward to facing him. I tell you we all did a bit of quiet thinking but didn't like to say we had the wind up.

Jack Henderson, who kept the Billabong Arms and batted third wicket down, asked me after the meeting if I knew if Cotter liked whisky.

That was how his mind was working.

However, Les Riley found a way out. The next meeting, he hopped up and said:

'After all this is only a picnic match. I suggest we put double matting down.'

We'd have agreed without any fuss had not Bill Reed, the barber, got up and said:

'Do you want Drought Creek to say we Billabongites are sissies?'

The fun started then. Harry Coffill who was the town's undertaker got up and said:

'Gentlemen, now that you are about to discuss a matter that might concern me, I think I should withdraw.'

And he did.

Anyway most of us had a down on Bill over the spoke he threw into the working-bee, and two mats it was.

Soon after that the big day drew near. Mayor Pook finally got his speech of welcome written with the help of the three parsons and the priest.

The beer arrived. Metho Bill was still sober.

Jones the postmaster and Mayor Pook were chosen as umpires. Tom's wife spent most of the last week before the match starching and pressing his white coat.

As I said before, at five to twelve on the big day he was the happiest man in Billabong and Mallee Mick Sloan the most popular.

By eleven o'clock on the big day the ground was packed. The cockies had come in from miles around in sulkies, buggies and drays. Mayor Pook had got his speeches over and everything was fine—even the weather, although we kept looking at the sky and hoping a dust storm wouldn't blow in off the mallee.

Victor Trumper won the toss and we took the field at ten to twelve.

Snowy threw the ball to Alf and the kids under the scoreboard let out a cheer. Victor Trumper came out twirling his bat and took block. Alf got ready and Mick winked at me.

Tom Jones was umpire at the bowler's end and Mallee Mick was at first slip. Snowy was behind the stumps.

Alf ambled up to the crease and threw up a lolly pop. It lobbed half way. Victor Trumper's bat lifted. You could see that ball already on its way to the boundary.

The ball ran very slowly towards Victor Trumper. He leapt out of his crease. His spiked right boot caught in the double matting and he sprawled across the pitch.

The ball ran up to him, gave a little hop, cleared his body and trickled into the stumps.

The right bail fell off. There was an awful silence. Snowy, quick as a cat, gathered the bail, popped it on innocently and casually.

Then Mallee Mick yells, 'Howzat?'

Tom Jones went pale.

'If you appeal,' he says, 'it's out.'

'I appeal', Mallee Mick says, speaking like a man in a dream.

He reckoned afterwards it wasn't his voice but someone else's, or that if he did speak it must have been nerves.

'Not out', says Tom loudly, but by this time Victor Trumper has got up off the ground and is back at the pavilion, pulling off his gloves.

It wasn't much of a day after that. Victor Trumper's team got themselves out fairly quickly and we got ourselves out very quickly, but it was no go for a second innings by Victor Trumper. At four o'clock a dust storm got up and that was the end.

By five o'clock Metho Bill wasn't the only one shickered. Mayor Pook, Tom Jones, and the whole team except Mallee Mick had joined him. Mallee Mick was probably shickered too but we didn't know because at twelve o'clock he had left the field and gone bush.

A couple of kids had heaved gibbers and a dead cat at him as he made off in Swampy Joe's buggy.

Stivens, *The Demon Bowler and Other Cricket Stories* (1979), pp. 71–7.

ON ONE LEG

Fred Shea of Essendon demonstrated in the early 1900s that injured players can be match-winners.

One final in particular I will never forget. Essendon was playing Carlton, there being no 19th man in those days. A minute after play began, Fred Shea, Essendon's talented flanker, was carried off the field owing to an injured leg, and Essendon was in sore straits. I have never been a believer in playing injured men, and set my face against Shea's reappearance after half-time. Like all footballers of mettle Shea was anxious to reappear, feeling that he had let his side down. It was left for me to decide, and I reluctantly agreed upon his re-entry, on the distinct understanding that he was not to move away from the goal-mouth. It was not that anything was expected of him, but that his mere presence on the field would prevent our opponents from having a loose man. In the dying moments Ernie Cameron broke his leg, and as the game hung in the balance it appeared as if Essendon was doomed. Cameron was a champion, expert in any position, though it was as a rover that he stood head and shoulders above his confreres. As he lay helpless on the ground he exhorted his comrades to see it out and leave him alone, and his advice acted like a tonic, as his mates made one despairing effort for victory. In the stress the Carlton full-back left his post, being sick to death of minding a wounded man, and at the psychological moment the ball was marked by Shea on his own a few yards in front. He steadied himself, gave pressure on his wounded leg to see whether it would stand the strain, kicked the ball, staggered, and fell. The bell rang, and Essendon won the day by a few points. It was his only kick in the match, and it won the premiership. Injured and all, he felt he had redeemed himself. Neither Cameron nor Shea ever played again.

Worrall, *Argus*, 3 October 1936.

'YOU NO-BALL MY GOOD BALLS'

An umpire no-balled an Aboriginal fast bowler, Albert Henry, once too often in 1904 and copped a tongue-lashing.

[Henry's] cricketing career became more inconsistent . . . in terms of not appearing regularly for matches and his bowling form deteriorating. In a club match he was no-balled on several occasions as the umpire considered his deliveries were doubtful. Henry's reaction to this was reported to the Queensland Cricket Association in the following way:

> Mr Henry, when the over was completed, deliberately went over to Umpire Cossart and said words to this effect, viz: 'You . . . you no-ball my good balls and the ones I did throw, you never. You know nothing about cricket'—at the same time shaking his hand in Umpire Cossart's face.

A month's disqualification was imposed on Henry, with bad language being involved as the basis for the sanction.

Blades, *Australian Aborigines, Cricket and Pedestrianism* (1985), p. 83.

'THEY DON'T WEAR ANY—'

A crack women's cricket team in Victoria in 1905 had a secret advantage over its rivals.

Ladies' cricket is booming in Victoria. The form shown by several of the club teams is really surprising, but one eleven in particular invariably triumph over their opponents. The secret of their success came out accidentally the other day. A gentleman who has been a good player himself, having witnessed three matches played by the crack team, said to a lady friend, who plays for one of the other clubs, 'They beat you all badly in fielding! None of you seem to get down to the ball like they do!' 'That's only because they don't wear any—'. Then she stopped and blushed, and finally added, 'I'm sure you don't think they "look" as well in the field as we do?'.

Piesse, The Great Australian Book of Cricket Stories (1982), p. 350.

POSEIDON AND JIMMY AH POON

The champion racehorse Poseidon became a close friend of Chinese market gardener Jimmy Ah Poon.

Poseidon was the idol of racing enthusiasts of his time, but it is doubtful if anyone outside the stable profited as largely from the horse's prowess as did a Chinese market gardener named Jimmy Ah Poon. Jimmy's garden was at Canterbury (NSW) and one of his customers was Mr Ike Earnshaw, trainer of Poseidon. Jimmy became associated with the trainer early in 1906, when he was engaged to supply carrots for Mr Earnshaw's horses. One of the horses to recognise Jimmy's part in providing the delicacy was the three-year-old, Poseidon. In time, the colt came to associate Jimmy with the carrots, and the market gardener's appearance was the signal for the colt to race around his exercise yard, whinnying his pleasure. The two became friends and always Jimmy brought a special quota for the colt.

Little wonder, then, that when Poseidon went out to contest, and win, the mile Welter at Randwick on 8 September 1906, at his first start as a three-year-old, Jimmy Ah Poon had £50 to £10 about his favourite. After Poseidon had won the Hawkesbury Handicap at 9/4 and the AJC Derby at 7/1, Jimmy had built up a bank of £1700.

The story, as told to the author by Mr J.F. Dexter ('Pilot' of *The Referee*) records that Mr Earnshaw, having heard of Jimmy's betting, spent time between the Derby and The Metropolitan talking Jimmy out of putting all his winnings on the colt in the handicap, and so reducing his bet to £700. Poseidon ran second. So to Melbourne, where Poseidon's run of four successes is reported to have grossed Jimmy Ah Poon £34 500, taking his total winnings from the £10 to £35 500.

Mr Dexter told the author more than forty years ago that Mr Earnshaw had been horrified when he heard that Jimmy had laid 4/1 on Poseidon in the Victoria Derby, and then put the 'bank' on the colt for the Melbourne Cup. He blasted the happy Chinese verbally, refused a proffered £500 to buy carrots for Poseidon until he should die and, when Jimmy told him he was 'going home', simply took it that the Chinese was going back to Sydney. Mr Earnshaw neither saw nor heard from Jimmy again, to his certain knowledge, though he was convinced that a parcel of Chinese delicacies that came each Christmas from Hong Kong for some years afterwards could only have come from Jimmy.

Ahern, A *Century of Winners* (1982), p. 142.

CONFRONTING MRS MESSENGER

Annie Messenger, the mother of 'Dally', was influential in the switch of the star player from Rugby Union to Rugby League.

Early in the day on 16 August 1907, Giltinan and Trumper, in company with Arthur Hennessy and Alick Burdon, had visited St Vincent's Hospital to see a prominent Rugby Union player and New South Wales captain, Harold Judd. Judd had a broken leg—the result of a football injury. Since he had received little compensation and was confined to hospital, the group thought they could persuade him to make the changeover to Rugby League. Judd told the men that he did not have the courage to make the break but that in any case they should not be wasting time on him. The player to get was Dally Messenger. Judd's influence had a decisive effect but by now they had become fully aware that they had to confront, not Dally, but Mrs Messenger.

At 7.30 p.m. the two men caught a cab from outside Trumper's shop in Market Street and headed for Double Bay. No doubt, as they rode along, Victor Trumper would have described to Giltinan many of the qualities of character of Annie Messenger.

She received them and offered them a cup of tea, and then Trumper, in suitably colourful terms, explained to her the plight of injured players like Burdon and Judd, the arrogance of the Rugby Union administration, and the necessity for a new code, such as had been started in Great Britain and New Zealand. They made their cash offer of £180 ($360) for the three matches. The discussion continued.

Every report from inside and outside the family was that the money Dally was given was not a factor in the decision, but his mother, no doubt in an effort to protect her son's future, later accepted it. For several hours, Mrs Messenger asked questions and the three speculated about the future.

Dally's mother had always been particularly concerned that her son might receive some permanent injury from football. To this Dally replied that he believed God had given him a special strength. In any case, the thought of permanent injury was the factor which most affected Mrs Messenger and finally influenced her in making her decision. Young Dally, who had kept out of the way, as had his dad, was called in. His mother said she thought he should make the change and he readily acquiesced. Trumper and Giltinan caught a cab back to the city at 11 p.m., elated at their success.

Messenger, *The Master* (1982), pp. 24–5.

'BANNED IN BOSTON'

Annette Kellermann, champion swimmer, was arrested on a Boston Beach in 1907 when she appeared in a one-piece costume. Kellermann was not perturbed by her arrest—indeed, she made the most of the situation.

Her performances in Europe led to a lucrative offer to travel to America for an appearance at the Chicago World's Fair. From there, she went on to New York to study ballet. While success in ballet represented her ultimate ambition, in 1907 she was enticed to perform one, final long-distance swim in Boston Harbor. During training for that race, she arrived one morning at Revere Beach attired in a one-piece boy's racing suit, only to be promptly arrested by the beach inspector for exposing her legs. Apparently, the sight of Kellermann's legs was a bit too much for modest Bostonians to tolerate. 'Banned in Boston', soon to become a popular slogan in the United States, reflected the delicate sensitivities of the good people of that city. Kellermann made the most of it. After some heated argument in court, a compromise was reached and Annette designed the first modern swimsuit for women, 'a tight-fitting jersey knit stockingette which came down to some inches above the knees'.

Being banned in Boston created international headlines and, in the United States at least, Annette was hailed as a heroine—a genuinely modern woman and a champion of women's rights. At about the same time, nearby Harvard University held a much-publicised contest for 'The Body Beautiful'. Annette was invited to enter and promptly won the competition from 3000 other young women. The publicity associated with these two events in Boston greatly enhanced her professional career. The New York Variety Theater offered her a contract for $1500 per week. This, in turn, led to a $4000-a-week contract with Universal Films. The youngster who began swimming in Sydney as a way of getting rid of the braces on her legs had become the world's highest paid variety artist.

Phillips, *Australian Women at the Olympic Games* (1992), pp. 18–19.

SHAMROCK SOLIDARITY

Dan Frawley was sent off by an Irish referee in 1908 but his quick wit saved the situation.

Dan Frawley was as quick with his wit as with his feet. He was also, perhaps, the finest of the early wingmen of Australian Rugby League.

In one match on the Kangaroo tour of England and Wales in 1908, Frawley clashed several times with his opposing winger. Cautioned twice, Frawley let go again with punches and was sent off by the Irish referee. As Frawley passed the referee, he said: 'And a great Irishman you've turned out to be. I never thought I'd see the day when an Irishman would send an Irishman off the field for jobbing an Englishman.'

'And what would your name be?' the referee asked.

'It's Daniel Frawley,' said Dan.

'Well, after thinking it over, Daniel, I think a caution will meet the case,' said the referee. And Frawley stayed on the field.

Lester, *The Story of Australian Rugby League* (1988), p. 50.

FEEDING FRAWLEY

The father of Eastern Suburbs star winger, Dan Frawley, reacted adversely to the crowd comments on his son in the early 1900s.

In a match against South Sydney, Dan Frawley, the star Eastern Suburbs three-quarter of the early years of Rugby League, was playing outside another great, Dally Messenger (the man they dubbed 'The Master'). Messenger, on that day, was trying to do too much himself and rarely passed the ball to Frawley. Upset, the fans began to chant: 'Why don't they feed Frawley?' His father was in the crowd, and eventually the chants of 'Feed Frawley' got on his goat. He turned to the barrackers and shouted: 'I'll have you know I'm his father. And young Dan gets a pound of steak every day except Friday.'

Andrews, *Great Aussie Sports Heroes* (1986), p. 102.

MADAME ISA BELL RUNS IN KNICKERBOCKERS

A professional race for women in Melbourne in 1908 attracted much comment and even controversy. Not unexpectedly, much of the media commentary focused on the costumes of the women rather than their athletic prowess.

The first Australian woman professional runner was Madame Isa Bell (Mrs Isabel Newton in private life), who in 1908 issued a challenge to race any woman for a sizeable wager in Melbourne. That challenge not only shocked Melburnians; people throughout Australia were scandalised to hear of a thirty-seven-year-old mother of five children who was prepared to discard her long dress and compete in a costume similar to that worn by men.

Staid Victorians vehemently opposed this hussy running in knickers for money. However, three women accepted her challenge—Miss Ivy Evans (Melbourne), Mrs F. Drennan (Sydney), and Mrs Ivy Leigh (Adelaide).

Two businessmen agreed to promote the race as the Australian Women's Championship. They selected Miss Ivy Evans to oppose Madame Bell, as she had a backer to wager £50. It was agreed that three match races over 50, 100, and 150 yards would be run. On 1 April 1908, on the South Melbourne Cricket Ground, three thousand people including the premier of Victoria, Sir Thomas Bent, turned up to see the race. Madame Bell wore a blue knickerbocker suit with a white sash and white stockings. The twenty-year-old Miss Evans wore black knickers and a loose jacket with sailor collar. Madame Bell was outclassed; Miss Evans won all three races.

Seeing the potential of women racing in match contests, an astute Melbourne promoter decided to hold a series of matches leading to an Australian championship at the Exhibition Oval. A couple of races were held; then some of the modest interstate champions refused to compete in knickers. However, running in long skirts impeded their movements, and deprived of the spectacle of scantily clad women, the cat-callers and wolf-whistlers stayed away. This brought female competition to a sudden end in Melbourne.

Mason, *Professional Athletics in Australia* (1985), pp. 172–3.

'A HOPELESS SLAUGHTER'

The fight between the black champion, Jack Johnson, and the great white hope, Tommy Burns, created enormous public interest in Sydney in 1908.

It was Boxing Day, 1908, when Jack Johnson, black and weighing 87 kilograms, fought Tommy Burns, white, and 76 kilos. Burns was 27, had fought 52 fights with three losses. Johnson was 30, and had lost three times in 62 bouts. At stake was the heavyweight championship of the world, held by the Canadian, Burns. More than 20 000 people crammed into the open air stadium at Rushcutter's Bay, Sydney, to watch the most famous fight in Australian boxing history.

The fight, black man against white man, was unique. All previous world heavyweight champions, such as John L. Sullivan and James Jeffries, had drawn the colour line, and Burns, too, had been accused of dodging Johnson, the 'coloured champion of the world'. It took Hugh D. McIntosh, the high-profile entrepreneur, to get them together.

'Fast or slow . . . I'm going to win,' declared an aggressive Johnson when he landed in Australia. He had been in Australia 18 months earlier, cocky and confident, and had thrashed a black man, Peter Felix, and then Victorian champion Bill Lang in quick time.

From the moment Johnson arrived, the sporting press and public were obsessed by the fight. Skin colour arguments provided the greatest drama, and there was real venom in the fighters verbal exchanges leading up to the big day.

Racism was rampant. 'Citizens who have never prayed before are supplicating Providence to give the white man a strong right arm with which to belt the coon into oblivion,' wrote one reporter in *Illustrated Sporting*. Sydney has rarely had a day like it. 'People set out before six in the morning,' reported the *Argus*.

When Burns stepped into the ring there was a deafening cheer from 20 000 throats. The bitter antagonism was aggravated before the fight when Johnson refused to fight unless Burns removed bandages he was sporting on his arms. McIntosh held his breath. Suddenly Burns ripped off the bandages, and another deafening cheer rose into the afternoon. It was the end of the cheering.

Johnson, towering over the champion, taunted and teased— and cut his man to ribbons. Author Jack London at ringside wrote: 'The fight? The word is a misnomer. There was no fight. No Armenian massacre would compare with the hopeless slaughter that took place . . . Burns never landed a blow.'

Johnson barraged Burns with fists and taunts. 'Ahh, poor little Tahmmy,' he jeered. 'Don't you know how to fight Tahmmy?' he taunted after knocking Burns down with a crashing uppercut in the first round.

The destruction of Burns lasted 14 rounds, at which point a Dr Maitland spoke to a police inspector as Johnson rained blows on Burns, and knocked him down again. By that time the cries of 'that's enough' from the crowd were insistent.

McIntosh stopped the fight, and declared Johnson the winner on points. Johnson, 'terrible in his insolence' in the words of one reporter, was, in the brutal beating he handed out, a striking symbol of black sporting power. The silenced crowd left within minutes of the handing over of the cheques.

Burns, remarkably, sustained no serious injury. 'I did my best, but Johnson was too big and strong,' he said. There were crude and racist accounts of the bout. Some papers likened the fight to a battle between a man and a beast.

Johnson held his title until 1915, when he succumbed in 26 rounds to the giant Jess Willard in a controversial bout. A famous photo shows him on the canvas, one arm raised over his head as the referee intoned the count.

Boxing authority Nat Fleischer was later to acclaim Johnson as the greatest heavyweight fighter of them all.

Heads and Lester, *200 Years of Australian Sport* (1988), p. 139.

RUM AND LEECHES

A Rugby League player, 'Bullock' Dobbs, finished a game with two black eyes and a damaged ankle. His team-mates' remedy did not improve his condition.

Pat Walsh and 'Bullock' Dobbs, two fine fellows . . . were mates on the 1908 tour, but there was nothing spared when they met when Glebe played Walsh's team in a game at Newcastle soon after the tour. Poor old Bullock finished with two black eyes and a damaged ankle. He looked like going to hospital but he was taken back to the hotel and put to bed there. Alongside the bed was a jug with four leeches in it, the idea being for Bullock to apply them to his eyes if he felt like it. His teammates went to the pictures and when they returned about 11 p.m., they checked the patient's condition—but could find no leeches. 'I drank all the water,' said Bullock, 'I must have swallowed them . . . get a doctor!' The players rushed downstairs to consult the proprietor about how to get a doctor quickly. They explained what had happened, and the publican settled the problem. Whipping out a bottle of rum he said: 'Here, give him this. It'll kill all the leeches in Newcastle!'

Heads, *The Story of the Kangaroos* (1990), pp. 14–15.

A PIECE OF GRANDSTANDING

'Dally' Messenger was not only a good footballer, he was also an eccentric entertainer, as he demonstrated in a match played in 1908.

Messenger was again singled out in this match, not only as a good footballer, but, in line with the Giltinan publicity philosophy, as an eccentric entertainer.

'Veteran', writing for the *Daily Despatch* of that day, details these exploits of Dally as well as an incident involving a brilliant piece of grandstanding. He had already kicked two goals, one of which had been extremely difficult, and his success had excited the crowd. He had also intercepted and gone over the try line just as the whistle blew in a penalty against Runcorn!

This was followed by an amusing incident.

Deane had marked and when Messenger went to take the kick he demanded a new ball. This brought a mixed reaction from the crowd. A mid-field consultation then took place between Messenger, Jolley and Mr Tonge, the referee. All the players had now moved closer to join in the 'stop-work' meeting. Mr Tonge decided that Dally should kick the existing ball and he would order a new one after the kick. Dally, on the half-way line, kicked the old ball well and accurately but it dropped short.

The new ball was then brought on and instead of resuming play Dally took it, put it down in the same spot, and before a stunned referee and players kicked it the same way as he had kicked the old ball. It soared between the posts. Dally had made his point and the crowd were ecstatic. The Kangaroos won the match 9–7.

Messenger, The Master (1982), p. 56.

TALISMAN WORTH 1000 RUNS

Playing in a match at Sydney in the 1908–9 season, batsman Syd Gregory was the recipient of a most unusual talisman from a spectator.

After a delay of 10 minutes on account of rain, the game was resumed. A man from the shilling portion of the ground climbed over the fence and walked to Gregory. Reaching out his hand, he made an obeisance worthy of a Chinese Mandarin. Then he placed at Gregory's feet a huge vegetable marrow, remarking that the customs of various nations in prehistoric and later times was to do homage to heroes by making some small offering. Gregory, who seemed unable to grasp the situation, handed back the trophy. At this the donor looked offended, but he placed it behind the wicket where Gregory was batting, saying, 'While that remains there it will act as a talisman. You will score 1000'. Just then a policeman rushed forward, and the man was soon marched towards the gate.

Piesse, The Great Australian Book of Cricket Stories (1982), pp. 56–7.

HORSES FOR COURSES

A 1910 interstate women's cricket match between NSW and Victoria was a rustic affair.

New South Wales started off very quietly, so quietly in fact, that two draught horses, oblivious that anything out of the ordinary was transpiring in the vicinity, began to browse near the pitch, and were not awakened to a sense of rashness, until a fast ball from Miss Rattigan whizzed past the wicket-keeper, under the skirts of the back-stop, and out of the reach of the second back-stop. Then, startled by the shrill cries of the fields and the screams of the barrackers, the horses tossed up their heels and cantered round the course.

Cashman and Weaver, *Wicket Women* (1991), p. 42.

'RECUMBENT NAKEDNESS IS TOO INDECENT'

The moral dangers of mixed bathing vexed many minds in the first decades of the twentieth century.

As swimming gained a hold on the lives of Sydney's citizens, many battles were fought in council chambers and sparked by fiery oratory from church pulpits.

Alderman Houston told the Randwick Council in the early part of the 20th century that the 'rapture of the lonely short walk, the quiet most essential to residential happiness, was sadly interfered with by surf bathers.

'I can no longer take my daughters for a walk by the waves because the recumbent nakedness is too indecent, the return to nature too pronounced.

'I have no words strong enough to express my condemnation of this form of aquatics; have no sympathy with it; do not hesitate to say that the old order has changed for the worse.

'The value of property is reduced and people are attracted to Coogee whom Coogee would afford to do without.'

There was widespread horror at the thought of the moral dangers facing those who indulged in mixed bathing.

In 1912, a Reverend Adamson spoke at a Methodist conference and was reported in the *Argus* as saying; 'No modest woman can be associated with mixed bathing and no man who respects the opposite sex could take part in it.

'I know arguments will be raised against me. Some excellent men have told me they have been associated with mixed bathing, enjoying it in the company of their daughters and wife.

'But another gentleman told me his wife absolutely refuses to be associated with the practice of mixed bathing. Married women ought to take up a strong position in this matter. If some of them who bathe could hear what is said about them, they would be startled.'

Clarkson, *Lanes of Gold* (1989), p. 13.

A KICK OF A HUNDRED YARDS

Champions such as 'Dally' Messenger produce their best when most needed. Dally's team-mate, Dinny Campbell, recorded the following triumph.

In 1912 Easts were playing Souths on the Agricultural Ground, and like all such games, this one was as keen as mustard.

Early on, with the help of Messenger, I scored between the posts—Easts 5, Souths nil. Darmody of Souths kicked a good goal and then kicked another just before the interval, which left Easts leading 5–4 at half-time.

Soon after resumption Darmody kicked a third goal, Souths 6, Easts 5. Gleeful South supporters were yelling out: 'How do you like it, Dally, being beaten at your own game?'

Dally, not to be daunted, kicked a good goal. Easts 7, Souths, 6. With about fifteen minutes to go, Darmody kicked his fourth goal to lead 8–7. The crowd was ecstatic.

Easts were all over Souths but could not penetrate. Then right on the bell, I broke through, came to Hallett, put the ball over his head. It was a great race between Hallett and myself and the dead ball line. The dead ball line won.

Was that the end? No.

Hallett dropped out from the 25-yard line and Dally, appearing from nowhere, caught the ball and called for a 'mark' a good five yards in his own half and right on the side line. I can still hear Pony Holloway, Dan Frawley and myself moan at his attitude. We wanted him to come round the open side and with a last effort endeavour to score a try. We claimed it was a million to one chance of his finding the goal posts.

As Messenger placed the ball, many people began to jeer and hoot. Because of the mark he had taken the ball back another five yards making 65 yards from the *corner* flag. Even some of his own supporters joined in the jeering at his seemingly high opinion of himself.

With still greater deliberation, he walked slowly back some six or seven yards, stopped, wiped the toe of his right boot on his left leg and with a quick run launched the mighty kick. The jeers were quietening as the ball started to lift across the ground, as the projection increased some gasps were heard, and the crowd went berserk as the ball flew between the posts and landed over the dead ball line, and Easts had won the match.

A kick of a hundred yards! Sure. The South Sydney players helped to carry him off the field. Easts, 9, Souths, 8.

The cheering continued for at least twenty minutes, and many a spectator, still dumbfounded, refused to leave the grounds for hours afterwards.

That was the greatest kick of his amazing career.

Messenger, *The Master* (1982), pp. 86–7.

DEATH OF A STUNT SWIMMER

Stunt swimmer Arthur 'Tums' Cavill was not afraid to flirt with death, but he met his match in the icy waters of Seattle Harbour in 1914.

[Amongst other feats,] Arthur Cavill . . . swam the entrance to San Francisco Harbour. He is believed to be the one who introduced the new crawl stroke to the Americans.

He was born on the night his father failed by only 50 metres to swim the English Channel and was christened Arthur Roland Channel Cavill. Generally he was known as 'Tums'.

By the time he turned 18 he was the NSW 500 and 1000 yards champion but was later disqualified from amateur swimming for pacing an entrant in a professional race on the Nepean.

Cavill later turned professional and was the Australian professional 220 yards champion before moving to the United States to become a coach in Portland, Oregon.

There was a lot of showman in Arthur Cavill. He once swam across the Bay at Tillamouk, Oregon, with his hands and feet tied. Several years later he was tied in a bag and lowered from a bridge into a river near Pittsburgh.

This stunt nearly went horribly wrong. He was bumped against the bridge pylons and the knife he carried, to free himself, cut into his body.

He managed to escape and kept up the hazardous exhibitions.

His luck finally ran out when he agreed to take on a 5000 metre swim across the Seattle Harbour in bitterly cold weather.

After 70 minutes he was dragged from the water a little more than a quarter of a mile from his goal and rushed to hospital but died shortly after.

The newspapers reported the tragedy and commented he had frozen to death in the swirling icy water.

Clarkson, *Lanes of Gold* (1989), p. 24.

A Boy Who Killed A Dove

Arthur Mailey's 'head was in a whirl' when he bowled to his hero Victor Trumper.

Vic, beautifully clad in creamy, loose-fitting but well-tailored flannels, left the pavilion with his bat tucked under his left arm and in the act of donning his gloves. Although slightly pigeon-toed in the left foot he had a springy athletic walk and a tendency to shrug his shoulders every few minutes, a habit I understand he developed through trying to loosen his shirt off his shoulders when it became soaked with sweat during his innings.

Arriving at the wicket, he bent his bat handle almost to a right angle, walked up the pitch, prodded about six yards of it, returned to the batting crease and asked the umpire for 'two legs', took a quick glance in the direction of fine leg, shrugged his shoulders again and took up his stance.

I was called to bowl sooner than I had expected. I suspect now that Harry Goddard changed his mind and decided to put me out of my misery early in the piece.

Did I ever bowl that first ball? I don't remember. My head was in a whirl. I really think I fainted and the secret of the mythical first ball has been kept over all these years to save me embarrassment. If the ball *was* sent down it must have been hit for six, or at least four, because I was awakened from my trance by the thunderous booming Yabba who roared: 'O for a strong arm and a walking stick!'

I do remember the next ball. It was, I imagined, a perfect leg-break. When it left my hand it was singing sweetly like a humming top. The trajectory couldn't have been more graceful if designed by a professor of ballistics. The tremendous leg-spin caused the ball to swing and curve from the off and move in line with the middle and leg stump. Had I bowled this particular ball at any other batsman I would have turned my back early in its flight and listened for the death rattle. However, consistent with my idolization of the champion, I watched his every movement.

He stood poised like a panther ready to spring. Down came his left foot to within a foot of the ball. The bat, swung from well over his shoulders, met the ball just as it fizzed off the pitch, and the next sound I heard was a rapping on the off-side fence.

It was the most beautiful shot I have ever seen . . .

Well, I never expected that ball or any other ball I could produce to get Trumper's wicket. But that being the best ball a bowler of my type could spin into being, I thought that at least Vic might have been forced to play a defensive shot, particularly as I was almost a stranger too and it might have been to his advantage to use discretion rather than valour.

After I had bowled one or two other reasonably good balls without success I found fresh hope in the thought that Trumper had found Bosanquet, creator of the 'wrong 'un' or 'bosie' (which I think a better name), rather puzzling. This left me with one shot in my locker, but if I didn't use it quickly I would be taken out of the firing line. I decided, therefore, to try this most undisciplined and cantankerous creation of the great B.J. Bosanquet—not, as many may think, as a compliment to the inventor but as the gallant farewell, so to speak, of a warrior who refused to surrender until all his ammunition was spent.

Again fortune was on my side in that I bowled the ball I had often dreamed of bowling. As with the leg-break, it had sufficient spin to curve in the air and break considerably after making contact with the pitch. If anything it might have had a little more top-spin, which would cause it to drop rather suddenly. The sensitivity of a spinning ball against a breeze is governed by the amount of spin imparted, and if a ball bowled at a certain pace drops on a certain spot, one bowled with identical pace but with more top-spin should drop eighteen inches or two feet shorter.

For this reason I thought the difference in the trajectory and ultimate landing of the ball might provide a measure of un-certainty in Trumper's mind. Whilst the ball was in flight this reasoning appeared to be vindicated by Trumper's initial move-ment. As at the beginning of my over he sprang in to attack but did not realize that the ball, being an off-break, was floating away from him and dropping a little quicker. Instead of his left foot being close to the ball it was a foot out of line.

In a split second Vic grasped this and tried to make up the deficiency with a wider swing of the bat. It was then I could see a passageway to the stumps with our 'keeper, Con Hayes, ready to claim his victim. Vic's bat came through like a flash but the ball passed between his bat and legs, missed the leg stump by a fraction, and the bails were whipped off with the great batsman at least two yards out of his ground.

Vic had made no attempt to scramble back. He knew the ball had beaten him and was prepared to pay the penalty, and although he had little chance of regaining his crease on this occasion I think he would have acted similarly if his back foot had been only an inch from safety.

As he walked past me he smiled, patted the back of his bat and said, 'It was too good for me.'

There was no triumph in me as I watched the receding figure. I felt like a boy who had killed a dove.

Mailey, *10 for 66 and all that* (1958), pp. 35–7.

THE RORKE'S DRIFT TEST

With three men out of action it seemed impossible for Great Britain's Rugby League team to hold on to a 9–0 half-time lead against Australia at the Sydney Cricket Ground in 1914, but the visitors won the celebrated Rorke's Drift Test 14–6. Great Britain's captain, Harold Wagstaff, told this story in his memoirs.

My first memory of the day on which that match, which came to be known as the Rorke's Drift Test, was played has to do with the fighting speech of our manager, Mr J. Clifford, who was so upset about the way in which arrangements for the match had been rushed through behind his back.

He called the men who were playing that afternoon into a room at the hotel and outlined the whole story of the revision of the fixture. Then he said that he expected every one of us to play as we had never played before. "You are playing in a game of football this afternoon," he told us, "but more than that you are playing for England and more, even, you are playing Right versus Wrong. You will win because you have to win. Don't forget that message from home: England expects every man to do his duty."

The men in my team were moved. I was impressed and thrilled as never before by a speech. You could see our fellows clenching their fists as Mr Clifford spoke.

We were prepared to go all out when we went on to that field, but before there had been a scrum Frank Williams on the wing twisted a leg. We took "Chick" Johnson out of the pack to help Williams on the wing.

We managed to lead 9–3 at half-time; Percy Coldrick scored a try and Alf Wood had kicked three goals. Immediately we started the second half Douglas Clark smashed his collarbone. He had broken a thumb in the first half and it had been bandaged tightly so that he could continue.

Early in the second half Clark got a pass and went racing clear, it seemed, for the line but "Pony" Halloway challenged him. Douglas put his hand out to push Halloway off then remembered his broken thumb. He withdrew the hand and went in to give Halloway the shoulder, but "Pony" stalled and Clark, unable to regain his balance, fell on the shoulder and the collarbone went.

Clark had the shoulder strapped and twice made efforts to return to the game, but in the end had to realise it was impossible for him to carry on. There were tears in his eyes as he left the field for the last time.

Frank Williams hurt his leg again and had to go off and we were left with 11 men. Then Billy Hall was carried off with concussion—he received the injury when he went down on the ball—and we had 10 men to face 13.

Ten men and 30 minutes to go! But never had I nine such men with me on a football field as I had that day. We were in our own half all the time and most of it seemed to be on our own line. But we stuck it. Our forwards gave their all. In the scrums the remnants of the pack that was left did its job and in the loose the men who had been brought out tackled as fiercely and finely as the backs did. As often happens in such circumstances, we continued to win the ball from the scrums. Holland, Ramsdale and Chilcott were heroes.

There were 20 minutes left when I managed to cut through when we were defending as usual, and going to John Johnson's wing I gave him the ball with only fullback Hallett to beat. "Chick", a forward on the wing, went away with it, but then none of us dreamt that we were to witness the scoring of as wonderful a try as Test football will ever produce. A few yards from Hallett, Johnson put the ball on the ground and began to dribble it. He had half the length of the field to go but he did it. And the ball never left his toes. It might have been tied by a piece of string to his feet so perfectly did he control it. No soccer international could have dribbled the ball better than did Johnson on the Sydney Cricket Ground that afternoon.

Alf Wood kicked the goal and there we were 14–3. Billy Hall recovered and came back for the last 10 minutes to help us in a defence that was successful until the last few minutes when Sid Deane scored Australia's second try to make it 14–6.

But the victory was ours and the Australian crowd gave us full credit for it. They swung around to our side in the second half and they were with us to the end, cheering us on in inspiring fashion. When the final whistle sounded we were done. We had gone to the last gasp and were just about finished.

Greenwood, *Australian Rugby League's Greatest Games* (1978), pp. 126–7.

DON'T COME HERE WITH YOUR SYDNEY TRICKS

A cricket umpire in a New South Wales country town was quick to justify a dubious decision.

While playing in a country town in New South Wales my brother's batting partner hit an easy two-er; when the second run had been completed he stood with both feet outside, but with his bat inside the crease. The ball was returned hard to the wicket-keeper who took it smartly and knocked the three stumps out of the ground. 'How's that?' he yelled—'Out,' said the umpire. The decision being so obviously wrong my brother turned and asked, 'What am I out for?' The umpire heatedly replied, 'You're out because you didn't have both feet inside the crease and don't come up here with any of your Sydney tricks.'

Noble, *The Game's the Thing* (1926), p. 244.

DUKE KAHANAMOKU'S
'FLOATING HUNK OF TIMBER'

The locals at Sydney's Freshwater Beach were enormously impressed by the feats of the famous Hawaiian Olympian, Duke Kahanamoku, on a nine foot long sugar pine board in 1915.

Snow McAlister, a veteran boardrider himself, now living in retirement at Pittwater Road, Manly, has the story:

'The famous Hawaiian Olympian Duke Kahanamoku who was the world's freestyle sprint champion was invited to Sydney for competition in the State titles at the old Domain Baths. On 2 January 1915 he won the 100 yards in the record time of 53 and four-fifths seconds.

'Duke's introduction of surfboard riding occurred at Freshwater Beach on 15 January 1915. He saw a good surf running so he decided to have a nine feet long sugar pine board made for him by a Sydney timber yard. At the time he was staying at the "Boomerang" camp at Freshwater and Donald McIntyre, an SLSA official and a member of that camp, encouraged Duke to give an exhibition.

'He eventually did and staggered the locals when he approached the water's edge. There was a boat and crew waiting to take the board out beyond the break. They had no idea how he was going to get this floating hunk of timber out to sea. He declined the boat crew's offer, laid on the board and paddled it out beyond the break.

'The good surf on the day allowed Duke to angle ride, standing up, across the bay. He continued to enjoy himself for over an hour and spectators and lifesavers had never seen a surfboard ridden before. All he was doing was riding the same way as he would back home at Waikiki.

'Duke eventually came ashore and asked Don McIntyre for a girl to ride a few waves, tandem style, with him. A splendid young 16-year-old body surfer, Isabel Letham, was told by McIntyre to swim out to Duke and then she and Duke amazed the crowd by riding the surfboard tandem style.

'After a half hour of display they returned to the beach and Duke and Isabel were cheered and clapped as they made their way to the clubhouse.'

Galton, *Gladiators of the Surf* (1984), p. 25.

'I HAVE SEEN SOME TERRIBLE SIGHTS'

Les Darcy, champion boxer, was renowned for his clean living. A 1917 letter to his friend and mentor, Father Coady of Maitland, suggests that there were plenty of temptations in America.

Now a word about how I have been living Father, and am not telling you this to make you think I am any different from ever I was but we arrived on 23rd and I went to Holy Communion on New Year's Day and I have been going about every month since and saying my prayers every day, on the Burlesque shows, thats where all the fighters and wrestlers fall, well we never had one night out late as soon as the show was over we went straight home to bed, I haven't been to a cabaret or dance since with Rickard the first night of arrival, there is a caberet in every restaurant but I mean danced or had anything to do with anyone belonging to them, up at Goshen we got bed at 8 p.m. here we can do the same. You can rest assured Father that I will be alright and nothing will happen to me. I have seen some terrible sights since I have been here Frank Gotch the greatest wrestler in the world ever saw a wreck now result Burlesque girls, gay life there is a fellow knocking around here in the last stages of syphlis he presses a hole in his leg with his finger and takes his finger away the hole stays there a wreck and cripple. There is no danger of me falling for that stuff.

Corris, *Lords of the Ring* (1980), p. 62.

'HOUNDED' TO DEATH

There was an outpouring of grief at Les Darcy's funeral in Maitland, New South Wales, in 1917. Darcy died in America at the age of twenty-two. Many believed him to be a casualty of the conscription debate, as he had stowed away to America on the eve of the conscription referendum in 1916.

From an early hour on the Sunday morning motor cars and every other kind of vehicle available were bringing country people to Maitland. After the arrival of the special trains from Sydney, Newcastle and the coalfields, East and West Maitland were crowded with people.

The whole of the line of route from the Darcy home (where the body had been removed) to the cemetery, nearly three miles away, was lined with spectators. The funeral moved off, headed by the mounted police, with the Maitland Federal Band and Singleton Band playing the Funeral March.

Nearly every organisation in the Hunter District, both sporting and administrative, was represented, and many prominent visitors were present from all over the State, including a great number of boxers, champions of the past and present. Upwards of 700 000 people lined the route to the cemetery that day.

Such a sight will probably never be seen in Maitland again.

The procession itself was over two miles long. As the funeral passed on its way all windows, balconies and other places of vantage were filled. There was a great crowd at every street crossing and on every vacant piece of land, while all hilltops were crowded.

On arrival at the graveyard, there were 4000 or more waiting for the last scene, which was a very pathetic one, and there were many outside of the family circle whose eyes grew dim as the seal was placed on the tomb.

Before the coffin was lowered into the tomb forever, the Very Rev. Father F. O'Gorman, P.P., said:

This is the first time I have ever spoken in a cemetery, and in all human probability it will be the last.

If my feeble voice could reach over this vast concourse of people, every hand would go up when I asked, 'Are you glad the remains of Les Darcy are at home, and that the land that gave him birth will hold him forever to her breast?' It will always be a pleasant recollection for the rest of my life that I had something to do in bringing this about. There never has been in Australia a similar demonstration of sympathy and respect. The hand of providence is plainly visible in all this affair.

Les Darcy, had you gone on and succeeded in the great future that was before you, you might not have had this glorious death, and to us that would make all the difference. Before the grave closes on you forever I say in your name we forgive those who hounded you to death. And may we learn some of the lessons of your life.

Ferry, *The Life Story of Les Darcy* (1937), p. 8.

'HE'S A BLOOMIN' HUMMER'

When M.A. Noble was the sole cricket selector for New South Wales he received advice from all quarters.

When I was sole selector for New South Wales—a position I hope no individual will ever be asked to hold again—people used to come to me with all sorts of ideas and suggestions for strengthening the State team. One in particular I shall never forget. The gentleman shall remain unnamed, but as he was then one of the best bowlers for the old Osborne Club, I thought his views would be worth listening to. All excitement, he whispered:

'Look here, Mr Noble, I've found a bloomin' hummer.'

'What's that?' I said, not understanding what he was referring to.

He repeated the remark in a louder tone, and added, 'I tell you, he's a bloomin' hummer.'

Although quite used to peculiar expressions, this one beat me, and I began to wonder what on earth was coming.

'He's a bloomin' hummer,' he repeated.

'Yes; but what's a bloomin' hummer?' I asked.

'Oh,' he replied, 'I've found a really good bowler.'

I was immediately all ears. 'Where is he?' I inquired.

'Well, he only plays junior cricket, but you can take it from me that he is a bloomin' hummer.'

'No doubt, but what sort of a bowler is he?' I asked.

'Oh, he's a beauty.'

'Fast or slow?'

'Oh, fast, very fast.'

'And what does he do?'

'I don't know where he works, but I can find out.'

'I don't mean how does he earn his living. What can he do with the ball?'

'Well, he breaks nearly a foot each way.'

'What?' I astonishedly asked, 'a foot each way, at a fast pace?'

'Yes,' came the quick reply; 'he breaks when bowling at his top speed. He's a regular bloomin' hummer.'

Anxious for further information I asked how he bowled and was informed that the prospective world-beater had a beautiful action right over the shoulder.

'But which way does he bowl?' I persisted.

'Oh, round the wicket; always round the wicket,' came the ready response.

'Is he a right- or a left-hander?' I asked.

This query proved a sudden staggerer, for the enthusiastic cricketer scratched his head and, in deep thought, replied:

'Well, to tell you the truth, I don't exactly know whether he bowls left- or right-handed, but you come out and have a look at him in harness. He's a bloomin' hummer; take my tip for it.' Then I collapsed.

Noble, *The Game's the Thing* (1926), pp. 237–8.

PICKED FOR AUSTRALIA

As Arthur Mailey discovered in 1920, Test cricket selection in Australia was quite an ordeal.

Having become more or less a regular member of the New South Wales team after the first World War, I was conscious that my fortunes were definitely on the upgrade. It was in the early summer of 1920 that I took my next step forward.

I had risen to the rank of water meter cleaner, a job I feel was sponsored by a cricket-loving foreman, who regarded a complimentary ticket to the Sydney Cricket Ground as a just reward for one who could close his eyes to the deficiencies of meter cleaners.

The MCC team skippered by Johnny Douglas had just arrived in Australia and was cleaning up the southern states.

The scene shifts to a coolabah tree near a suburban fowl-house. I sat under its branches cleaning a water meter. Cricket was in the air and Australia's team for the first Test was about to be chosen. As I unloosened the bolts of that meter I allowed myself to wonder whether I had an outside chance of wearing the green cap. A white Orpington which had just produced an egg chuckled as it blinked its way across the yard, while a large Rhode Island rooster threw his beak to the heavens and crowed majestically. Thought-reading is not confined to humans.

I seemed to make little headway with meters that day and was preparing to snatch a quiet nap in the afternoon shade when I heard: 'Piper . . . piper . . . Test team picked. Piper.' I had a few coppers in my pocket and was prepared to spend one for such news even if it meant having to walk one tram section to my home.

I got the paper and deliberately looked at every page but the one on which I knew the Test team would be printed. I was longing to know if I had made the Australian team but had no wish at all to learn that I had been left out. As I went on feverishly turning the pages even the fowls seemed to be jeering at me. Go on, Mailey, you coot. Can't you take it? What a fine Test player you'd make—you're just a bundle of nerves.

I made an effort and slapped the paper open at the fateful page. Although there was a mass of print before my eyes the names of the team hit me as if they were printed in headline size. MAILEY, NSW . . . yes, I was in.

I cannot be sure whether I reassembled the water meter. After all, it was thirty-six years ago. Perhaps the poor old lady in the cottage hasn't had any water since. But I do remember what happened in the tram-car on the way home. All the men on the tram were greedily devouring their papers. I felt I must talk to somebody to convince myself that it wasn't all a dream. Opposite me a big burly chap was reading a racing guide.

'Did you see the team?' I asked.

'Wot team?'

'The Australian Test team. It's just been picked. It's in the papers.'

'Give us a squint,' he demanded.

He ran his eye down the names.

'What do you think of it?' I asked.

'B——lousy. I dunno why the 'ell they picked Mailey.'

I left the tram, the bloke and the paper at the next stop.

Mailey in Buzo, *The Longest Game* (1990), pp. 126–7.

'GIRLS', 'WOMEN' OR 'LADIES'

In a 1920 letter to the Geelong Advertiser, *A.R. Campbell of Melton questioned whether females had the resilience to play three advantage sets in competition tennis.*

Sir,

As an old member and player, I ask your permission to say a word or two about Number 6 on the Programme of the Geelong Lawn Tennis Club's Easter Tournament, the Women's Championship. Why Women's? In my tennis day, the term Lady was used. A lady, according to my dictionary, is a 'woman of refined and gentle manners; a well-bred woman' . . . But that is by the way.

The real purpose of my letter is to protest against what in my opinion is the excessive strain imposed on the contestants in the Women's Singles Championship by requiring the best of three advantage sets in each round thereof. The thing is cruel. It is not tug-of-war, nor yet a go-as-you-please, in which the only qualities that count are strength and endurance . . . As now played . . . the best player is often defeated, and the triumph rests with the toughest specimen. But with girls it is even more marked . . . Not long ago, a leading member of the medical profession in Melbourne issued a warning against making contests for girls needlessly strenuous, and told of the bad effects resulting therefrom.

Geelong Advertiser, 6 March 1920.

THE CANNY LITTLE DIGGER

Prime Minister Billy Hughes hated to lose a golf ball.

Malcolm Fraser, as Prime Minister, had his troubles at Royal Canberra merely trying to hit the ball.

It seems that another Prime Minister, Billy Hughes, never liked losing one.

'The Little Digger' gained a reputation at the club as an indefatigable ball searcher.

In a book published to celebrate Royal Canberra's jubilee in 1979 came this gem about Hughes:

'One of Billy's partners, tired of waiting and searching with him, and having one and then another foursome pass through them, dropped an almost new ball into the rough and shouted, "Here you are, Mr Hughes, here it is!"'

'Billy having examined the ball carefully, replied, "No, that's not it," pocketed it, and resumed his search for another five minutes.'

Ramsay, Golf (1985), p. 49.

A THIRTY-TWO FOOT LEAP

Bill McKay was a popular trainer whose horse Molly eventually became a star attraction.

In the early 1920s there lived in northern Victoria a farmer who had among the horses running on his property a mare known as Molly. The breeding of this rather plain looking mare was somewhat obscure, but not her reputation. Molly had gained a considerable amount of notoriety because of her wildness and her efforts to go to any lengths to avoid being caught. No one had ever laid a hand on Molly. It was not for the want of trying. Not even the high fences on the farmer's horse yards had been able to contain her for long.

With drought conditions not uncommon to the district, the farmer decided upon trying to conserve some of his grass by having the mare shot. It was only the pleading of his wife that had saved Molly from this fate, as the farmer had agreed the mare could go to the first person to catch her. At first it was the neighbours who had taken up the challenge, but after numerous attempts had all ended in failure, Molly's reputation began spreading far and wide throughout the district. By this time the mare had become a source of entertainment for the farmer as Molly met each challenge with every trick in the book, and a few of her own to boot. The farmer made no rules to these 'contests', other than have each of the challengers that now came forward, to make the attempt on their own.

One day a young man came riding up to the homestead leading two spare horses. When the young fellow calmly announced he had come to catch the mare, the farmer's first reaction was to smile broadly at this display of quiet confidence from one not much bigger than a jockey. The stranger certainly lacked the physical strength of most of those who had tried and failed before him. The farmer took the young man to the paddock in which Molly was running in company with other horses. After pointing her out to the newcomer, the farmer took up a vantage point from where he could watch the fun.

He looked on curiously as the young man quietly worked the mare away from the others where he was able to direct her through a gateway into the adjoining paddock that had not long been ploughed. Then, using his three horses as relay mounts, the young man kept after the mare with no effort to catch her. Each time he changed mounts he did so without delay, giving Molly no chance to rest. Up and down and around and around they went over the rough ground. Finally, the mare had had enough, and she stopped running from sheer exhaustion as her tired legs refused to carry her further, her head bent low in defeat, and her sweat-soaked flanks heaving like a giant bellows from having covered so many miles through the ploughed ground.

The farmer's curiosity had given way to admiration as he watched the horseman dismount and slowly approach the mare, speaking quietly and reassuring Molly that everything would soon be right. Calmly he placed a halter around her head and then led her to where the surprised farmer stood. 'Well, I'll be damned,' he spluttered. Remaining true to his word, the farmer opened the gate for Molly and her new owner. The mare was going quietly, but the farmer and the young horseman knew that this had been only the first round, and that other contests between the two were certain to follow. As the farmer bid farewell to the mare and horseman, he asked: 'What did you say your name was again?' The young man drew rein and replied quietly, 'McKay . . . Bill McKay.'

On arriving back at his Boort home with Molly, McKay discovered numerous shot gun pellets in her tough hide, a testimony of earlier attempts to have had the mare shot. Molly responded to McKay's methods, though he discovered she had to be kept boxed for the first months as she could jump her way out of his stock yard with surprising agility. It was this natural ability to jump extraordinary heights that led the horseman to prepare her for a jumping career in the show ring. At this stage the name of Bill McKay was already well established on the show circuit. But his only connection with the sport of trotting was through his brother Jack, who had become private trainer at Inglewood to Jack Isaacs, owner of a number of trotters.

Molly took to show jumping like a duck takes to water. She particularly appeared to enjoy the challenge of the high jump, and her success in tackling the tall timber brought her to the forefront of the various shows. On one visit to the Melbourne Royal Show, Molly became the star attraction when she startled even experienced horsemen with an official leap of 32 feet 10 inches over the water jump for McKay.

Agnew, *Australia's Trotting Heritage* (1977), p. 161.

SHORTEST-EVER TEST BATTING CAREER

It was unfortunate that Mrs Roy Park dropped a ball of wool when her husband, Dr R.L. Park, came to bat in Melbourne in the 1920–21 series. She thus missed her husband's entire Test batting career.

Victorian cricket followers, with whom [Dr R.L. Park] was enormously popular, were outraged when he was left out of the first two Test matches in that summer of 1920–21.

He got his chance in the third Test at the MCG.

He was given a thunderous standing ovation all the way from the players' gate to the crease when he came in with the score at one for 116.

He was out the first ball, clean bowled by Harry Howell.

Again the Victorian crowd rose and cheered him as he began the long walk back to the pavilion. They were still clapping when the next man in reached the wicket.

Such was the popularity of Dr Roy Park.

Australia won the third Test without having to bat again. In the next Test, Park was 12th man. After that he was dropped and never picked again.

In his next Shield match, he made a century against South Australia.

This week, for the first time—and nearly 60 years too late—the story behind Dr Park's momentous Test match duck emerged.

He didn't tell anybody at the time—he didn't let on until years later when he told his son-in-law, Ian Johnson—but Roy Park had not been to bed the night before his Test debut.

He had been called out to a maternity case at Footscray. It was a difficult birth and Dr Park stayed with his patient all night.

'That was typical of the man,' said Mr Johnson, secretary of the Melbourne Cricket Club and one of the bursary's four trustees.

'Not only did he place the welfare of his patient first, but he never told anybody. He didn't make excuses.'

The story goes that Dr Park's wife, who was knitting in the stand, dropped a ball of wool as the bowler ran in. She bent to retrieve it—and missed her husband's only Test innings!

Melbourne *Herald*, 9 June 1979.

No SBW (Skirts-before-wicket)

A match between the lady passengers and an assortment of enthusiastic male cricketers on one voyage between England and the Cape ended in controversy when a dismissal was challenged.

On one voyage to England via the Cape I remember we had many enthusiastic cricketers on board and played many games. Amongst the players on that occasion were a parson, a musician, an actor, and a general who had played an important part in the First World War. The parson was a fine player who had played pennant cricket in Sydney. He was most enthusiastic and led us in games against various sections of the crew. Once we played a match against a team chosen from the lady passengers. The game was played with a tennis ball and the men had to bat with a section of broom-handle. At that time, even at sea, short skirts had not yet come into vogue and it was somewhat of a feat to drive a tennis ball with a broom-handle through a side of long-skirted women spread over a narrow field. The captain of the ladies' team was an actress of high repute. When the general who was acting as umpire gave her out leg-before-wicket she, following in W.G. Grace's footsteps, refused to go as she argued that the ball had not hit her legs but only her skirt, and that there was no skirts-before-wicket rule in cricket as far as she knew. Then the general said that she would have to pull up her skirt, but she told him to be a gentleman. Then she said she would do so if she had good legs, but as she hadn't she wouldn't. Fortunately at that stage the afternoon tea gong sounded and she fled.

Mickle, *After the Ball* (1959), p. 31.

A Bronzed Hunk

Sydney swimming fans were captivated by the celebrated deeds of Andrew 'Boy' Charlton in the 1920s.

On January 12, 1924, 6500 fans squeezed into Sydney's old Domain Baths to see a bronzed hunk of an Australian teenager, Andrew 'Boy' Charlton race Sweden's record-smasher Arne Borg over 600 metres. With spectators packed like sardines, thousands more were turned away.

Borg, 22, was the sensation of world swimming, holder of most of the world records from 400 metres up to 1500 metres. He was known as the 'Electric Flash'.

Charlton was 16, tall and tanned, a real Sydney beach boy who developed tremendous arm power ploughing through the surf at Queenscliff. Before the race the Swede was icy-cool: 'I expect to beat Charlton easily, by 15 to 20 yards,' he said. 'I'll do my best,' said Charlton.

It was a magnificent and thrilling race. Borg led early, but Charlton pegged him back to draw level at the half-way mark. Urged on by 6500 voices, Charlton was unstoppable. He passed Borg by the 250 yards turn, and powered right away to win clearly in a world record equalling time of 5 minutes, 11⁴/₅ seconds. Pandemonium erupted as Borg, gracious in defeat, rowed Charlton up and down the pool in an old boat.

Five days later Charlton again beat Borg, this time over 800 metres. Their careers were linked forever after those two momentous races. Borg was there at the Paris Olympics in 1924 to chase Charlton home in the 1500 metres.

Charlton carried many nicknames: He was the 'Flying Fish', the 'Jazz Age Hero', and the 'Flapper's Idol'. He was also called the greatest swimmer the world had seen.

Arne Borg trained relentlessly in the years between the Olympics, determined that he would beat Charlton. And he did, winning the 1500 metres at Amsterdam, 1928.

'Boy' Charlton's tally in three Olympics (Paris, Amsterdam, Los Angeles in 1932) was one gold, two silver and one bronze. After Los Angeles he retired from swimming to work a 4860 hectare grazing property near Goulburn. A quiet, modest man, he shunned the spotlight. 'That is something that happened in my life and is finished and done with,' he would say of his time in swimming.

In 1968 he was enticed to Sydney to be guest of honour at the opening ceremony of a new pool to replace the old Domain Baths, scene of his great triumph. The pool could, of course, have only one name, 'The Andrew "Boy" Charlton Baths . . .' recalling a great swimmer and a wonderful day.

Heads and Lester, *200 Years of Australian Sport* (1988), p. 172.

'UP THERE CAZALY!'

This famous phrase from Australian Rules Football, immortalised in Michael Brady's 1979 song, was the battle cry for Australian soldiers during the Second World War.

The cry will live as long as the game of Aussie Rules: 'Up there Cazaly!' It's a call that transcends sport . . . a part of the Australian psyche, still heard today, as it was in Melbourne in the 1920s. Its subject, Roy Cazaly, — 'Cazza' as he was affectionately known, was born in Melbourne in 1896, the 10th and youngest child of English-born James Cazaly and his wife Elizabeth.

As a young man Roy Cazaly was obsessed by physical fitness: he was a teetotaller and non-smoker, and followed a strict diet. He came to big-time football with St Kilda as a 15-year-old, a tough-fibred kid with natural ability and an uncanny football brain. Cazaly stayed 11 seasons with St Kilda, then switched to South Melbourne. It was there that the cry that immortalised his name evolved.

Cazaly developed a wonderful understanding with rover Mark 'Napper' Tandy and with 'Skeeter' Fleiter. The three became known as the 'Terrible Trio'. Fleiter's constant cry of 'Up there Cazaly' was soon taken up by the crowds. Magnificent photos remain of Cazaly's sensational leaps to pull down marks. Cazaly said he had learned the art of breathing correctly from his father, and whenever he leaped for a mark he would take a deep breath which helped him to 'fly'.

The cry that was born at South Melbourne became part of the Australian idiom. In the battle zones of the Middle East during World War II, 'Up there Cazaly!' was the yell that accompanied Victorian Battalions into action. It was used as a password by Australian soldiers in the leafy darkness of the New Guinea jungles.

Roy Cazaly left South Melbourne after five seasons, and began a long and successful pilgrimage into coaching, where he imposed his own tough formula of physical fitness and discipline on countless young players. He was a wonderful testimony to his own beliefs on fitness and lifestyle. In 1951, at the age of 55 he played a full match in Hobart, and did so effortlessly.

Heads and Lester, *200 Years of Australian Sport* (1988), p. 163.

BELTING BOYS IN BAGS

Stadiums Limited, which had a monopoly on all aspects of boxing, condoned some brutal rituals.

In the 1920s at Rushcutters Bay, the Thursday afternoon weigh-ins and medical inspections were enlivened by 'blind' fights between boxing-mad youngsters. Fred Imber, later a sporting journalist, recalled his days as a peanut-seller and aspiring fighter without rancour:

About eight boys at a time were bundled into the ring, equipped with gloves and a chaff bag which was pulled over the head and tied tightly around the neck. The idea was for the blind boys to walk out at the bell and let fly when they bumped. Stadium officials would poke them with prop sticks and broom handles and laugh their heads off when they started throwing punches.

On one occasion nine of us shaped, chaff bags and all. In about three minutes eight of us were flattened, and some were right out to it.

The reward for these 'contests' was a free ticket to the bleachers. Interestingly, newspaper reports of similar 'blindfold bouts' being conducted in Queensland in 1978 brought a storm of protest. The 'blind' fights between the peanut and program sellers in the 1920s must have been common knowledge to journalists and sportsmen of the day, but they were accepted as an amusement.

Corris, *Lords of the Ring* (1980), pp. 103–4.

'WORLD'S HARDEST WICKET'

A salesman made a remarkably accurate prediction about the future success of Don Bradman.

A couple of years ago I was in a sports depot in Sydney and a wiry sunburnt young bush chap came in, and started looking over the goods. I've had so much to do with athletes I can generally pick a man fairly well, and I said to the salesman, 'That's a hard-looking young fellow and he's very light on his feet. I should say he had done some boxing or was accustomed to riding rough horses. They have to be pretty active for that game.'

So the salesman laughed and said, 'No, you're a bit out. But he's a somebody all the same.'

I said, 'Who is he?'

'Oh,' he said, 'that's Don Bradman, this new boy wonder cricketer they have just discovered.'

You see he was only Don Bradman, the Bowral boy then, and hadn't been to England. He's Mr Bradman now, and many congratulations to him.

So the salesman brought the boy over—he seemed only a boy to me—and after we had exchanged a few remarks, Bradman went out. So then I asked the inevitable question: I said, 'How good is this fellow? Is he going to be as good as Trumper?'

Now, the salesman had been a first-class cricketer himself and he gave me what I consider a very clear summing up of the two men.

'Well,' he said, 'when Trumper got onto good wickets he developed a beautiful free style, like a golfer that plays a full swing with a good follow-through. He trusted the ball to come true off the wicket, and if it bumped, or shot, or kicked, he might be apt to get out. But this Bradman takes nothing on trust. Even after he has got onto good wickets, he won't trust the ball a foot, and he watches every ball till the last moment before he hits it. His eye is so good and his movements are so quick that he can hit a ball to the fence without any swing at all. That makes him look a bit rough in style compared with Trumper, and he hits across his wicket a lot. They say that's a fatal thing to do, but I never saw him miss one of them.'

So I said, 'You wouldn't remember W.G. Grace, can you remember Ranjitsinhji?'

'Yes,' he said, 'Ranji had a beautiful style, but he was a bit fond of playing to the gallery. If he'd liked to stonewall, they'd never have got him out, but he used to do exhibition shots—late cuts, and tricky little leg glances—and out he'd go. There's no exhibition shots about this Bradman.'

I said, 'How will he get on in England? Will he handle the English wickets?'

'Yes,' he said, 'don't you worry about him on English wickets. He'd play on a treacle wicket or on a corrugated iron wicket. He's used to kerosene tin wickets up there at Bowral. He'll never be the world's most artistic cricketer, but he'll be the world's hardest wicket to get.'

Well, it's not often that a prediction works out as well as that, is it?

Paterson, *Songs of the Pen* (1983), pp. 486–7.

Borotra Knocked Out By A Volley

In the Inter-Zone final of the Davis Cup in 1925, Australian Gerald Patterson demonstrated his ability literally to flatten an opponent.

For Australia the story ended with France in a match played at Forest Hills, Patterson and Anderson shouldering the singles burden, and the tried and true pair, Patterson and Hawkes, taking over when the first day's singles stood at one-all. The doubles, before a huge gallery, was very close. And it was memorable for its centre-court drama. When the match was well advanced, the burly Patterson, stationed at the net, intercepted a return from La Coste. His cracking volley hit Borotra on the temple, felling him. But Borotra was known for his pranks on the court. Patterson, hoping his unintentional shot had done no harm, proceeded to test the situation. Wire-photo services around the world carried a picture of the centre-court consternation, Hawkes and La Coste advancing concerned from the ends of the court, linesmen and referee starting from their chairs and Patterson leaning over the net to prod Borotra with his racket for signs of life. But Borotra was temporarily unconscious. In fact, he was 'out' for several minutes. Yet he recovered after a spell, and the Frenchmen fought on to wrest the doubles from Australia at 10–8 in the fifth set.

Kinross-Smith, The Sweet Spot (1982), pp. 97–8.

Mighty Manfred

In the 1925 AJC Derby, the renowned racehorse, Manfred, gave his rivals a huge advantage at the start. This made his win even more dramatic.

The Manfred legend grows with each year of its telling. But it happened, all right. More than 75 000 people were at Sydney's

Randwick on the day in 1925 that the mighty three-year-old missed the start in the AJC Derby by half a furlong . . . and won! One experienced 'clocker' reported that Manfred stood at the post for seven seconds before moving off in pursuit of the field.

Manfred went out a hot favourite for the Derby, 2 to 1 on, in a small field of seven. When the barrier strands flew up, the colt, to the alarm of punters and jockey Billy Duncan, stood stock-still. Clerk of the course Tom Luckey reacted quickly. He galloped his pony full bore across to Manfred, and cracked his stockwhip. His was a swift and brilliant piece of horsemanship — but Manfred was still giving his rivals at least 101 metres start.

Passing the nine furlongs post Manfred was still 45 metres behind the leader, Avron. At the mile favourite backers started to swallow nervously as he edged up to 22.5 metres behind. By the home turn Manfred was up sharing the lead with 3 to 1 second favourite, Amounis. On the turn he raced wide — and Amounis dashed clear. But, hard ridden by Duncan, Manfred refused to concede and a mighty roar erupted as he joined the lead at the leger — and then raced clear!

Manfred won the Derby by a length and a half, running the 2.4 kilometres in 2.35, which meant that his *actual* time was a brilliant 2.28. A muddling pace helped him. But there could be no accusations that the horses he beat in that mighty performance were below standard. Amounis, which finished fourth, won a Caulfield Cup, two Epsom Handicaps and a Futurity Stakes, with 10.4. Third place getter Tibbie, ran a place in the Sydney Cup.

Manfred went on to win the Victoria Derby by 12 lengths and then finished second to Windbag in the Melbourne Cup. The following season he won the Caulfield Cup with 59 kilos.

The great Manfred had only one fault — his waywardness. But it was because of it that he has a place in racing history.

Heads and Lester, *200 Years of Australian Sport* (1988), p. 168.

MAILEY IN TAILS

Arthur Mailey was caught arriving at a Test match in 1926 in white tie and tails, but he answered his manager in the best possible way.

There was Mailey himself, arriving for the final Test of the '26 tour still unchanged, in the white tie and tails he had worn to dance all night. As he emerged from his taxi, he bumped into his team's manager, who drew a deep breath. 'Not now,' pleaded Mailey, 'not till after stumps.' He then changed and prayed that Australia would lose the toss, and he would take six wickets. He wouldn't dare take only five: the manager might have had something to say—but there could be nothing to say to a man who'd taken six. He took six (including Hobbs')—and spent the following night dancing.

Batchelor in Mullins and Derriman, *Bat and Pad* (1984), p. 203.

TOO SMALL FOR VFL

For whatever reason, star Aboriginal athlete and Australian Rules footballer, Doug Nicholls, was not accepted at Carlton Football Club.

At 5' 2" (157.5 cm), Nicholls was short, but he was a gifted footballer. As an apprentice horse-team driver, the fifteen-year-old Nicholls appeared as a guest player for local teams as he travelled around southern New South Wales. The tiny fellow became known as the 'flying Abo' in recognition of his ability to leap high to contest marks with players who towered over him. Nonetheless, he also had to rise above the racist taunts from opponents and spectators alike.

In 1925 Nicholls was invited to play on the wing for the Tongala club, which was coached by former Victorian Football League star Leo Stockdale. A talent scout from Carlton spotted

Nicholls and suggested that he try out with the Blues. In 1927 at 16, Nicholls showed extraordinary self-confidence when he set out for Melbourne on the back of a cattle truck to make his mark in the big league. An Aborigine on the main streets of Melbourne was a rare sight in the 1920s and it was even more uncommon in the city's major football clubs. He made it to the Blues' final list, but in the end he was told he was too small for VFL football. Size was not the real issue. The Carlton players had complained about playing alongside an Aborigine and claimed that the young fellow stank.

Harris, *The Proud Champions* (1989), p. 28.

REVIVING NECTAR

Teetotaller Hubert Opperman was persuaded by his father to imbibe a secret brew in 1927. The results were disastrous.

A whisky firm approached me with a lucrative monetary offer to sign a testimonial concerning the uplifting efficacy of their products during strenuous cycling effort. At the same time Tom Carlyon, an astute entrepreneur owner of the Green Mill dance hall, located near Princes Bridge, requested my paid presence when one, Desmond McMinn, was attempting a non-stop 100 hours' dance. While the monetary aspect of the offer from the liquor firm was a lure, I was quite adamant where such stimulants were concerned. My mind automatically back-pedalled into an early incident when, most inexperienced in the ordeals of long distance events, I thought that anyone who had advice to give based on the flimsiest of knowledge were oracles of cycling wisdom. Because of this naive assumption, I had steered into some hazy but educational miles towards the end of the 1921 Bendigo to Melbourne. My father, with the best of paternal intentions, following a half-hour of persuasive discussion influenced me into accepting a sure recipe for rejuvenation during a prolonged event. He wrote mystic symbols on a piece of paper, and said, 'Now take this into the bar of the hotel and ask them to mix it for you, about half-way sip a little at a time and remember, only sip it.' I promised faithfully I would ration this reviving nectar of the sporting gods and requested the mixture at the bar. As a teetotaller I was in strange surroundings but covered embarrassment with youthful cockiness as the barmaid, serving with a Menzian uplift of the eyebrows queried, 'You want this, sonny?' and replied, 'Too right, it's a good drink!' She shrugged and when I pedalled out of Bendigo an hour later with my group, I had enough food for a long-weekend, plus the bottle stowed away in the calico shoulder bag. The collective effect of the weight, the stepped-up speed of a strong backwind and the fixed wheel bouncing on an atrocious surface, snapped over-burdened tapes and only a slip-field grab retrieved the bottle. I clutched it with the frantic grasp of a sinking sailor on to a lifebelt and hurriedly tucked it into the front of my knickers. I suffered unmentionable bumping hurts on a delicate place, until Bruce came alongside with his motorcycle and sidecar. 'Here, take this!' I yelled, 'Give me a drink after Gisborne.' At Gisborne the scratchmen caught up and we simultaneously took the lead with them. By then I had been riding solidly for 3½ hours without food. The day was hot and my tongue stuck drily to my palate. Bruce roared up, I shouted for a drink and rapidly uncorked the bottle. Completely forgetting instructions I allowed all of the liquid to disappear down my throat. For a mile or so I felt like Shelley's *Blithe Spirit*, then wondered why two swarms of bees had settled in my ears. The bicycle steered stiffly and awkwardly, and I became authoritarian. When asked to pace I brusquely stipulated I would not be 'jumped' by the next relayer. It was L.C. 'Bowie' Stephens, about four stone heavier than I. Being a race, he was perfectly justified in endeavouring to drop me off with his fast sprint to the front, but when he sped past I took umbrage, upbraided him in nautical terms and offered to fight him on the spot. As he swivelled his head in amazement, I steered straight at him, but he switched away swiftly, as I tore out front-wheel spokes on his pedal. I managed somehow to gouge a swaying erratic course to the finish, with the front tyre rasping and wearing at every turn until one yard over the line, still in 5th place, I collapsed completely. I was grabbed and stretched out on a car footboard by sympathetic and pitying spectators. Lying prostrate and unable to utter a word I heard, 'Poor kid, he's all in' and 'Listen son, you're too young for these races—you'll strain your heart,' 'We've sent for a doctor.' He arrived, knelt down, felt my pulse, rolled back my eyelids, seemed puzzled, bent closer and perhaps catching my breath abruptly rose to his feet. 'What's wrong, Doc?' someone said as he walked away. 'Well maybe,' he replied, 'maybe bike riding makes a man this way, but in my opinion, in your sporting phraseology, he's as full as a boot.'

The next day a horrified father reminded me he had told me to sip it, not gulp. In my innocence regarding spirituous liquids I had put away on an empty stomach a melange of Russian bitters, brandy and probably some other ingredients of a devastating cocktail so for the first and the last time in my life I was steering a bicycle under the control of Bacchus. It was an early and valuable lesson, for from then I viewed any suggestion of such artificial stimulus with the antipathy of a vegetarian for a hamburger.

Opperman, *Pedals, Politics and People* (1977), p. 77–8.

OPPY PISSES *EN PASSANT*

Champion Australian cyclist Hubert Opperman endeared himself to the sophisticated French because of his unique style.

In 1928 the French sporting journal *L'Auto* conducted a poll to discover the most popular sportsman in Europe. More than one and a half million votes were cast and the Australian cycling idol, Hubert Opperman, convincingly beat France's own tennis champion, Henri Cochet.

'Oppy won because the public admires and appreciates his courage, his perfect loyalty and his eternal smile,' *L'Auto* said. There is the possibility that the eternal smile was there because he did not know what the French were saying to him.

Alf Stumbles, an old Malvern Star colleague, says there was one particular reason why Oppy became so popular with the French, he learned to relieve himself while actually riding his bike. In events like the Paris-Brest-Paris marathon it was vital not to lose a minute. So Oppy didn't—he openly urinated while free-wheeling.

'As far as I know he was the first cyclist to learn to do the trick, and it made front page news. The sophisticated French loved him for it.'

Dunstan, *Sports* (1973), p. 270.

MAROUBRA'S KILLER TRACK

A seven furlong motor track at Maroubra was very steep in parts. During the 1920s, five men died at this speedway in under three years.

The 'killer track' at Maroubra, south of Sydney, was a spectacular and tragic place. Five men died at the speedway in just two and a half years—the brief lifespan of this entrepreneurial failure of the 1920s. The seven furlong concrete motor track was built in a natural hollow in the Maroubra sandhills. It cost the promoters, Olympia Motor Racing Ltd $140 000 to build, and drew crowds of up to 70 000 people.

The track was so steep in parts that it was impossible to walk up it. Racing there was nerve-wracking. The site, only a few hundred metres from one of Sydney's most famous beaches, was infested with snakes, and no one ventured off the concrete without thick boots. The snakes would slither in from the grass in their dozens to bask in the sun on the concrete track.

The first meeting, on December 5, 1925, drew an enormous crowd of 72 000. But accidents happened often, and Maroubra Speedway soon gained the reputation of being of being a 'killer' track. Company directors Leo Salmon and Albert Vaughan died racing there early in 1926. On January 8, 1927, Phil Garlick one of the great racing drivers of his era, blew a tyre before a crowd of 15 000, shot over the rim of the track at 90 m.p.h. and was killed instantly when his Alvis hit a light pole. Garlick was 39, and an idol. His funeral on the following Monday was huge. On February 6, Fred Barlow broke his back when his car slewed off into the marsh in the middle of the track. He died in hospital.

The death of the famous Phil Garlick, in particular, signalled the beginning of the end for Maroubra Speedway. By 1927 it was all over; the gates were locked and Maroubra became a ghost track—although it was used briefly by the Light Car Club in the early 1930s.

From then the track was left to the wind, the sand and the snakes. Today no trace remains, although it is probable that concrete slabs from the 'killer track' still lie beneath Coral Sea Park and the suburban cottages which now stand on the spot.

Heads and Lester, *200 Years of Australian Sport* (1988), p. 166.

THE DIMINUTIVE LONG-DISTANCE AIRWOMAN

Australia's 'Chubbie' Miller was the first woman to take to the air in a big way.

Australia's 'Chubbie' Miller first made the headlines in 1928 when, as a passenger in Captain Bill Lancaster's tiny Avro Avian biplane, she became the first woman to fly from England to Australia. Later the same year, a chance meeting with the American crewmen of Kingsford Smith's Pacific-conquering *Southern Cross* led Chubbie and Bill to Hollywood to make a flying film. The venture fell through; but shortly after settling in California Chubbie gained a licence and entered the first Women's Aerial Derby.

Her performance (in the long distance race and in winning a speed event at the 1929 National Air Races) attracted the attention of the Fairchild Aircraft Company. They invited the diminutive airwoman to fly their latest machine in the 1929 8000 kilometre Ford Reliability Tour. Chubbie was the only woman pilot to complete the gruelling course and finished in eighth place.

Lancaster and Mrs Miller decided to settle in America, partially it seems to escape the gossip that had been generated in Australia concerning their relationship. For both were already married but living apart from their spouses. Lancaster got a job flying commercially while Chubbie went record chasing.

In 1930 she approached the manufacturers of the Alexander Bullet with a plan to attack the trans-continental record. The Bullet had a reputation as a 'killer'. Two test pilots had died during its spinning trials, and the aircraft had not yet been granted a type certificate. However Chubbie was able to convince Don Alexander that her flight would be at full speed and would never come near to the low speed situations likely to cause a spin. He eventually lent her the remaining Bullet.

On 12 October 1930 Chubbie left New York, heading west for Los Angeles. She made five refuelling stops and, despite bad weather over the midwest, completed the flight in 25 hours 44 minutes air time—beating the existing record by nearly five hours. A few days later she headed back to New York setting a new record for the eastward crossing. In America she became an overnight heroine and was headlined as 'The Australian Aviatrix'; yet in her homeland Chubbie's exploits went virtually unnoticed.

In 1935 she was again in the headlines when she went missing while returning to America from a promotional flight to Havana. A massive search was mounted and eventually she was found on an island in the Bahamas where she had force-landed, lost and out of fuel.

The adventurous pair next made the news in Miami. There, Chubbie, Lancaster and a young American writer, Haden Clarke, had become involved in a classic love triangle. It ended when the writer was found shot in Chubbie's house. By his body was a dubious suicide note. Lancaster was charged with murder and a sensational trial ensued. Lancaster was eventually cleared and the pair rushed to England to escape the glare of publicity.

In 1933 Lancaster disappeared over the Sahara Desert attempting to beat the London-Capetown record. A year later Chubbie Miller was named as an entrant in the 1934 England–Australia air race but later withdrew. She eventually married a British airline pilot and settled quietly in England.

In 1962, a few years before her death, Chubbie Miller again hit the headlines. Bill Lancaster's mummified body had been found in mid-Sahara alongside the wreck of his Avro biplane.

He had survived the crash landing 29 years earlier and had written a pitiful diary in his aircraft log-book during the week he lay dying of thirst. One of the last messages Lancaster had written before tying the book to the aircraft's wing, was to his beloved Australian companion. It read, 'Chubbie give up flying, you won't make any money at it now.'

Maybe Lancaster's disappearance 29 years earlier had convinced the 'Australian Aviatrix' to do so, for following her brief blaze of glory in America Chubbie Miller's name never again appeared among the air racers.

Gwynn-Jones, *The Air Racers* (1983), p. 185.

THE INFLUENCE OF SOUP ON CRICKET

A lot of things can influence the selectors of a Test cricket side—including table manners.

There must have been a lot of tragic—and funny—stories about men who almost played for England or Australia but didn't quite make it, or who almost toured for their country and didn't quite make it.

They had the ability but somehow the selectors passed them over—and not always for reasons directly related to cricket.

In at least two cases, the attitude of a cricketer to soup caused him to be 'missing' when the Test team was listed.

How is that possible?

Well, take the case of Les Jackson, a top-class fast bowler who did make it into the English side, but only twice.

A certain fellow cricketer (another fast bowler in fact) recalls that, on one occasion, at the height of his career, Les was at a cricket dinner on some big occasion.

The waiters served that refined French cold soup.

Les called out to his fast-bowling mate: 'Hey, Fred! They've forgot to warm up the soup.'

The Amateurs and Gentlemen present were not amused and made a note of the transgression.

Anyway, Les Jackson never again played for England, though plenty of good judges thought he should have.

Of course, I can't vouch for the actual gospel truth of Les Jackson's case, but I can when it comes to the reason why Bert Ironmonger, the Victorian bowler, never ever got a trip to England.

Bert Ironmonger was, by profession, a garbage-carter in one of the less affluent suburbs of Melbourne, and not noted for his table manners.

Nor for his batting. He always used to go in number eleven and never reached double figures in his long career. (On one occasion, his wife rang him at the Melbourne Cricket Ground. A voice answered the telephone and said: 'He's just gone in to bat, Mrs Ironmonger. Hold the line: he won't be a minute.')

Bert Ironmonger was perhaps the greatest orthodox leg-break bowler who played in living memory. He would have been suited to English conditions—but the selectors passed him by every time the team was announced to visit the Old Country.

Well, the old Bert eventually retired from cricket and, after twenty years, just about everyone had forgotten him—when he turned up as a star guest on a radio programme called Fifty and Over.

The format of the programme was an interview with some person over fifty who had, at one time, been in the public eye.

Well, the interviewer asked Bert Ironmonger a lot of questions about his career as a cricketer, needless to say, and Bert did his best.

Until, at last, he asked Bert: 'You never ever got a trip to England with an Australian touring team. In view of your outstanding record, how do you explain that?'

'Oh, I used to make a noise drinking my soup,' Bert Ironmonger replied, without as much as a grin on his face.

Which just goes to show that a lot of things can influence Test selectors—including soup.

Trueman and Hardy, 'You Nearly Had Him That Time . . .' (1978), pp. 81–3.

When Lindrum Ripped A Priceless Cloth

Walter Lindrum, destined to become the unbeatable world champion of billiards in the 1930s, was stopped from playing billiards as a boy because his father thought there were already too many billiards players in the family. One day Walter stole the key to the billiard room and engaged in a secret session.

I was having the time of my life and I attempted a shot I had seen Fred playing. I shudder even now when I think of it. I ripped a priceless cloth almost a yard square. I was panic stricken. I hid myself behind a bedroom door and cried myself to sleep. Police and black trackers were out looking for me when I awakened and the family heard me crying. I got a good spanking for ripping that cloth but it was worth it as the family saw the uselessness of trying to keep me out of that room.

Sporting Globe, 16 July 1938.

Catching An Old Foe Flush On The Knee

Walter Lindrum was punished as a boy when he absented himself from school to watch a billiards match. Some time later, Lindrum gained his revenge on the teacher.

One incident that occurred during the Lindrum–Stevenson match had a more agreeable ending. It stemmed from Walter's school days when he used to play truant in order to watch the good players who patronised Billiards Limited in Sydney. Unfortunately Walter's teacher found out about these little escapades. Apart from getting six whacks with the cane Walter had to write out the word 'billiards' 500 times each night for a week. Shortly after this experience Walter happily left the school and that teacher. It was during an evening session of the Stevenson match that Walter renewed his acquaintance with his old foe. As he was potting the red ball into the middle pocket Walter spotted his former teacher seated in the front row of spectators. He bided his time, waiting for an opportunity to settle an old debt. Finally, when he had the balls along the side cushion, Walter forced the cue ball off the table and caught his old foe flush on the knee. The spectators all laughed, thinking it was simply a bad shot. After the session the teacher went to the dressing room and asked if Walter remembered him. 'Remember you,' said Walter, 'What do you think I whacked you on the knee for?'

The pair had a hearty laugh, agreed the score was even as far as hitting was concerned, and became great friends.

Ricketts, *Walter Lindrum Billiards Phenomenon* (1982), p. 47.

'FURTHER BACK THAN WALLA WALLA'

The champion pacer Walla Walla, who overcame seemingly impossible handicaps, was a crowd favourite.

The phrase 'further back than Walla Walla' has been part of the Australian vernacular since the 1930s. It recalls a champion horse—the famous Walla Walla. Foaled in 1922, the son of Globe Derby and Princess Winona, he was trotting's Phar Lap. Like his contemporary Phar Lap he was a horse of tremendous public appeal, who drew huge crowds to the Agricultural shows circuit.

He raced at the annual shows of Sydney, Melbourne and Brisbane, smashing records as he went. On the Sydney Showground saucer he trimmed the mile record from 2.8.6 down to 2.6. The phrase that instantly recalls Walla Walla immortalises some amazing performances when he was given 'impossible handicaps'. He won a Harold Park handicap from 164.5 metres behind, and was third in a Goulburn Cup from 263.3 metres behind. He won the Brisbane and Launceston Thousands in

1929, and the last Harold Park Thousand in 1930—in the Australian record time of 3 minutes, 17 seconds for the one and a half miles.

At Harold Park he ran a race record of 2.6 from a standing start—breaking the previous record by five seconds. In a time trial at the track in 1933, he lowered the Australian mile record to 2.2.4. A granite headstone at Goulburn Racecourse was constructed after his death in 1952 in memory of a horse who did more than any other to put trotting on the 'map'.

Heads and Lester, 200 Years of Australian Sport (1988), p. 184.

THE WILL TO WIN

Some golfers are reluctant to declare any ball unplayable no matter how difficult the situation. Winifred Witham, honorary secretary of the Katanning (WA) Golf Associates, takes up one such story.

We were playing as a three in a ladies 'open day' competition at the picturesque little Woodanilling golf course (in the Great Southern Area). It was a bitterly cold windy day, with light rain and sleet. When playing the last hole before luncheon (a par four hole) one of the ladies sliced her ball into the timber and it fell into a fallen tree area. Whereas I would have myself declared it unplayable, she and the other lady in our three decided to shift the branch of the fallen tree. This in itself was a mighty effort. There was the ball sitting beside a 'bob-tail' goanna in its winter nest. So the other lady picked up the goanna and held it by the neck (she said that goannas were a farmer's best friend), while the owner of the ball got in and hit the ball well out on to the fairway. They put the goanna in its nest, pulled the fallen branch back and left it in peace! (I was keeping well away from the goanna.) On we went and she finished with a par four for the hole. With wind, sleet and almost snowing, I felt this was indeed an example of sheer tenacity of purpose and the will to win! We've often had a good laugh about the incident since.

Maclaren, ANZ Golfer's Handbook (1975), p. 141.

LEAPING THE SACRED PICKETS AT THE SCG

When an interstate women's cricket game was played at the Sydney Cricket Ground in 1930 (the first for many years) male officials frowned on the ebullience of the players.

Certainly a picnic spirit prevailed, and officials of the Sydney Cricket Ground were horrified when several players leapt the picket fence instead of making the conventional sedate exit through the gate to the dressing room. And Victoria took the field like a football team, running on, and passing the ball from one to the other.

Cashman and Weaver, Wicket Women (1991), p. 47.

EDDIE GILBERT'S THUNDERBOLTS

Bradman lasted only five balls against the Aboriginal fast bowler Eddie Gilbert in 1931 but not everyone praised Gilbert's performance.

Just before Christmas, 1931, Gilbert had Bradman out for a duck after five balls of what Bradman said was the fastest bowling he ever faced. Gilbert hit Bradman with the fourth delivery and had him caught by wicket-keeper L.W. Waterman off the next ball. A few minutes earlier Waterman had caught Wendell Bill off Gilbert. At the end of the match the New South Wales team manager, A.L. Rose, accused Gilbert of throwing and claimed his bowling was a blot on the game. Rose said four of NSW's leading players were emphatic that Gilbert threw. Bradman wrote later that Gilbert's bowling looked fair from the pavilion but that 'when batting against him if he did not actually throw then he certainly jerked it.'

Pollard, Australian Cricket (1988), p. 471.

Amateur Golf Champion Of Australia At Sixteen

Harry Williams, a left-hander who played with nonchalant skill, was an Australian golf sensation in 1931.

Harry Williams a tall, slim youth from Victoria, caused a sensation in 1931 when he captured the Amateur championship of Australia at the age of 16. He is unchallenged as the youngest winner.

Unquestionably, the most remarkable recovery staged during a major Australian final occurred in 1932 at Royal Adelaide when Williams, still only 17, defended the Amateur crown against Dr Reg Bettington, a triple Oxford blue and captain of the NSW cricket team.

Dr Bettington, a lovable bear of a man, trailed three down with seven holes to play after Williams casually holed a birdie putt from 15 yards to win the 29th. Williams appeared to have the title safely in his keeping when he hit his tee shot to six feet at the par-3 12th, the 30th hole of the contest. Bettington followed to 24 feet, and courageously holed the putt before stepping back to watch Williams miss.

Dr Bettington gave the ball a hearty thump from the tee, but his strong point was his magnificent putting.

Smith's Weekly noted: 'He is huge and hairy, and known to caddies at Royal Sydney as Tarzan. Although Dr Bettington swings and slogs like a navvy, he has a delicacy of touch around the greens that would make us unhesitatingly place our life in his hands.'

Dr Bettington birdied the next two holes, stymied Williams on the 33rd green and birdied the short 34th with a six foot putt to be two up with two holes to play. Four birdies and a stymie to take five holes in a row at that stage of a national title fight! They halved the par-5 35th and Bettington was champion. Williams was square with par for the last seven holes, yet lost five of them.

A left-hander, Williams played with nonchalant skill and was a master of the short pitch shot. Gene Sarazen wanted to take him to America, promising earnings of at least $100 000. Williams was not interested.

In 1937, he regained the Australian title. By then, however, he had lost heart as well as interest following the death of his father.

Betting on horses became an addiction with Williams and he quickly blew a $60 000 inheritance.

In 1961, he committed suicide. The kitchen where he died was gas-filled. The refrigerator was empty, except for a single lettuce leaf.

Smith, *Australian Golf* (1982), pp. 27–8.

THREE YEARS AT THE CREASE

Dame Pattie Menzies was not as enthusiastic about cricket as her husband. She was easily bored by the game because nothing much seemed to change in a cricket match—including the batsmen.

Dame Pattie Menzies, wife of the Hon. R.G. Menzies, Australian Prime Minister, unlike her husband is not a cricket addict.

After the South African v. Australia Test match in Melbourne [season 1931–2], I asked her if she had seen the game.

'No,' she said, 'I've only seen one Test match in Australia, away back in 1924. England was playing Australia, and my husband suggested I should go at least one day of the match. When I arrived at the ground Hobbs and Sutcliffe were batting, and after watching them for a couple of hours, I became bored, and went home.'

'And that was the last game you saw?' I asked.

'Oh no, I went to England in 1926, and Bob suggested that I should see at least one match in England. So I went to the Oval where England was again playing Australia, and what do you think? When I arrived at the ground, there they were again, Hobbs and Sutcliffe. They were still batting.'

Piesse, *The Great Australian Book of Cricket Stories* (1982), p. 193.

WHEN LINDRUM WAS FURIOUS
WITH HIMSELF

Walter Lindrum set himself extremely high standards. Even after creating a world-record break of 4137 in 1932, he could not accept missing a difficult cannon shot.

Lindrum scored his still world-record break of 4137 and had his greatest moment, at London's most famous billiard shrine Thurston's. He was playing England champion Joe Davis from a handicap of 7000. At the end of the first day's sessions Davis (receiving 7000) was 8834, Lindrum 2224. Walter had reduced his leeway by less than 1000. The next day he got down to business, scoring 701 unfinished in 30 minutes in the first session and 2450 still unfinished in the second in 105 minutes to be 3151 'not out' overnight.

His own world-record break was then 3905, made in London the previous year, 1931. He was anxious to break it, to go beyond 4000, even 5000, and take the lead from Davis.

On the third day, 20 January 1932, Thurston's was packed long before play was due to be resumed.

Lindrum had left himself an awkward opening position and appeared to be uncustomarily uncomfortable about it. He narrowly avoided missing several difficult open play shots before he manoeuvred the balls into a good position at the top of the table. Then, amid 'breathless' silence, he scored 112 and 123 with runs of close cannons.

The crowd gasped with dismay at 3484 when the red almost stopped on the brink of the pocket, hovered then trickled in. Lindrum passed 3500 after 15 minutes of the session, added 100 in three more minutes and went to 3700 in another 150 seconds.

A spell of open play took him equal with his previous record on 3905. He paused to chalk his cue, made the important shot. The spectators cheered wildly and demanded a speech. Lindrum thanked them briefly for their appreciation and went on past 4000.

At 4137, scored in two hours 51 minutes, he missed a difficult cannon and was reported 'to be furious with himself'.

Inspired by this mammoth break, which contained 1295 nursery cannons (2590) Joe Davis went to the table and scored a break of 1247. This was the first time opponents at billiards had made successive four-figure breaks.

Whitington, *Great Moments in Australian Sport* (1975), pp. 20–1.

'YOUR LENGTH IS LOUSY, BUT YOU BOWL A GOOD WIDTH'

Celebrated barracker Stephen 'Yabba' Gascoigne kept the cricket crowds entertained with his deft comments in the 1930s.

Looked at in cold print Yabba's wit and wisdom may not seem so extraordinary but it needs to be remembered that much of the humour derived from the situation of the game, the timing and the inflection of the barracker. Even so there was a delightful irony in his comment to the Indian prince, Pataudi, who played in the English side, when he rechristened him Irishman Pat O'Dea and advised him to return to Africa.

Yabba had a great fund of expressions and the ability to add some new twist to an existing phrase or an old idea. Cricket followers still remember his 'Your length is lousy, but you bowl a good width' as a classic response to a wayward bowler . . .

Some typical Yabbarisms: 'Strewth, he's alive!' and 'Whoa, there, he's bolted!' when a batsman emerged from a scoreless period with a single, or 'We'll get Grace Bros' (or Anthony Hordern's Removalists) 'to shift you' when confronting a stodgy batsman;

'Hurry up, Herbie, (Collins) declare the innings before he gets set and scores a century.'—advice to the NSW captain when the side was over 500 and a rookie batsman crawled to five in 30 minutes;

'I think you boys had better call on Nurse Mitchell (a well-known abortionist) to get the bastards out';

'Put Arthur (Mailey) on and don't waste time—poor Johnnie (Douglas) is wanted on the telephone'—as Douglas, who always had trouble with Mailey, came to bat;

'Put a penny in his meter, George . . . he's stopped registering.'—to the umpire George Borwick, a gas-meter inspector, in response to a slow Pataudi innings.

Cashman in Pollard, *Middle & Leg* (1988), pp. 202–3.

WHEN THE CROWD TOOK A WICKET

Dr E.P. Barbour, a New South Wales batsman, allowed the barrackers on the hill at Marrickville Oval to get under his skin in 1932.

Until World War II large crowds turned up at district cricket matches and barracking was sometimes a problem for visiting batsmen. The *Sydney Morning Herald* of 15 February 1932 reported that barrackers on the Marrickville 'Hill' were blamed for taking the wicket of Randwick and New South Wales batsman, Dr E.P. Barbour:

> Barbour usually had no problem in dealing with barrackers, but was disconcerted by a section of the crowd who were silent as the bowler ran in but who shouted 'Hit it' just after the ball left the bowler's hand. He appealed to the umpire and home captain but no action resulted. When the barracking continued Barbour stepped away from his wicket, just after the ball was delivered, and was bowled. Barbour remained at the wicket for a minute discussing the matter with the umpire, who had given him out, and left for the pavilion: the scorecard read 'b. Amos' but it could have read 'b. Marrickville barrackers'.

Cashman and Meader, *History of Marrickville*, vol. 2 (in press).

THE DEATH OF PHAR LAP

The death of the mighty Phar Lap in 1932 was greeted with stunned disbelief, gloom and an outpouring of grief.

The news of Phar Lap's death left Australia in an extraordinary state of bereavement. One moment Phar Lap was the total conqueror, the mighty winner of the Agua Caliente, the horse that was going to conquer all America, the next moment he was dead.

The first cables told of Woodcock's misery:

Woodcock threw his arms around the horse's neck and wept unrestrainedly. Mrs D.J. Davis, wife of the part-owner, was hurriedly summoned and tried to comfort the trainer. Finally he was dragged away from the horse. Woodcock said: 'My friends in Australia know how I loved the horse. He was almost human and he could almost speak. At home they will realize what his death means to me.'

Something like disbelief was the first reaction. *Truth* reported:

Every sportsman and non-sportsman was staggered . . . It cast a gloom over the whole Continent and in the Dominion across the Tasman. Every man who had wagered on the champion whether it was five shillings or £100 felt pangs of remorse steal chokingly at his throat.

The artist Daryl Lindsay said:

It's like the Prince of Wales is dead. I went into the store and bought a paper. It was a long time before I could take in the significance of the headlines. People were standing about the store with long stunned faces. Phar Lap was dead.

Dunstan, *Sports* (1973), pp. 70–1.

THE PHAR LAP MYSTIQUE

Phar Lap was mourned long after his death.

It was Hickey's devotion to Phar Lap that triggered the mystery ritual of placing a wreath outside Randwick racecourse to mark the anniversary of the champion's tragic death at Menlo Park, California, in April, 1932.

It all started when Private Hickey, then serving with the 2/13 Battalion in New Guinea, sent £1 to the *Sunday Telegraph*'s sporting editor with the request that a wreath be purchased and hung in Phar Lap's memory outside Randwick Racecourse on Doncaster Day, 1944.

Hickey, in his accompanying letter, wrote: 'I know this appears a fantastic favour I ask, but I think it will meet with great approval from those interested, as I am, in the Sport of Kings.

'Phar Lap put Australia on the map among the leading countries of the world for horse racing. We all know how great he was, yet we never show it.

'America celebrates the occasions of their champions, such as Man O'War. Why don't we? There are many boys like myself who think and talk of nothing else but racehorses. It breaks the tedium and horror of war.'

The sporting editor carried out the request, having a wreath of roses, frangipani and autumn leaves made up by Searls, the florists in King Street, Sydney. Attached were red, black and white ribbons, the colours that Phar Lap's jockeys wore in most of his 37 victories.

A *Sunday Telegraph* reporter took the wreath to Randwick Racecourse and nailed it to a post outside the Alison Road entrance. Thousands of racegoers saw the tribute as they passed through the gates and wondered. A ritual was born.

It was continued the next couple of years by friends commissioned by Hickey while he was in the Army. Once, and once only, the wreath was hung outside Rosehill when a meeting was held there on April 6, 1946.

The following year it was back at Randwick when this small item appeared in the *Sun* on the Saturday afternoon:

'Somebody today placed a wreath at the main entrance gates in memory of Phar Lap who died in America 16 years ago.'

Such is fame! Phar Lap had died actually 15 years before.

Lillye, Backstage of Racing (1985), p. 38.

400 Fans Move Each Quarter

Star players, such as Australian Rules footballer Ken Farmer, have always had dedicated followers.

Ken Farmer was without doubt the greatest drawcard at the time and it was a common sight at North Adelaide games to see four hundred people change ends every quarter in order to appreciate his every move at close range. To keep Farmer in Adelaide a fund was launched on his behalf in 1932 and a postcard featuring a playing photograph of him was sold at all matches at Prospect Oval.

Whimpress, The South Australian Football Story (1983), p. 86.

Football With Six-inch Spikes And Chromium-plated Spurs

Poet Kenneth Slessor, writing after Australia had lost a Rugby League Test to Great Britain by 8–6, made some imaginative suggestions about how the local players might provide stiffer resistance.

What I did see of these footballers — and I saw several of them on two or three occasions during the afternoon — has completely changed some rooted ideas I used to have about big men. I used to think that if a cove stood about seven feet in his gum-boots, and weighed about 19 stone, with or without socks, it was perfectly safe to insult him at a distance of anything over 200 yards, provided you were nippy on your feet and could hurdle a back-fence. Now I wouldn't do it under a quarter of a mile, mounted on a motor-bicycle. Not only are these footballers all over seven feet and 19 stone, but they can run like water-spiders. If that's your big man, I say, he might as well be loose, or in the Williamson grand opera company.

Now for a few technical pointers about the game. In the first place, reading the reports of the match in the daily papers, it is perfectly obvious that the Australian team has been got at. I shouldn't wonder if this was some more of the sinister work of the Privy Council, similar to that already exposed by Mr Lang. Well, the obvious retort is to declare an immediate moratorium on all of the English goals and tries.

In fact, from what I saw of the leading English kickers in many instances they shouldn't have got goal, but gaol. Another fellow, named Ellaby or Wallaby or something, wasted at least 10 minutes right at the start, just when the serious gouging should have been getting under way, by scoring a so-called try. This may be considered football in some interested quarters, but it isn't my idea of the grand old game.

You ask me what *is* my idea?

Well, for a start, the Australians could easily be equipped with real man's boots, including six-inch spikes and chromium-plated spurs. Then they could try ringing in a football of solid cast-iron. This would cause considerable confusion, and in places actual discomfort, to many of the younger and more enthusiastic English lads, whose naive idea it is to kick a football whenever they see one.

Then, again, for certain selected players I suggest a revised costume, consisting of layers of pneumatic-tyre furnished with bumper-bars front and rear, and, if considered necessary, tail-lights. By inflating these chaps to bouncing point, they could be hurled at suitable moments over the heads of an opposing team, or, in fact, a good strong kick would be sufficient to propel them, with football attached, over the bars of the rival goal.

Speaking about goal-posts, I see no reason why the Australian posts should not be built like telescopes, on the extension-ladder plan, so that they could be raised in the nick of time to frustrate any more of this English kicking obsession.

Finally, to simplify everything, I would like to throw out the suggestion that these games should be decided not on a mere trumpery adding up of more or less mythical points for so-called goals and tries, but by the sturdier, more British, process of jumping on the captains. Let each team take alternate turns at leaping on the stomach of the opposing captain, who would be held in a recumbent position by a gang of umpires. Whichever captain got sick of it first would lose the match for his side.

I don't want any thanks for these ideas. I don't expect any. They are just volunteered for the love of the grand old game. And if the Australian authorities decide to try any of them, then—and not until then—shall I be willing to play in another Test match.

Smith's Weekly, 11 June 1932.

AMBIDEXTROUS HOLES-IN-ONE

Golfers dream of holing-in-one, but how many ways are there of doing it?

Noel Craig, of Wagga Wagga Country Club in New South Wales, holed-in-one three times playing right-handed and three times playing left-handed. Craig simultaneously held two single figure handicaps, left-handed one, right-handed three. Playing right-handed he holed the Steelworks Club's seventh hole-in-one in 1934, the Lismore Club's seventh in 1936, and Royal Queensland's fifth in 1938. Playing left-handed, he holed the Wagga Wagga Country Club's second in 1948 and 1960, and its 18th in 1965.

Pollard, Australian Golf (1990), p. 3.

BRADMANMANIA AT BIRCHGROVE

Bradman was such a celebrity in the 1930s that lesser batting lights were literally swept aside by the fans who mobbed 'the Don'.

The next grade match was a promoter's dream because it pitted Bradman's team, St George, against Mailey's team, Balmain, at Birchgrove Oval. Many believed, at this time, that Mailey had a hoodoo over Bradman. Special trains were put on for the two Saturdays to transport the record crowd which provided the Balmain Park Trust with sufficient operating revenue for 12 years. Bradman did not disappoint the crowd this time as he scored 134 and in the process 'massacred' Mailey, who had dropped a 'sitter' at the beginning of his innings. Such was the crush at the ground when Bradman was batting that he decided it was better to remain at the wicket during the tea interval rather than fight his way back to the stand. As the Balmain side trooped off the oval at tea Winning thought it only polite that someone stay with the visiting captain and the umpires. He moved towards Bradman but ended up nowhere near him because he was elbowed and pushed aside to somewhere near the boundary by the huge crowd which swarmed on to the ground attempting to get close to Bradman, to get his autograph, or to touch him or his bat.

Cashman, *'Ave a Go, Yer Mug!* (1984), p. 91.

A FAST POOL

North Sydney has always been regarded as a 'fast pool' and the number of records set there supports this contention.

No swimming pool in the world has been the host for as many world records as the North Sydney Olympic pool.

Opened on April 15, 1936, as the venue for the 1938 Commonwealth Games in Sydney, the pool cost a mere $70 000 but it would be impossible to put a price on its history.

Over the years there have been 82 world records set in the pool, many of them during the golden era of the '50s and '60s.

NSW swimming official and honorary recorder Stuart Alldritt, who has kept an account of the records over the last 30 years, doubts whether any pool in the world will ever be the venue for so many world records.

Unlike many modern pools, there is a lot of water in the North Sydney pool. This is probably one of the reasons why it has always been regarded as a 'fast' pool.

Clarkson, *Lanes of Gold* (1989), p. 202.

108 IN THE SHADE, 120 ON COURT

Jack Crawford featured in three finals at the 1936 Australian Tennis Championships in Adelaide, and he and Adrian Quist played ten sets with only a twenty-minute break in seering heat.

Of all the players from his era, Quist retained the most accurate account of details. In his typically eloquent way, Quist relived that final: 'Naturally I remember it because that was my first national title. But most of all Jack and I recall the heat. It was 108 degrees in the shade, closer to 120 on court. So hot that Jack wore a white floppy hat. That was unusual for such a staid character as Jack. Games were continuous and you didn't sit down in chairs because there were no bloody chairs. Five advantage sets was normal procedure in every national or state final. We started at midday and the temperature was no exaggeration.'

Following the singles marathon, which Quist finally clinched 6–2, 6–3, 4–6, 3–6, 9–7, the pair were granted 20 minutes rest before being ordered out to the boiling Memorial Drive centre court for the doubles final. Quist and Turnbull beat Crawford and McGrath 6–8, 6–2, 6–1, 3–6, 6–2. 'After the singles Jack and I came into the little dressing-room, absolutely buggered, both of us. We had just taken off our clothes and were sitting down when Ray Hone, a doctor friend of ours who was referee came in. I remember him saying "Come on fellows, we don't want to keep the crowd waiting." I pleaded for a little more time and he replied, "Oh all right, another five minutes." So we played ten sets with a 20 minute break. No chairs on court and certainly no 90 seconds at the change of ends.'

Matthews, *Game, Set and Glory* (1985), pp. 50–1.

BLACK SUNDAY

A diabolical scene occurred at Bondi Beach on Sunday, 6 February 1938. But for the heroism of some lifesavers, the tragedy could have been even greater than it was on 'Black Sunday'.

Sunday, February 6, 1938, was a glorious day for the beach. The sun shone brightly over the whole of Sydney and an estimated 60 000 people flocked to the world-famous Bondi Beach to enjoy its charms.

Whole families made the trip to set up umbrellas and picnics and play games on the seashore. Almost every speck of sand was taken up by sun-baking bodies and, although the surf was quite difficult, hundreds frolicked in the water. A sandbank had formed offshore from which many people were swimming, while more adventurous souls rode boards further out.

The scene was pure Australia—mass content in the sun.

At work on that day was Carl Jeppesen, captain of the Bondi Surf Bathers' Life Saving Club. Soon to become one of the most popular and respected members of the surf lifesaving fraternity, Jeppesen had been captain of the club for only a year when, on this day, he was caught in the middle of the worst day in Bondi's history—Black Sunday.

The day that had started brightly was to end in disaster with the death of five swimmers. It was also a day that helped cement the legend of the tough and heroic Australian surf livesaver.

In mid-afternoon, almost in an instant, the summer idyll changed as the water went eerily quiet. Then, three huge waves rose up out of nothing to swamp those in the water and on the sandbank, placing them in immediate difficulty. A powerful backwash was created by the waves and, in less than 10 seconds, more than 200 bathers were dragged out to sea.

The waves hammered into the beach and dragged back scores more who were desperately scrambling ashore. Raised arms, the signal of distress, shot up all through the water and frantic screams rent the air as people thrashed about in terror.

Much of the crowd on the beach fell into panic as people saw friends and relatives simply disappear. Members of the crowd were bolting in all directions. The situation seemed hopeless.

Yet through this diabolical scene came calm and purpose. More than 70 Bondi lifesavers, who just a few minutes earlier were preparing for a surf race, sprang into action. Countless hours of training and drill came into their own as teams of brave lifesavers ignored fears for personal safety to race into the raging sea and rescue the desperate swimmers.

All manner of equipment and craft were used to reach those floundering, including rubber floats, surf-skis and surf boards. The rubber floats were especially useful as up to six exhausted surfers could cling to them while waiting to be rescued.

The belt and reel, which was developed only a few years earlier, was also used to good effect, despite the over-zealous efforts of would-be civilian rescuers. In their panic and haste to be of assistance, many pulled frantically at the seven lines and the extra strain caused some to snap.

The men were the chief panic-merchants. While most of the women in difficulty waited patiently to be rescued, many men screamed and thrashed pathetically in the water.

Some lifesavers were almost drowned as the people they were trying to rescue clung to them and pushed them down in the water . . .

One man commended by police was Ashur Hart, a 21-year-old lifesaver who had contracted infantile paralysis when he was 14. The disease wasted the muscles of his hips and stomach, which affected his legs, but he developed extraordinarily powerful arms which helped him win scores of races.

Those arms helped him save many people on Black Sunday.

Another who was heavily involved in the rescue effort was Aub Laidlaw, beach inspector at Bondi from 1929 to 1969, who later became famous for ordering bikini-clad swimmers off the beach.

Telegraph Mirror, 6 February 1993.

'BLOODY BEAUTY!'

Bill Tallon, bowling for Queensland in the late 1930s, got three prize scalps all caught by his brother Don. The third victim wasn't quite as routine as the first two.

This story comes from Neil Hawke, former Australian Test all-rounder, who now lives in Lancashire.

Neil says he heard Wally Grout, who used to bend bananas up in Queensland and kept wicket for Australia in his spare time, tell it at a cocktail party years ago in Australia.

Wally claimed to have heard it from Bill Tallon. Bill's main claim to fame was that he was a brother of Don Tallon, the great Australian wicket-keeper. The Tallons were also banana benders. Wally Grout succeeded Don as Queensland and Australia wicket-keeper.

Bill Tallon himself played a few seasons for Queensland as a medium-paced bowler. He didn't leave any figures in the record books but he had one day of glory on the Gabba Cricket Ground when he opened the bowling for Queensland against South Australia.

Here is how Bill Tallon told the story.

'There I was opening the bowling. I've got the new ball and I'm running in to bowl the first ball to a bloke named Nietzsche, a left-hander. Bloody good bat. It was an in-swinger and he got an outside edge.

'Bloody beauty! Me brother, Don, caught it in front of first slip.

'One for none!

'So out came Badcock. He was a bloody good bat, too, but I had the new ball and I could swing it a bit. So I ran up and bowled to Badcock and, all of a sudden, he went for the cover drive and got a thick edge.

'Bloody beauty! Me brother Don caught it in front of second slip.

'Two for none!

'So out came the great Don Bradman. I felt a bit nervous: I'd never bowled to Bradman before. But I had the new ball. And there I was bowling to Don Bradman himself. I'm swinging the ball both ways and getting a bit of bounce; when, all of a sudden, I dropped one short and he went for the hook. He hit it so high that fine leg ran for it, square leg ran for it, mid-on ran for it, I ran for it meself and I got a sunburnt mouth waiting for it to come down.

'Bloody beauty. Me brother, Don, got under the ball first and caught it.

'Three for 284!'

Trueman and Hardy, 'You Nearly Had Him That Time . . .' (1978), pp. 31–2.

TAKING A NO. 1 WOOD TO A MOSQUITO

A golf club has many uses, including some off the golf course. Harry Williams, a protégé of Norman Von Nida, demonstrated one such use in 1939 in the Philippines.

One night The Von was asleep at their hotel when he was awakened by strange noises in the next room. The Von burst through the door to find Harry standing on a bed with a driver in his hands. This was how Von Nida described it:

> He had the look of a big game hunter in his eyes. All of a sudden he let go. The swish echoed round the room. 'Got it that time, Norman', he said. He had, too. Harry had killed a mosquito with a No. 1 wood. That's how accurate he was. He used to hit his shots a mile but I don't think anyone else in the world could take a driver to kill a mosquito.

Pollard, *Australian Golf* (1990), p. 375.

BALM FOR THE SOLE

In the 1940s Geelong tennis players had to devise their own remedies for sore feet.

The Colas-Wood courts in Corio Terrace were very hard and hot on the feet after a day's play in warm Easter weather. The heat of the court came searing through the rubber of the Narm tennis shoes popular in those days. Sore feet were common, players hobbling to a cool surface to take off their shoes and bathe their feet in nostrums they had developed to soothe the skin. For Ernie McCann, it was usually a mixture of olive oil and methylated spirits. This balm helped to harden the sole. Then, with a change of socks, he could play further matches on the hot courts. In fact, on one such day the stalwart W.S. Carr had nothing to relieve his burning feet. In the absence of Ernie McCann's remedy, the players resorted to Jack Hawkes, who usually had some Grant's Whisky in his locker. Perhaps a gentle application of that would relieve fiery soles. But no—the glass seemed to contain too much for that purpose alone. Bill Carr, with a wink, drank off the half of it, and used the rest as a balm. Moderation in all things!

Kinross-Smith, *The Sweet Spot* (1982), p. 138.

THE THREADBARE BALLS OF WARTIME

The shortage of raw materials during the Second World War had deleterious effects on sport and how it was played, including tennis at Geelong.

Rubber was at a premium. Tennis balls were in short supply. The GLTC [Geelong Lawn Tennis Club] appealed to the Minister of Supply for its share of any that were available, stressing that 'most members were engaged in essential services'. Balls had been

9d. per pair during the Depression, and two pairs were usually consumed on each of the asphalt courts in an afternoon's play. Now, in war-time, the boys waiting for the used balls to be thrown over the fence waited longer. Balls were used until they were threadbare. At Jarman Bros Sports Store, old balls were repressurised in a special drum to give them an extension of life. The pressure was put into the drum by a hand- or foot-pump. And threadbare balls could be recovered with a second nap to give them extended life.

There was also the problem of tennis shoes—few new pairs were available, even at 7/6d. a pair. So members did their own repairs to the thinning rubber soles—everyone had a tin or tube of Renu, a none-too-effective rubberised mending solution, and applied it many times to the same shoes until the upper canvas gave out. And many members, using skills they had learned during the Depression, strung their own racquets with gut bought in hanks at Hawkes Bros store. Price 12/6d. per hank; two hanks required to restring a racquet.

Kinross-Smith, The Sweet Spot (1982), p. 143.

THE WORST WHINGER AT THE WICKETS

While many cricketers experience bad luck and often offer this as an excuse for a 'bad trot', a few players seem to relish misfortune.

I first met this bloke—the worst whinger who ever went to the wickets—during a country week match on the Melbourne Cricket Ground in the 1930s. He had a reputation of being a first-class batsman who had little luck.

'How would you be?' I asked him.

'How would I be? How would you expect me to be? I've had three innings in Country Week this year for three ducks. First day I got in the middle of a hat trick; second day I got me duck in a run-out decision which was so doubtful that the supporters of the opposing team booed the umpire; third day a bumper hit me in the chin, knocked me out cold and I fell on the stumps. I'm batting again today and there's a rumour that Harold Larwood is playing against us as a ring-in. Be just my luck for the rumour to be true and Larwood turn bloody body-line on me. And you ask me how would I be.'

Next I heard of him, his cricket career seemed to be going well: he had shifted to Melbourne and was playing district cricket—and knocking at the door of the Victoria team. But when I met him again he was working in a sheep shearing shed. I asked him the innocent question: 'How would you be?' Well, he dropped the sheep he was shearing, spat, and fixed me with a pair of bitter eyes and he said: 'How would I be? How would you expect me to be? Get a load of me, will yer? Dags on every inch of me hide; drinking me own sweat, swallowing dust with every breath I take; shearing sheep that should have been dogs' meat years ago; working for the lousiest boss in Australia; frightened to leave because me wife is waiting for me in Melbourne with a maintenance order. Was a certainty to be picked for Victoria this season but they heard that I made a noise drinking me soup. And, talking of drinking, I haven't tasted a beer for weeks and the last glass I had was knocked over by some clumsy coot before I finished it. How would I be? How would you expect me to be?'

I met him next in 1940: we were in an army camp on the Caulfield Racecourse in Melbourne. 'How would you be?' I asked him. 'How would I be?' he replied. 'Well, I made it into the Victoria team at last, as you probably read in the papers. And in me first knock I had to strike that Eddie Gilbert, the Queensland Aboriginal, who bowls faster than Harold Larwood. Well, he takes the new ball, knocks the bat out of me hand and the middle stump out of the ground. The next week, Gilbert's declared to be a chucker and banned from first-class cricket; a week later, inter-state cricket is called off for the duration of the war; and I'm called up for the bloody army. And get a load of this outfit they've issued me with. Look at me flamin' hat: size nine and a half and I take seven and a half. Get an eyeful of these strides—you could fit a blasted brewery horse in the seat of them and still have room for me. And take a gander at these boots, will yer? There's enough leather in 'em to make a full set of harness. And it'll be just my luck to be sent overseas and bloody killed. How would I be? How would you expect me to be?'

Well, he did get sent overseas—and so did I. And the next time I met him was in Tobruk. He was sitting on a box, tin hat over one eye, cigarette butt dangling from his bottom lip, rifle leaning on one knee, cleaning his finger nails with his bayonet. I should have known better but I asked him: 'How would you be?' He swallowed his cigarette butt and stared at me with a malevolent eye. 'How would I be? How would you expect me to be? Shot at by every Fritz in Africa; eating sand with every meal; expecting to die in this God-forsaken place. And I'll tell you something else: they've organized an inter-unit cricket match for next Sunday. I'm playing for our mob as opening bat and it'd be just my luck for those idiot brasshats to lay the matting wicket over a landmine and me be the first man to make a run over it. How would I be? How would you expect me to be?'

Well, he didn't run over a landmine but he was fielding in the outfield and, just his luck, a stray sniper's bullet picked him off. They abandoned the match and buried him with full military honours.

Then, one night in Tobruk, I had a nightmare: dreamed I died and went to heaven. It was as clear as a cinema screen. I saw him there inside the Pearly Gates and I asked him: 'Well, how would you be now?' He eyed me with an angelic expression and he says: 'How would I be? How would you expect me to be? This joint's not all it's cracked up to be. Get an eyeful of this nightgown, will yer? A man trips over it fifty times a day and takes ten minutes to lift it up to scratch his knee. And take a gander at me right wing: feathers falling out of it, I must be moulting. Cast your eyes over this halo: only me big ears keep the rotten thing on me skull. And just take a Captain Cook at this harp: five strings missing and there's band practice in five minutes. And I tried to organize a cricket match but I'm in a ward full of Yanks who've never even heard of cricket. "How would I be?" you ask. "How would you expect a man to bloody well be?"'

Trueman and Hardy, 'You Nearly Had Him That Time . . .' (1978), pp. 126–8.

SACRED TURF

The patch of ground on which sporting teams play can assume immense symbolic meaning.

A soldier, one of the gamest players in the VFL, came home on leave from the murderous business going on in New Guinea. His club, in dire war-time straits, welcomed him exuberantly and asked him to strip that very next Saturday afternoon. He played that day—played as if his life depended on it. When the siren sounded the boy went down and scooped up a handful of grass and earth from his home ground. Curious team-mates asked him why . . . 'Well, I'd like to take a bit of our ground and the game I love back with me next time,' he replied. He never came back.

Dunstan, *Sports* (1973), p. 223.

A SAWN-OFF FINGER

Some Australian Rules football players, such as Carlton's Bob Chitty, relished their reputation for toughness.

Carlton had Bob Chitty, who in my opinion was the toughest player who ever pulled on a boot, in their side, despite the fact that he had cut his finger off at work. When he turned up at training on the Tuesday the selectors naturally thought that he wouldn't be able to play, but he astounded them by announcing: 'I'll be able to play all right, I'm getting a metal guard to put over the top of it.'

Sure enough, he ran on to the ground on the Saturday with a special metal guard over his finger. When he came off at half-time the selectors asked how his finger was. He growled: 'No bloody good. This metal guard is getting in the way.' With that, he flicked the metal guard off, and when he came back at the half-time interval he was sporting his sawn-off finger in the raw!

Richards in Hutchinson, *The Great Australian Book of Football Stories* (1983), p. 206.

GOLFING CURIOS

The hazards facing golfers in a country as geographically vast and varied as Australia are legion.

However sympathetic they may be to the difficulties golfers endure because of Australia's unique fauna and flora, the Royal and Ancient cannot legislate for every possibility. Nobody can frame rules for an incident when crows, watched by the greenkeeper at St Michael's in Sydney, seized members' golf balls and dropped them on the cliffs expecting them to smash open so that they could eat the food inside, and when this failed, pushed the balls under a bush. The watching greenkeeper later found 144 balls there.

At the 1946 Queensland Open, Eric Cremin's drive disturbed an ants' nest on the Brisbane Golf Club's course. Realising he had to move smartly, Cremin rushed the nest, swung at the ball while on the run, and landed it close to the pin. Equally impressive was Norman Von Nida's chip in the 1952 McWilliams Wines tournament at The Australian, when his ball landed on top of a beetle, who proceeded to wobble the ball. Von Nida chipped off the beetle for a par.

Pollard, *Australian Golf* (1990), pp. 7–8.

SHARK-BAIT!

About 100 lifesavers literally ran to the shore of the Manning River on one occasion during the 1940s.

Those were fun days around the carnivals [of which] Dick (Richie) Wilson, formerly of Newcastle and now at Southport, tells this story: 'Pre-war, I took Cook's Hill boys to Taree in my Dodge Flying Four Tourer 1929 model. Next day about a hundred visiting lifesavers decided to have a race out to an oil drum in the middle of the wide Manning River at Taree. It was great fun and everyone milled around the drum, treading water and skylarking, until an old character rowed out in a leaky boat and yelled, "Git away from that bloody drum". A hundred voices told him what he could do with his drum. Then the old man came closer, "There's half a rotten pig on a shark hook tied to that drum . . . I'm trying to catch a sixteen footer what's been seen up the river 'ere." I kid you not . . . one hundred visiting lifesavers got up and RAN on deep water all the way back to the shore.'

Galton, *Gladiators of the Surf* (1984), p. 59.

A FRAIL AND TINY PAIR

Lew Hoad recounts his very first match with future tennis partner, Ken Rosewall, who played with a racquet which seemed too big for him.

When I was twelve I won all the tennis events open to me in the Balmain District, and the word went around the area about all my wins. We kids had been admitted to the Hereford Club by then. Up in the Illawarra District of Sydney, the other boy of my age had won everything too, and people were saying what a terrific little player he was.

I think it was Alec McPherson who thought it would be a good idea to organise a match between us and put it on as a curtain-raiser to exhibition matches at Rockdale between Australia's best players and the American Davis Cup team, which had just beaten Australia 5–love at Melbourne in the first post-war Challenge Round.

For days before the match my mother fed me raw carrots to improve my eyesight. She always sent me on to the court immaculately dressed, shorts neatly pressed, and she must have spent hours at the washtub on my things. She even ironed my shoe laces. We were all very excited at Wigram Road about the match.

We were talking about the match one night with Aub Griffiths— 'Griffo'—and for practice I challenged him to a match at White City. 'Griffo' bought new shoes, shorts and a shirt to fit the occasion, and we played seven sets. I beat him, but I never had such a good match in my life. At Wigram Road afterwards, when everybody wise-cracked at 'Griffo' for losing, he said, 'Anyway, I've played at White City, which is more than you lot have ever done.' He was very proud to have played on the show courts of the State.

Mum and Dad took me to Rockdale. When we arrived on a very hot Sunday, about two thousand people had been packed into the stands; hundreds more had been turned away. My father was so pleased my name was in the programme that he rushed to buy one for a souvenir. He was startled when the programme-seller asked for seven shillings and sixpence. This was a dodge to get over the law forbidding paid Sunday sport.

Scared he might not have that much, Dad dug into his pocket and paid up. I was completely unconcerned about meeting such a great player as Jack Kramer, my future professional manager. About one in the afternoon I went out into the sun to the off-yellow hardcourt in my freshly laundered clothes, carrying a racquet we'd polished.

My opponent's family were all there too in the seats which rimmed the court. When I looked at my opponent for the first time, I saw that he was dark and that the racquet seemed too big for him. We were a frail and tiny pair, smaller than the ball-boys. I brushed back my blond hair. The umpire introduced us and we shook hands. When the applause stopped, I looked over the net at him.

His name was Ken Rosewall.

Hoad, The Lew Hoad Story (1958), pp. 29–30.

OVER THE BARN TO WIN THE PGA

When Jim Ferrier pulled off a miracle shot to win the prestigious American PGA title in 1947, his opponent was flabbergasted.

Ferrier's big break-through occurred in 1947 when he won the American PGA championship at Plum Hollow Country Club in Detroit. In the final, he beat Chick Harbert 2 and 1 and did not need to take a second putt at any hole because his opponent conceded any that didn't drop. Ferrier said he wasn't surprised by his superlative putting, explaining: 'I have been doing that for a long time.' He looked like a praying mantis as he hunched his huge frame over a putter that was four inches shorter than normal. Ferrier had used this putter ever since trading three golf balls to a Manly member for it in 1930.

Ferrier's tee shots during the final didn't match his putting. He hit no less than eight spectators. Yet he was 27 under par for the 203 holes he played. Ferrier beat Claude Harmon 1 up to get into the quarter finals, and surged into the final by disposing of Lloyd Mangrum 4 and 3 and Art Bell 10 and 9.

The turning point of the final against Harbert, in which the big hitting American won the first two holes, was Ferrier's miracle shot at the 21st hole. In his own words, this is what happened:

'The 21st or 3rd hole at Plum Hollow is 442 yards in length. To the right of the fairway is an out-of-bounds fence flanked with shrubs. I was a little bit quick with my drive, pushing to the right, and the ball went into the bushes just inside the fence. Chick's drive was a beauty, 300 yards down the middle.

'We found my ball lying on a tarpaulin which had been hung between two bushes. This was right alongside a golf equipment shed. The ball was at least a foot off the ground. Byron Nelson ruled that the ball could be lifted, the canvas removed, and the ball dropped exactly where it had come to rest, without penalty.

'I was in a tight spot. My ball was lying so close to the bushes that I couldn't swing to hit towards the green. I could take a putter and hit back into the fairway, but that would give the hole to Harbert. A rather strong wind was blowing, coming in a bit from the left and into my face. If I could play a wide hook out of bounds, over the fence, over the barn, and then bring the ball back into bounds, it might be possible to take advantage of the head-wind and get somewhere near the green.

'It was a do-or-die chance, and I decided to risk it. I took a 5-iron, stood for a wide hook, and hit hard. It had to be a crisply hit shot to get anywhere against the wind. That ball travelled as if it had eyes. It got up fast, cleared the trees, sailed out over the barn and then came in towards the green. As it met the full force of the head-wind, the ball dropped almost straight, right onto the green and almost dead to the pin.

'Chick was flabbergasted. Nelson said it was such a shot as he had never seen and never again expected to see. From that minute I knew I was going to win. I dropped the putt for a birdie and won the hole.'

Smith, Australian Golf (1982), p. 32.

MOTORCYCLING ON MELTING TAR

Riding in the 1949 Isle of Man motorcycle race was particularly hazardous.

[George] Morrison moved to Ballarat in 1936 and opened a motorcycle dealership. The first road races held in Victoria after the war were at Victoria Park, Ballarat. Here Morrison became friends with visiting Sydney rider Harry Hinton. George was not selected for the 1949 Australian Isle of Man TT team, but his international performances that summer soon made a mockery of that non-selection.

Morrison and Hinton created an immediate impression on the Isle of Man. Other riders pussyfooted over the first-gear jump at Ballaugh Bridge and through the right-hand corner that follows. Harry and George took the jump with a rush, sending both wheels well off the ground, and almost brushed the wall with their handlebars as they took the right-hander. 'They all thought I was mad,' George said. He finished 27th in the 350 TT. In the 500 TT he won plaudits for his riding and his tenacity:

Halfway around the Isle of Man course there's a village called Kirkmichael. The corner coming into the town is a long, sweeping bend which we could take at about 90 m.p.h. On the outside of the corner was a footpath, about three feet wide, then a low stone wall. During the races people would sit along the wall.

British roads have low-melting point tar, so it won't crack during the winter. The temperature that day was up around 90 on the old scale, and so, unknown to me, the tar started to melt.

The first time through Kirkmichael, my bike started to creep across the road. I couldn't work out why. The next thing the bike hit the gutter on the outside of the corner and bounced up onto the footpath. Fortunately, the footpath was concrete, so I had some grip. I didn't back off! There were about 40 spectators sitting along the top of the wall, with their legs dangling in front.

When I took off down the footpath, the blokes and ladies just flopped backwards over the wall to miss my handlebars. There were legs and bloomers everywhere. I rode the footpath until I was lined up for the next corner, then aimed back into the middle of the road and waved back to say thanks for getting their legs out of the way. The Poms thought I was Superman to do that and not back off!

Cox and Hagon, *Australian Motorcycle Heroes* (1989), p. 40.

THE SPORTING WIDOWER

One Melbourne spectator was not prepared to miss the Grand Final for anything.

At an Australian Rules Grand Final match, two men sat at the Melbourne ground with an empty seat between them. They got yarning together about the difficulty of acquiring seats for the great game. One told how he'd slept outside the ground for six successive nights in order to be at the head of the ticket queue. The other told a similar tale of hardship.

'Doesn't seem right, does it, this empty seat between us going to waste?' observed the first man.

'Oh, that's mine, too,' said the second. 'I bought it for my wife, but she died.'

'Too bad. Couldn't you have brought a friend?'

'Just wasn't possible, mate. They've all gone to her funeral.'

Fearn-Wannan, *Australian Folklore* (1970), p. 21.

POSTPONING THE WEDDING

The opportunity for a humble D pennant player to advance in tennis was obviously highly prized.

The player who perhaps best typifies the club spirit of the post-war years was a humble D pennant player, who must remain anonymous. His great ambition in life was to rise to the status of C grade. To this end he practised tirelessly and took countless lessons from Leo Guiney—to little effect. A city office worker, he was often seen by other members (who, to their shame, pretended not to know him) practising his shots on Flinders Street railway station. Then came his one opportunity! An outbreak of influenza decimated the higher ranks of pennant players. The club secretary rang up the D grade battler:

'We were wondering whether you could fill in a place for C pennant tomorrow afternoon?'

'I'm getting married tomorrow afternoon.'

'Congratulations,' said the secretary. 'Not to worry. We'll find someone.'

'No. No,' replied our man. 'I'll postpone my wedding.'

Johnson, *Amazing Grace* (1989), p. 88.

Never Again!

Keith 'Spas' Hurst was part of a plan to row the North Bondi surfboat 917 kilometres from Sydney to Coolangatta for the National SLSA Championships at Greenmount Beach in 1950.

The crew was Hurst, who was then 21, Jack Watson, 29, Keith Woods, 19, Billy Pointing, 21, and Colin Guthrie, 22.

They left Bondi on 3 March and made it to Coolangatta a month later—after picking up a tow from a launch on a 145 kilometre stretch, and then getting a short lift by road.

Along the way they lost a sail near Killcare; all the crew became seasick and had to be towed off a sandbar at Port Macquarie; they were dumped by a big wave near Forster and the crew and all their gear went into the water; and they were dumped again near South West Rocks, with Guthrie trapped under the boat unconscious. Furthermore, the surfboat was attacked by a shark, holed by a swordfish, a whale surfaced near the boat and almost caused it to capsize—and the sharks were with them all the way.

A truck gave them a lift from Nambucca Heads to Urunga after they had trouble getting through the Nambucca Bar. While Spas flew back to Sydney for the State titles, the surfboat was towed from Coffs Harbour to Evans Head.

Another shark attacked the boat near Ballina and Hurst fell overboard but apparently frightened the shark away.

The surfboat averaged four knots doing 32 kilometres a day and the crew averaged six hours of sleep each night. All along the way they were royally entertained which often made rowing the following mornings very hard to face. They left some lasting memories at some of their stops. One of the crew said, 'In some towns they didn't want to see us back.'

Two thousand people turned out at Coolangatta to welcome them when they landed at Greenmount Beach but the surfboat failed to gain a place.

Of the trip, Spas has this to say, 'I would never do it again unless it was for the good of the country.'

Galton, *Gladiators of the Surf* (1984), pp. 86–7.

A Makeshift Pair On A
Borrowed Bike

*Lionel Cox and Russell Mockridge were ill-prepared for the tandem
cycling event at the Helsinki Olympics in 1952.*

Lionel Cox and Russell Mockridge's tandem cycling victory must
rate as one of the most remarkable in Australian Olympic
history. Until seven days before their gold medal ride, Lionel
Cox had never ridden a tandem bicycle, and in his preparation
for the Games had trained only for sprints.

Australia had competed in Olympic cycling since the 1920
Antwerp Games, but had never entered the tandem—an event
that was neither popular nor well-known in Australia ... Russell
Mockridge had ridden a tandem for the first time at the 1952
nationals ... The bike they rode was given to Mockridge by the
English manufacturer, Sandy Holdsworthy just before his de-
parture for the Games, and both he and the bike arrived in
Helsinki seven days before the Games began.

Mockridge and Cox immediately set about trying to familiarise
themselves with the bike. They were both 'clueless about what
gears to use.' As Mockridge wrote in *My Life on Wheels*:

> by carefully taking note of the sizes of sprockets and chainwheels on
> the other competitors' tandems during training, we came to the
> conclusion that about 100 inches seemed to be the popular gear for
> such an event. It was the gear that we used in our three battles to get
> into the final.

Other disadvantages for the Australian cyclists were the lack of
a sectional manager to help them and the absence of a mechanic.

A few hours before the tandem final, Mockridge had won the
exhausting 1000 m time trial. This win, he wrote, gave him
confidence for the tandem:

> I suppose it would be logical to think that the time trial would have
> tired me so much that it would have put me off for the tandem race.
> Normally, it did take two days for the edge on my speed to return
> after a hard 1000 metres time trial. This time I recovered very
> quickly after the morning ride.

... For the final, the South Africans were favoured over the inexperienced Australians. They were more rested and had also recorded a faster finish ...

The Australians had won their previous races by riding from the favoured rear position, but in the final completely reversed their tactics.

From the start they hit the front and stayed there. In an all-out burst over the last 300 metres they resisted every challenge from the South Africans. They won by inches, but it was enough to give them a gold medal ...

It was a remarkable win by a makeshift pairing, on a borrowed bike, with no available technical assistance and very limited previous experience. Only the natural talent and the determination of the two gifted riders made this gold medal victory possible.

Howell, *Aussie Gold* (1984), p. 135.

LITHGOW'S MINUTE OF NOISE

When Marjorie Jackson won an Olympic Gold Medal in the 100 metres sprint in 1952, her home town of Lithgow celebrated with sound.

Jackson tells of her feelings after the race: 'When I went through that tape my grin just must've swallowed the whole of the world because I was so, so excited. And just excited for everybody, because there was so much sacrifice on a lot of people's parts for me to be there and to my wonderful parents who sacrificed everything and the people of Lithgow who had built me a running track to train on before we went to Finland . . . and Jim Monaghan who had trained me. I really felt that that first gold medal was for all of them. I know Australia went mad. Lithgow had a planned minute of noise at three o'clock in the afternoon when I won and everything that could make a noise made a noise. They had fire engines tearing up and down the street and even the little triangles in the primary school, all the kids went out and donged those. And to know, so many thousands of miles away from home, that they were just so proud of me, it made me proud to be an Australian, and to see our flag go up was a very moving thing for me. It was a moment in time that was mine, that can never be taken away from me. I'll always cherish it and always remember it.'

Cadigan, *Blood, Sweat and Tears* (1989), p. 164.

KEITH MILLER — JUST ANOTHER DAY AT THE OFFICE

Keith Miller had a unique technique for concentrating in the field.

It was another club match at Chatswood against Gordon. Sid Carroll, a fine player, was batting against a young Alan Walker, who in these days before he went to England was very, very quick.

Dud Fraser was keeping, Eddie Robinson at first slip, Miller at second slip, and Philpott in the gully. Fraser, Robinson and Miller were talking about the races, Keith with his usual animation on that subject, and I was frozen in terror-stricken concentration as Walker hurtled his thunderbolts short of a length, and Carroll slashed hard at every one of them. A full-blooded cut or jet-propelled snick was due any ball.

When it did come, Miller was in mid-conversation with Robinson. He barely missed a word. As the ball flew at a thousand miles an hour, Keith casually reached out a left hand, caught it, flicked it to the keeper, and continued his discussion of the horses.

Disconsolate, Carroll trailed off the ground, while a very young gully fieldsman still could not quite get his jaws back together.

Philpott, *A Spinner's Yarn* (1990), p. 100.

WHEN THE CHECK STARTER
WAS ACCIDENTALLY SHOT

A makeshift gun at a Tamworth swimming carnival in the 1950s put the check starter out of action.

At Tamworth, the check starter was accidentally shot. The starter had been using a sawn off rifle to start the races. Midway through the first race, when conferring with the check starter, the starting gun discharged. The disc of lead hit the check starter in the side, finally lodging against his spine.

The police took the starter, and the gun, away. The mayor had to leave the carnival to bail him out. Meanwhile, the championship continued, with an alternative starter.

Later the check starter, a Newcastle businessman, asked his Sydney solicitor to claim damages from the association.

It turned out that the solicitor was also the association's honorary solicitor and he was able to talk the Newcastle business man out of taking any legal action.

Makeshift starting guns were outlawed following the incident.

The association had to get starting pistols from the police department. They, or the starter's personal pistol, had to be used with blanks.

Clarkson, *Lanes of Gold* (1989), p. 159.

'MOPSY'

Richmond forward of the 1950s, Don 'Mopsy' Fraser, was long practised in the art of upsetting his opponents.

I did a few shabby things, and probably the worst was at Footscray.

They had a backman named Kelly, who had beautiful hair. It made me envious. Always looking for some means to upset an opponent, I seized on a couple of hair clips he had pinning back his locks. 'You must be a sheila,' I laughed at him and, for good measure, gave a tug.

What a shock! I thought I had scalped him, because his complete mop of hair came away in my hand and left nothing on his head but gleaming skin. Honestly, I didn't know it, otherwise I'd have pulled it off earlier. You should have seen that fellow fume. It had the desired effect and put him right off his game. But I'll tell you something about the fellow. He was tough, and there was nothing girlish about him. He was just self-conscious about his naked nut.

Not that I should scoff about a man's hair or lack of it. I had a thick crop and on wet days I had to use hairpins to keep it down. The well-known press cartoonist Sam Wells always depicted me as a long stick with a mop on top. From that came the nickname Mophead, later to become Mopsy.

Dyer and Hansen, *Wild Men of Football* (1968), p. 198.

BRIGHTER CRICKET—
THE BARNES VERSION

Cricketer Sid Barnes had his own unique way of livening up a cricket match in 1952.

Controversial player Sid Barnes had his own idea of brightening up cricket during a drinks interval at an Adelaide Shield match reported the *Sydney Morning Herald* of 30 November 1952. 'Dressed in a grey suit, with a carnation in his buttonhole, and sporting dark glasses' and with a 'towel folded over an arm' twelfth-man Barnes escorted the uniformed steward on to the ground. He then proceeded to brush the players with a clothes brush, comb Keith Miller's hair and then hold up a square mirror, before he sprayed both players and umpires with a scent, offered round cigars and chocolates and towels soaked in iced water. In some respects Barnes anticipated the gaily adorned accessory-laden trolley of the late 1970s but officials at this time were not amused and this behaviour adversely affected his selection prospects. The crowd of 9155, on the other hand, roared with laughter and some of the players thought the event was very funny. A few of the spectators became impatient with Barnes when it took him a long time to remove his gear from the wickets but, after the event, Barnes received many phone calls of appreciation: many said it was the most humorous event that they had ever witnessed on a cricket field.

Cashman, 'Ave a Go, Yer Mug! (1984), p. 108.

THE PROFESSIONAL BLEMISH

Former federal politician Don Chipp was an athlete of some ability who fancied his prospects as an Olympic sprinter. However he did not get far because Victorian amateur officials questioned his status.

While still a callow youth in my mid-twenties, I fancied myself as being reasonably quick on my feet. I therefore decided to test my ability, and with the boundless conceit which accompanies our youth I decided I should set myself for the 100 or 200 metres at the Olympic Games. In attempting to register with the Victorian Amateur Athletics Association I received a rude shock. I was informed that because I was a professional footballer (I was with Fitzroy at the time) I could not be admitted as an athlete. I stoutly complained that I had deliberately maintained my amateur status and not taken any money for my games with the club. The amateur official quickly retorted that that did not matter, I had taken football knickers and a football guernsey and therefore had lost my lily-white status; however, if I cared to fill in the requisite number of forms, wait a period of up to a year, the stain on my blemished record could, as an act of grace, be wiped clean. I promptly suggested that he put my amateur status underneath my football guernsey (I could have been even a little bit rude) and proceeded to register as a professional athlete with the Victorian Athletics League.

Mason, Professional Athletics in Australia (1985), p.v.

SLASHER — A TOTAL NERVE CASE

*There was an unprecedented interruption in a match between New
South Wales and Queensland at the Gabba in the 1950s. Batsman
Ken 'Slasher' Mackay was not impressed.*

Then there was the Mackay incident in Brisbane. 'Slasher' had
picked up a duck in the first innings from a beautiful Davidson
delivery which left him late. When Mackay walked out in the
second innings, he was chewing his gum at a hundred chomps per
second, and the pressure was really on with Davidson bowling
again.

But before Slash could face a ball, the game came to a
temporary halt. The loudspeakers announced that play would
cease for the broadcasting of the Melbourne Cup, and the players
lounged on the turf for a welcome spell from the Brisbane heat.
All except Mackay, of course, who was neither helped nor
impressed by such a delay.

For it was unheard of. To interrupt the day's play for a horse
race—even THE horse race—was never before contemplated.
Only one man could have thought about it, then made it happen.
That man was the NSW captain, Keith Miller.

When play resumed, Slasher was a total nerve case, as he had
now been waiting out on the ground for nearly ten minutes,
sitting on 'a pair'. Davidson's first ball swung away late again,
took an outside edge, and found the safe gloves of Ossie Lambert.
In a frenzy of action, Davidson lept in the air, and, instead of
appealing, shouted, 'It's the best ball I've ever seen!'; Mackay left
the field loudly deploring the delay; the crowd was roaring, the
players hardly knew whether to laugh or cry; and Miller was still
excitedly discussing the race.

Later, Mackay, not at all happy with his pair or the events
surrounding it, threatened future revenge. As it turned out he did
have the last laugh, for in the return match in Sydney, Slasher
scored a remarkable double century. But that, of course, was in
the future; for the moment, the Sport of Kings, and the King of
Sports, reigned supreme and unchallenged.

Philpott, A *Spinner's Yarn* (1990), p. 100.

A Stiff Beer

A resourceful railway guard found an odd method of keeping beer cold for a New South Wales lifesaver travelling from Sydney to Melbourne in the 1950s.

There is another story told of a New South Wales lifesaver, Rothe Bassingthwaighte, also headed for Perth in a much earlier era. He had been presented with a dozen bottles of beer in Sydney and then travelled to Melbourne to join the train which was also carrying Victorian members. He asked the guard if he could find a cold place for the beer.

Along the way he made friends with one of the Victorian officials and offered him some interstate hospitality with the promise of a cold beer.

'Where can you get cold beer on this train?' his travelling companion inquired. 'I'll get it,' Bassingthwaighte replied and headed off for the guards van. Back he came with a 'coldie' and they quickly finished it off.

The two men repeated the exercise several times and each time the beer was cold.

Finally, even Bassingthwaighte had to ask the guard where he was keeping the beer cold. He was told very reverently, 'I have it packed in where we carry the bodies across in ice.'

Galton, *Gladiators of the Surf* (1984), p. 92.

The Whizz Kids

Teenagers Lew Hoad and Ken Rosewall had a memorable five-set doubles victory over the American champions, Savitt and Mulloy, in 1952.

As we started the fifth set, the tension was so thick on the Centre court you could almost touch it. Hearing of our effort on

Wimbledon's Bush Telegraph, more than thirteen thousand people had jostled into the stands. They sat, crushed together, on the stairs; and we knew they were all for us. Unfortunately, they even applauded the American's errors. There was a great hush, and then we were into it.

We played so well that Savitt, who had hardly smiled in the tournament, began a big grin whenever Rosewall and I banged a winner past him. Everything hung on which team could get a service break. Several times our racquets clashed together as Rosewall and I scurried for returns, but our luck held.

The eighth game went to deuce on my service and then to advantage for Savitt and Mulloy. I hit two successive aces and the stands vibrated from cheering. Savitt flubbed a shot and it was 4–all. We were still in it.

The Americans won the next game, to lead 5–4. I was thoroughly enjoying every hit. In that tenth game the Americans had match point on Rosewall's serve. There was that hush again. Rosewall swung into his serve, and we took the point and the game to level the score. We had been playing more than two and a quarter hours.

Every point seemed to bring fresh excitement; and in the eleventh game of the set we ran to a 40–love lead. Then Savitt and Mulloy won two desperately thrilling rallies and made it 40–30. At that point Ken Rosewall played two of the greatest backhand shots in the history of tennis.

The first he hit with a lot of angle from wide of the baseline, a remarkable piece of retrieving, from a splendid swinging service from Mulloy, which carried the ball back to Mulloy who fell as he volleyed. I pushed it into the open space this created, and it gave us the breakthrough.

The second Rosewall backhand will go down as one of the most amazing shots ever seen at Wimbledon. Savitt lobbed over Rosewall's head for the first time in the match, and we both ran back and shouted, 'Mine!' Rosewall was better placed, however, and as we sprinted side by side, I veered away from the ball; and he turned side-on and from several yards behind the baseline, almost into the back-stopping, hit a fabulous winner between the Americans as they closed into the net to volley away our return.

I served for the match in that twelfth game, and though Savitt and Mulloy pressured us for the break-back, we won the game to love to win 6–4, 8–6, 1–6, 3–6, 7–5. Rosewall threw his cap in the air with joy. It was the greatest match either of us had played until then, and whatever we have since done, or do in the future, that match will always live with us and the crowd, who rated it one of Wimbledon's greatest. It transformed us from two promising juniors into players everyone wanted to watch. We were accepted internationally for the first time.

The entire crowd stood and clapped and stamped their feet for several minutes. They tossed their paper hats into the air as, very tired, we gathered up our last reserves of energy and moved into the net to shake hands. Savitt had the big grin on his swarthy dark face, but Mulloy appeared very surly. We picked up our racquets and towels and walked wearily into the tunnel and up to the dressing-room. The audience was still cheering when we went out of sight.

Immediately the pressmen, who gather at Wimbledon from all over the world, asked for a press conference with the winners and losers. Old 'Gar' Mulloy was asked what he thought of it all. He laughed and said, 'Great, that's what those kids are—great!'

At Glebe when the radio came on again at 7 a.m. and they heard the former Wimbledon idol, Fred Perry, give the result on the BBC, my father and mother were so excited they couldn't concentrate on anything else all day. The house was full of visitors from around the neighbourhood, who kept popping in to congratulate them. Next morning Dad said he went to work on the tram car and read his paper's report on the match five times. He was almost in tears, and there was a lump in his throat.

Hoad, *The Lew Hoad Story* (1958), pp. 61–3.

DAVIS CUP FEVER 1953

The 1953 Davis Cup Challenge Round between Australia and the USA has gone down as one of the most dramatic in history. It led to 'Davis Cup fever'.

A new, though not completely unexpected, disease was noticed yesterday by a *Geelong Advertiser* reporter who saw many signs of the latest 'epidemic' as he moved about the streets.

This new outbreak could be accurately named 'Davis Cup Fever', and the public is warned that wireless sets are the greatest spreaders of this disease. City shops, offices and hotels, as well as private homes and motor cars parked in the streets, all contributed to the spread of the fever by broadcasting descriptions of the Lew Hoad–Tony Trabert match throughout the afternoon. The loudspeaker at the Eastern Beach held the attention of a big crowd of 'sufferers'. The climax of the fever was reached when Hoad won the third singles match and was signified by spontaneous cheering . . . It was clear, from a visit to the Hospital, that the ailment was baffling medical science, as many patients and members of the staff were absorbed in descriptions of the game. One staff doctor seemed less affected by the result of the tennis than most people. The cause of his gloom, however, was the fact that he had sold his seats for the Davis Cup match and had missed one of the greatest singles displays in the history of the sport.

Geelong Advertiser, 31 December 1953.

NORMAN MAY — THE COMPETITOR

Norman May was a prominent sportsman before he joined the ABC as a broadcaster. One of his major events was the surf lifesaving rescue and resuscitation.

Norman May . . . had an impressive record with Freshwater, being a member of the winning Senior R & R in 1953 and 1954 and the 1956 Senior Teams. He also won the club's Senior Surf in 1951 and the club's Senior Belt in 1952 and, considering his opposition included such men as Ray (Soccer) Matheson, he knew what it was all about. Norm also tried the boats and has been another of those favourite characters around the carnivals.

It was his lifesaving experience that led Norman to a career in broadcasting. He had been working in insurance with Max Riddington.

Born in Carlton (Melbourne) and originally with Coogee Club where he won the Club Championship, he trained in rock pools with people like Olympian Evelyn de Lacey. He and his brother, Alan, moved over to Freshwater but Alan subsequently transferred to Manly where he coached teams to win both Senior and Junior Championships of Australia.

Norm competed in five Australian R & R Championships, won an Open Surf race at the Australian carnivals but decided to join the ABC after his team failed to qualify in 1957. Dick Healy, then the principal ABC commentator and later a State MLA and Minister, lived up the road from the Mays and invited Norm to join the broadcasting team for a carnival at Dee Why. Norm went on to become one of the best known of all ABC personalities, covering Test Cricket, Olympics, Commonwealth Games, surf carnivals and every major sport. Each year he hosts the ABC programme 'Sportsman of the Year'.

His nationwide television coverage each year of the Australian Surf Lifesaving Championships has become one of the movement's greatest promotional assets. In 1972 the SLSA recognised this personal contribution by May with a special presentation during the Australian Championships.

Norm says it was funny when he left Freshwater competition: 'When I retired to join the ABC I told Freshie they would never replace me. They did, with Olympian Bruce Bourke and Freshwater went on to win 27 contests straight.'

Galton, *Gladiators of the Surf* (1984), pp. 109–10.

ONE OR TWO GOOD POINTS TO MY CREDIT

Olympic champion Betty Cuthbert had a distinctive running style which included a high action, a long raking stride and an open mouth — her trade mark — which drew much comment.

I knew nothing at all about the art of sprinting when June started coaching me. I apparently had a lot of natural ability but my style was not very usable. It was ungainly and uncoordinated. I had a dreadful action with my arms, holding them too low and letting them flop about in all directions. My stance was far too upright and, in fact, I actually leaned backwards when I ran. It looked as if I had been sitting back on a chair and somebody had pulled it out from under me. Action photographs taken of me later in my career show that this upright posture was something I never entirely did away with, despite all June's hard work and coaxing. It became more noticeable when I was tired or in my first few runs after coming back from a spell.

But I did have one or two good points to my credit. I had a good high action with my knees, which has always been a big help on a firm track. That's the main reason why I've always liked running on cinders and have found soft tracks hard to handle. I also had a long, raking stride. Well, that's what June had to work on: a little girl with quite a bit of speed, but lots to learn before full use could be made of it. But she had plenty of time to teach me ... 13 years as it turned out. I had one other little thing I haven't mentioned. Even then I always ran with my mouth wide open and later on it became a sort of trade mark of mine. Down through the years many people have criticised me for doing this, saying it forced me to take in too much air and also increased my wind resistance. But it didn't seem to affect my performances too much. I've often been asked if I ever caught any flies in my mouth. I've trapped a few now and again but a few flies and a handful of critics didn't make me change what came so naturally to me.

Cuthbert, *Golden Girl* (1961), pp. 31–2.

A 'HOT DOG' OR A 'BIG GUN'

Malibu surfboards quickly became popular in Australia.

The first hot-dog board to reach Australia arrived in 1954 with Peter Lawford, the film star, who brought one with him when he came to take part in the film *Kangaroo*. But Australians didn't get a really good look at the new board until two years later, when a team of Hawaiian and American surfers arrived and put on a display at Avalon Beach, Sydney, which really had the local riders doing some hard thinking. The visitors called their boards Malibu boards, after the Californian beach where they were so popular, and although they weren't so fast out through the break as the long, hollow boards we had all been using up till then, they were a lot better for wave-riding.

I remember that at first some of the crowd on the beach laughed at the Americans when they set out through the break lying down to paddle, and got left behind by the Australian surf club boys. You know the sort of thing—'Bloody Yanks,' and all that. They were beaten in the surfboard race, all right. But then a few of us took a good look at what they were doing to the waves on their way in: zipping one way and then the other, stalls, abrupt turns, beating the break nearly all the time. And a few days later Gordon Woods and other local board-builders were building copies of the Malibu boards for interested local riders.

The first of these were made out of plywood, because balsa was hard to get in Australia. Then the builders began importing balsa from America, and finally they switched to polyurethane. Nearly every surfboard built in Australia these days is a foam board, either hot-dog or big gun, and has been developed from those early Malibu boards we saw at Avalon.

I guess those blokes on the beach have stopped laughing by now.

Farrelly, *This Surfing Life* (1965), p. 112.

THE TANTRUMS OF 'THE VON'

Norman Von Nida—'The Von'—seemed destined always to be in the thick of golfing controversy during his career.

One of Von Nida's most famous tantrums occurred when Queensland staged its first Australian Open in 1955. Officials at Gailes golf course bustled about the clubhouse with paint brushes right up until the tournament started. When Von Nida went to the toilet before his first round he emerged with a ring of white paint around his buttocks. He grabbed some brand new towels to clean off the paint only to find they had never been laundered and were still full of fluff. He had to go out and play with paint and fluff sticking to the inside of his trousers. Bobby Locke won the tournament and when Von Nida stepped forward to accept the prize for second which he shared with Ossie Pickworth he told the audience the conduct of the tournament had been a disgrace to Queensland. At this point his brother Dudley, a staunch Gailes member, offered to take Norman behind the clubhouse and fight him. Sanity prevailed and the punch-up did not occur.

Pollard, *Australian Golf* (1990), pp. 356–7.

SURFBOATS ON ROOFTOPS

Lifesavers manned their surfboats in 1955 to carry out heroic rescue work in the Maitland floods.

It was during the 1955 season that the boat crews from Newcastle, Nobbys, Swansea-Belmont and Swansea-Caves helped save 1800 residents when floodwaters engulfed the New South Wales town of Maitland. They had done something similar in the 1949 floods.

They used the surfboats made by Tom Humphreys and all of those saved can thank the rigorous hours of boat training and the steel-hearted spirits of the boatmen who stuck to their tasks against terrible odds.

A report from the Newcastle Club's *75 Years History* by John Jenkins tells part of the story of both 1949 and 1955: 'As the floodwaters rose rapidly during the cold winter of 1949 there was no State Emergency Service and a call went out for assistance … and every club in Newcastle responded magnificently. Club members dropped their pens and tools and within a few hours surfboats were in High Street, Wallis Creek, and the surrounding flood plains, helping the police and Army in a massive rescue operation.'

Jim Jenkins recalls some of the details: 'The damage was appalling but the spirit of the victims was amazing—and we who were there to help were really moved by their attitude. The boats rescued many people from rooftops, verandahs and isolated ground in the first day or two. In the following days we supplied isolated houses with food and even carried feed for the cattle. The cold winter wasn't the best time of the year to be out in such weather but it was a great experience and none of us would have missed it for quids. The 1955 flood was an even greater disaster and once again the surfboats came to the rescue carrying out similar duties as in 1949. There were several hair raising experiences including rowing into some live powerlines during the night and witnessing the terrible crashing of a helicopter into powerlines resulting in the death of two airmen. On each occasion there were light-hearted moments, particularly regarding the methods used and the circumstances under which we were able to get a drink. We found one hotel where the beer taps were only one inch above flood level and it was a real work of art filling a glass. We also sampled jail life one evening when we slept in cells at Maitland Police Station.'

Surfboats also played an important part in flood rescue work at a number of other New South Wales centres, including Kempsey, the Richmond River and outer Sydney areas. They also featured in Queensland flood rescue work and have frequently been called into sea rescues of stricken ships.

This proves another point about surf lifesavers. They are a very useful back-up force to be brought into sudden emergencies such as floods or sea disasters. Many have also played their role as bushfire fighters.

Galton, *Gladiators of the Surf* (1984), p. 107.

No Sleep, But Plenty Of Rum

Keith Miller could not have had a worse preparation for a match at the Sydney Cricket Ground in 1955 but he turned in an astonishing performance, as Peter Philpott describes.

The stories told of Keith Miller are numerous and legendary, but one in particular is told more than any other. I have heard it from many speakers, all over the world, and I have heard many versions of it, for it is not unknown for a story-teller to embellish his tale.

Once and for all I want to get this story straight, put it on paper as it occurred, and so document the definitive Miller story. For, apart from Keith himself, I am the only one who really knows—the only one who was there with him throughout the entire day.

It all happened on Saturday, the 19th of November, 1955. NSW was playing SA in a Shield game at the SCG. As usual in such circumstances Keith was to give me a lift to the SCG, as my home in Balgowlah was en route to Sydney from Keith's home in Newport. As usual, I waited at the corner of Sydney Road and Hill Street at about 9.30 a.m.

Keith is a wonderfully kind and generous man: he has done many things for me, and never let me down in any way. But on this day I thought he had. For at 10.00 a.m. he had not arrived, and I began to worry. By 10.30, my concern had turned to despair, as the game was due to begin at 11.00, and I was on the other side of the city. It was now too late for a cab to save me, and I began to contemplate the effect on my youthful career of a failure to turn up at a Shield game.

I need not have worried, for suddenly, up Sydney Road from the direction of Manly, a car came speeding. It screeched to a halt beside me, Keith apologised for the delay, and off we went. His war-time airforce experience came in good stead that day, as we flew very low, and landed inside the SCG gates just after 11.00 a.m. Mid-flight, he explained to me that his fourth son had been born the previous evening, and that he had come straight from the arrival and the consequent celebration. Sleep had not found a spot on the agenda, but I could tell the rum had.

We raced into the NSW dressing-rooms to find the situation rather confused. Richie Benaud had assumed the captaincy and had the team ready to take the field, but was one short. Fortunately overnight rain had delayed the start briefly, and with a rush we could just make it and join the team.

Keith had no trouble, he was used to last-minute changes. He kept on his white dress shirt, simply discarding the tie, pulled on creams over normal underwear, ripped on a pair of socks, donned his boots as yet with untied laces, and was ready to go.

'Come on let's get going,' he said, totally unconcerned, as I scrambled far less successfully into my gear.

We went.

The ground was still a little damp, and the wicket itself appeared to have sweated under the covers, though it was not rain-affected. There was no doubt that Keith, now stooped tying up his laces in the middle of the wicket, had had no sleep that night and was, to a certain extent, hung over.

He went through the normal Miller routine, well known to most of us, but always memorable for newcomers.

'Right, who bowls in this team?' he said, looking around and smiling.

'Oh, you bowl a bit, Pat. You take that end.' And so tall, lean and very pacy Pat Crawford measured out his approach from the southern or Randwick end. He had a blustering sou'easter behind him, humming over the scoreboard hill, the skies were overcast with scudding clouds, and the humidity was high. A not unusual Sydney day.

Les Favell and Dave Harris resumed for South Australia with the score at 0–2. They had batted for ten minutes on the Friday evening, after Miller had declared the NSW innings at 8–215. Crawford steamed in. As usual the wicket was quick: there was bounce and seam, and the ball was swinging around, but as yet there was nothing extraordinary to view.

With the over completed, Miller looked around again. 'Who else bowls?' he said. 'Oh, Davo, you can bowl a bit. You have a go.'

So Alan Davidson began to measure what were to be fifteen famous paces from the Noble Stand end, but before he had completed this, the Miller mind had changed.

'No, I'll bowl. Give us the ball,' and walking back about 10 yards, with no measurement of run-up, he was ready to fire. He looked around, placed his field as he often did ('Scatter!'), waited until the fieldsmen had scattered efficiently, and bowled.

I was at second slip, and I can still remember that first delivery clearly. The seam was perfectly upright, the rotation perfectly even, about half-pace—which, with Miller, was still fairly brisk. It hit just outside off-stump, cut back from the off, and whistled over Favell's middle stump, almost cutting him in half. Every player on the field shook his head and stared, particularly the batsman and Miller himself. What did we have here?

Miller proceeded to bend his back. He was really quick, but that was not the major problem. It was the searing lift combined with the seam and cut which whisked the ball feet either way. Much of what he bowled that day was unplayable, and he only needed to bowl another 6.3 overs in order to get the rest he was after.

The scoreboard is worth reproducing in full. You will notice that the South Australian batting side was fairly useful: they were certainly not rabbits.

Les Favell b. Miller	....	2
Dave Harris ct Crawford b. Miller	....	1
Col Pinch b. Crawford	....	4
Dean Trowse b. Miller	....	0
Phil Ridings b. Crawford	....	8
Graeme Hole b. Miller	....	1
Gil Langley b. Miller	....	6
John Drennan b. Crawford	....	0
Don Gregg ct Benaud b. Miller	....	0
Jackie Wilson b. Miller	....	3
A. Bailey not out	....	1
Extras	....	1
South Australia all out	....	27

Crawford had bowled 8 overs to take his 3–14, and Miller, in all, had bowled 7.3 overs with 3 maidens, to take 7–12. Furthermore, there is little doubt in my mind that he had only begun to bowl at all in order to lift himself physically after a hard night.

South Australia did follow on, but the story so often told, that Dave Harris had collected a pair before lunch on Saturday, is not true. In fact, Dave scored 1, then 48 in the South Australian second innings of 252. This left NSW 65 for a win, and these were obtained on Monday morning for the loss of one wicket. That Monday was November the 21st, 1955—my 21st birthday.

Miller showed little interest in bowling during that second innings. He bowled only 6 half-effort overs, leaving the bulk of the work to Benaud and Davidson.

Herein lies an essential message, without which we cannot begin to understand Keith Miller. He had annihilated South Australia as few bowlers have annihilated any first-class innings, yet on a wicket almost as responsive he showed little interest in repeating the dose.

Philpott, *A Spinner's Yarn* (1990), pp. 101–5.

THE MOST SENSATIONAL MILE RACE EVER

John Landy sacrificed the certainty of a sub-four minute mile at Melbourne's Olympic Park on 11 March 1956 when he stopped to assist Ron Clarke, who had fallen in his path. Although he lost some 60 yards, Landy caught the field and won.

Those who watched Landy's chivalry and recovery called this race 'the most sensational mile ever run in Australia'.

As the 13 runners came to their starting blocks the huge crowd began to seethe with suspense. The field was top class, but it was Landy, as he trotted down the track to second outside position, who raised the loudest roar.

From the gun John Plummers, of New South Wales, raced to

the front and after 50 yards Landy lay eighth. At 220 Morgan-Morris passed Plummers and led at the quarter mile from national junior mile champion Ron Clarke, New South Wales mile champion Alec Henderson, Plummers and Landy. The time for the lap was 59 seconds.

Landy improved his position to fourth at the 660 yard mark. He was behind Morgan-Morris, Henderson and Clarke. At the half mile in 2.2 Morgan-Morris led Henderson by a yard. Clarke was third and Landy had eased in behind him.

Half way through the third lap, at 1100 yards of the 1760, Clarke clipped the heels of Henderson and fell. 'I got caught up with something in front of me, just what I'm not sure,' he said after the race.

Trying to hurdle the spreadeagled Clarke, Landy spiked his right arm as he descended from his leap. Fearing Clarke was seriously hurt, Landy stopped and trotted back along the track.

Clarke called to Landy, 'I'm alright. Run on.'

Landy turned and looked for the field and was 'horrified' to see they had rounded the bend. They were more than 60 yards ahead of him and he did not believe he could catch them. What followed has been called 'the most amazing scene ever witnessed in Australian athletics'.

The New South Wales runners, one of them Herb Elliott's respected rival Mervyn Lincoln, had clapped on speed. Suddenly a cry of 'He's off' shattered the stunned silence. Landy had begun his chase. Running more brilliantly and desperately than in any of his other races in Australia, he hurtled around the track — narrowing the great gap.

Henderson led at the bell for the final 440 yard lap. Time for the 1320 yards had been 3.6. Four yards behind Henderson came Lincoln with Plummers half a yard away third. Landy was still 25 yards from Plummers, but he was gathering even greater speed. Coming to the final bend he closed on the leaders with 220 yards to go.

At that bend he raced around Henderson and, amid stentorian cheering, ran to the tape with the speed of a top-class sprinter to win by 10 yards.

Lap times were 59, 63, 64 and 58.2. Race time was 4.4.2. Landy's time for the last lap was estimated at 55. Henderson ran second in 4.5.8, seconds faster than his previous best. Lincoln was third in 4.8.8.

It is clear that Landy sacrificed the certainty of an under-four minute mile by returning to inquire about Clarke and his action was described as 'heroic sportsmanship in the finest Olympics tradition'.

Whitington, *Great Moments in Australian Sport* (1975), pp. 9–10.

ME A WORLD RECORD-HOLDER!

Olympic sprinter Betty Cuthbert didn't feel like running on 16 September 1956 but was pleased that her mother persuaded her to participate.

I ran well in the competitions and then came that eventful 16th September. On that particular Sunday morning I didn't feel like running later in the day at the Sydney Athletic Field. I could feel a cold coming on and wanted to do anything else but compete. But it was a lovely warm day, one of the only ones we had for the meetings, and Mum talked me into going along. I'm glad she did. I won the 100 metres in 11.8 s and then lined up for the 200 metres.

There was nothing very special about the race. There was no title at stake and Marlene [Matthews], who had some leg troubles, wasn't competing so I didn't have to worry about keeping my clean record against her intact. I was drawn in lane five and Fleur Mellor was in the adjoining lane. I'd always had to keep a close watch on her in races, but this particular day she seemed more determined than ever to beat me. I can remember rounding the curve and feeling Fleur going for her life just a stride or two behind me. It sent a bolt of fear through me and I shot off as if I'd had a firecracker dropped under me. I flew down the straight like I'd never done before and was going so fast when I hit the tape that I ran into the retaining fence about 20 yards behind it and almost tumbled over the top of it. I'd left the other runners yards behind me.

Then they announced the time at 23.2 s., a world record.

I couldn't believe it. Me a world record-holder! I was staggered to think I'd sliced 0.7 s. off my own previous best time and 0.2 s. off the world record Marjorie Jackson had set up at the 1952 Helsinki Olympics. My time was flashed round the world.

Cuthbert, *Golden Girl* (1961), p. 44.

DEMONSTRATING R & R IN THE MIDDLE OF COLLINS STREET

Noted sports broadcaster Norman May describes what it was like in Melbourne at the time of the 1956 Olympics.

In 1956, the Surf Life Saving Association deferred the Australian Titles to the end of the year so they could be held in conjunction with the Olympic Games. This meant that two Australian titles were held in the same season, the first in December and the second in March. As a swimmer with the Freshwater Club in Sydney, I was competing in two events, the rescue and resuscitation and the four man surf team race.

On the early morning of opening ceremony day, I set off with two of my team-mates to travel to Melbourne by utility truck. Dick Evans was the driver and Clarrie Williams was the other passenger. We listened to the Opening Ceremony on the radio on the way down the Hume Highway. After an overnight stop at Tarcutta, we arrived in Melbourne in mid-afternoon on the first day of competition. This was my first experience of an Olympic city and I still remember that day 28 years later.

We had arranged to meet our clubmates at Scotts Hotel in Collins Street and were lucky to find a parking space because the streets were crowded with people and cars. It appeared that the whole of the city of Melbourne was gripped with Olympic fever. Everyone was happy and friendly and anyone who looked like a visiting athlete was greeted with a smile, a handshake or a pat on the back.

It was the effect the Olympics had on the people of the host city that struck me more than anything else, and in later years I saw that same expression on the faces of the people in Tokyo 1964, Mexico City 1968, Munich 1972, Montreal 1976 and Moscow 1980.

I can remember an amusing moment in Collins Street just after our arrival. We were carrying the club surf reel on the back of the utility and a group of burly Turkish athletes (either weight-lifters or wrestlers) couldn't work out what was this strange object on the back of the small truck. There aren't too many beaches around Ankara and it's not easy to explain a surf reel in sign language and broken English. It was all in good fun and at one stage we almost gave a demonstration of R & R in the middle of Collins Street.

We were scheduled to go to Geelong which was on the way to the beach at Torquay, but decided to stay in Melbourne to go to a party in a semi-detached house which was quite close to the Main Stadium, the Melbourne Cricket Ground. Around 10 o'clock Dick Evans suggested that we should walk over and see if we could get inside for a 'peek' at the Olympic stadium. Somebody scoffed at the idea but we decided to give it a go.

The members gate was open and we walked straight through and out on the track. The floodlights were on and there was not a soul in sight. Dick and I kicked off our shoes and had a sprint down the running track. I even had a go at the long jump but my effort was well below the Olympic record. Careful to sweep away our footprints, we returned to the party without sighting another person.

Television had started in Australia a month or two before the Games and with tickets almost impossible to get, the next best thing was a hotel lounge. All the pubs did a roaring trade with their new TV sets installed in lounges and bars. They were only smallish black and white sets but everyone thought it was marvellous. I was watching in a large lounge the day Shirley Strickland won the 80 metres hurdles. There must have been 400 people in that room and when the victory ceremony took place the service stopped, the cash registers stopped tinkling and everyone stood up in silence for 'God Save The Queen'. It was like that in Melbourne for the whole of the Games.

May, *Gold! Gold! Gold!* (1984), pp. 47–50.

MARATHON'S ONLY FALSE START

While false starts are common in sprint events, they rarely occur in longer races. An eagle-eyed starter created Olympic history at Melbourne in 1956.

The starter of the marathon championship at Melbourne provided a packed stadium with probably its best laugh of the 1956 Games. He judged that one of the 46 runners in this 26 miles 385 yards event had moved slightly before he fired the gun—and he insisted on recalling the entire field. It is now generally accepted that this is the only instance in world athletic history of a false start in the marathon race.

Guiney, *The Dunlop Book of the Olympics* (1957), p. 101.

'MIDGET'

Bernard 'Midget' Farrelly was 'shook up' by the performance of lightweight surfboards at Manly Beach.

I was pretty small in those days, even for my age—it was about this time that I picked up the nickname Midget—so after a while I began to leave the board at Manly to save the drag of having to lug it down to the beach every time I wanted to use it. Then one weekend it was smashed up in a storm, and I thought the end of the world had come. But my parents had realized how keen I was on surfing, and they helped me to buy a racing-style board that was built specially for me. It was about fourteen feet long and twenty-one inches wide—a beautiful board with plywood decks, cedar rails, a shining stainless steel plug and stainless steel tailhook. I kept this board for quite a while. I used to go surfing with it at the Bower, trying to improve my technique by watching other surfers, and learning how to turn it a bit on the wave.

Then one morning as I was walking down the Corso at Manly I noticed some surfers in the water who were slicing sideways across the waves instead of driving straight in towards the beach. I had not seen this done before, not at such an acute angle to the wave, and it really shook me. These fellows were starting somewhere near the point at Manly and coming way down into the centre of the beach. It was really something different. I stayed to watch them, and when they came in I had a good look at their boards. They were short, and light, and looked as though they couldn't even float. The year was 1956, and the surfers, though I did not know them then, were the visiting Olympic team of American surfers—Tommy Zahn, Greg Noll, Mike Bright, and others.

Farrelly, *This Surfing Life* (1965), p. 88.

BIG BILL BARRED

Big Bill Edwards, President of the Queensland Lawn Tennis Association, found himself with an Equal Opportunity problem during the running of the Australian Tennis Championships at Milton in 1956.

Not even the women avoided the controversy which raged through the tournament. Sydney player Mary Carter and Queenslander Daphne Seeney refused to budge when Edwards attempted to move them from centre court during their semi-final. The burly president wanted to start a men's match on centre court, much to the dismay of the indignant women. The sight of the 20 stone Edwards trying to herd the two paperweights to an outside enclosure remains vivid for those who witnessed the comical stand-off. The women stood up for their rights, went on strike and then locked themselves in the dressing-rooms. Eventually a compromise was reached and the pair finished the match on centre court the following day with Carter winning 6–3, 7–5.

Matthews, *Game, Set and Glory* (1985), pp. 50–1.

'So Many Bloody Double Faults'

Mervyn Rose was puzzled why he served so many double faults at one end of the Milton courts in 1956. Later he discovered the reason.

Rose couldn't understand why he served so many double faults at one end of the centre court as he and Candy, now Pam Shriver's coach, beat Queensland pair Roy Emerson and Anderson in an early round doubles match. For two hours the three journalists, Don Lawrence, Alan Trengove and the late Ken Moses, were refused entry to inspect the centre strip which had left Rose crying 'short court'. Lawrence said: 'Each entrance to the centre court was blocked by one or two burly Queenslanders who looked as if they had just ridden in from the outback. They stood there with their arms folded as we darted vainly from one entrance to another. Finally the tournament chairman, the late Alf Chave, made a balcony speech that rivalled Romeo and Juliet.' From the balcony of the club's private house at Milton, Chave announced: 'It's a free country, we cannot stop you.' The hefty custodians at each entrance stepped aside and the writers hurried on to court as darkness descended on the Milton stadium. For more than two hours Trengove, now editor of *Australia's Tennis* magazine, had tucked up his sleeve a 15-inch ruler he had 'lifted' from the office of club secretary Frank Land. 'Until Chave's famous balcony reprieve, tournament referee Edgar Stumbles had refused us permission to measure the court and he flatly refused to do it himself,' Lawrence said. 'Once we were on the centre court Trengove whipped the ruler from his sleeve and we set about checking the incredible story circulated by Rose and the other players. Several times we ran the ruler from the service line to the net. We could not believe it, the court was 25 inches short at one end.' When the trio told Rose of their findings, he retorted: 'Of course it was. I have never served so many bloody faults in my life. And they were all into the same end of the court.'

Matthews, *Game, Set and Glory* (1985), p. 51.

THE LITTLE SNOWY-HAIRED BASTARD

Many of the great players in any sport have a confidence that borders on arrogance. Rugby League footballer Johnny Raper had no doubts about his own ability.

Channel Ten sportscaster and rugby and rugby league international Rex Mossop related a Raper story which told as much about Mossop's giant ego as it did of Raper's character. 'I found Raper to be an arrogant young man when I first played against him in '57,' Mossop said. 'He was playing for Newtown and I was with Manly where I had a penchant for running down the blind side. This little snowy-haired bastard kept cutting my legs from underneath me everytime I ran down the blind. With 20 minutes to go and only a point in the game, he got me so frustrated I began throwing punches. Normally I'd run 30 or 40 yards down the blind but he was stopping me after five. I punched him and got penalised. After the game I put my arm around his shoulder and said, "Well played, son. What's your name?" He said, "John Raper, and you'll hear a lot more about me."'

Masters, *Inside League* (1990), pp. 169–70.

THE OTHER J. CHRIST

J(oyce) Christ was inevitably a prime target for barrackers, one of whom was in top form at a 1958 Test match.

Rain . . . saturated the St Kilda Oval and there was no play on the first day of the Second Test but a damp and treacherous wicket set up a very intriguing second day. Sent in to bat, Australia could only manage 38 runs with Betty Wilson top scoring with 12 and leg spinner Mary Duggan taking 7–6 off 14.5 overs. One Australian barracker at least had a good sense of humour. When

Australia subsided to 5–17 and the name J. Christ went up on the board the loud comment was heard around the ground: 'Thank God, we've got a chance. J. Christ is out there now.' The first name of the Australian Christ was actually Joyce.

Cashman and Weaver, *Wicket Women* (1991), p. 119.

GRETEL'S HUGE ROLLERS

When Gretel secured a win in an America's Cup race in 1959, it was the first win by a challenger since 1934. The Australians celebrated appropriately.

In the second race, *Gretel* started from behind but began a tacking duel and gained, until *Weatherly* broke it off and maintained only a loose cover. (Mosbacher knew better than to mix it up with the Aussies if he could avoid it. *Gretel* had a huskier crew, and a Payne-designed device to link two 'coffee grinder' winches together, so four men could haul in a sheet rather than two.) Then, on a downwind leg sailed under spinnakers in a 25-knot wind with *Weatherly* only slightly ahead, Mosbacher's crew was startled to hear a banshee-like scream from the other boat. Next it was rushing past them as if they were dead in the water! *Gretel* had caught a series of huge rollers just right and surfed into the lead. *Weatherly*'s afterguy parted at almost the same moment, and that was the race: *Gretel* by 47 seconds.

It was the first win by a challenger since 1934. Australians and their partisans, who included many Americans, celebrated until dawn at a waterfront bar. It was one of the biggest and certainly most raucous celebrations Newporters had ever seen.

It was all downhill for them from then on, however. Mosbacher won the third, in light air, as well as the fourth and fifth, by superior tactics or better luck, although he won the fourth by only 26 seconds—the closest time yet in a Cup race.

Riggs, *Keelhauled* (1986), pp. 102–3.

THE FEATHER-DUSTER CLUB

Lou Richards, ex-Collingwood captain and rover, backed his predictions as a football commentator with some bizarre promises from the time he became a broadcaster in the mid-1950s.

When you stick your neck out, you've got to be prepared to take the consequences—well I did and I have!

I said that I'd sweep Collins St with a feather duster if Footscray beat Melbourne—OUCH!

Will Footscray Football Club please send a nurse to massage my sore and sorry knees and a seamstress to repair the two pairs of pants I wore out yesterday doing my street-cleaning?

That Jack Collins, Footscray's fighting secretary, certainly drives a hard bargain. Collins and those Bulldog players Arthur Edwards, Jim Gallagher and Bernie Lee made me eat my words or that's what it felt like after I'd swallowed half the dust in Collins St and that dashed duster!

I thought I'd get away with it by sweeping just a small section at the top of Collins St but those Bulldogs made me kneel my sweeping way down to Swanston St.

And if you don't think it's busy at the corner of Swanston and Collins Sts at 11 o'clock any morning, ask *Sun* photographer George Bugden and me.

I reckon we both deserve medals from Footscray FC for risking our lives in the middle of cars, buses, trams, pedestrians and policemen. I lost George at one stage and found him perched on the front of a tram heading for St Kilda Beach.

I see that the Bulldogs, or Feather-Duster club, are meeting my old mates, South Melbourne, for whom I once wore a straight-jacket, next Saturday.

OK, I'll stick my neck out again!

If this match is a tie, and there won't be much between the two teams, I'll go for a swim in Albert Park Lake with the two skippers my old mates 'Smokey' Clegg and Ted Whitten!

Melbourne *Sun*, 11 August 1959.

An Old Bush Custom

Rugby League, before the six-tackle rule, was a tough and bloody game on and off the field.

One of the happier occasions of 1959—and that was a great year for me—was the birth of my second daughter, Donna. I had a heavy representative season and I suppose Eugowra suffered by my absence but we still made the semi-finals. Just before the County-City game at the end of the year Parramatta came up to Eugowra. Apart from Noel Kelly I had two great rivals in NSW for the tour hooking spot, Bede Goff of Western Suburbs and Billy Rayner of Parramatta. Billy was there that day, though he didn't play.

After the game we put on an exhibition for the visitors. Some blokes were shearing sheep—I sheared a few myself. Then Frank Toohey, our club president, said to me 'Castrate a lamb for the boys, Ian!' I jumped the yard and grabbed one. Well, it's an old bush custom to do this job with your teeth. You cut the top of the purse, get the testicles in your jaws and pull them out. It doesn't look so good; you've got blood everywhere, dripping from your mouth and so on. But the old-timers reckon its quicker. The traditional saying is that you 'swallow the hundredth to keep count'.

Anyway I marked this lamb with my teeth and afterwards I spat one of the testicles at Billy Rayner's foot. He looked mighty sick. 'There's no risk, Walsh,' he said, 'you DID bite that Englishman in Orange!'

Masters, *Inside League* (1990), p. 48.

A Perpetual Orbit Of Victory

Champion squash player Heather McKay took up the game simply to keep her legs in shape for field hockey.

An English men's touring squash team had visited Australia in the late 1950s and thrashed the locals. That ignominy set off a squash mania that reached into Queanbeyan . . .

At first, eighteen-year-old Heather and her friends looked on the courts as a place to keep their legs in shape for field hockey, which ranked as their number one sport. 'Hell, we were just out there hitting and running,' Heather recalls. But she could hit and run better than anyone else, and during Easter week of 1960, she was persuaded to travel down the road to Woollongong and enter the New South Wales Country Championships. To the surprise of one and all, she won the Country Junior Championship and the Country Women's Championship. In June, she went to Sydney for the New South Wales Open Championships. She won the junior, and in the women's tournament she lost to the eventual champion, Yvonne West, in the quarter finals, one of the two smudges on her otherwise perfect lifetime record.

'I might have won,' Heather says. 'I was two games up on Yvonne and leading her 8–2 in the third, and then I got pooped. I'd already played a hard junior match that day, and I didn't have any energy left. But I went home happy. I hadn't expected to do anything in the tournaments at all.'

Her performance earned Heather a position on the New South Wales team to play in the Australian Championships in Brisbane in August, and the squash world began its long acquaintance with Heather McKay. Within twelve months after she'd taken up the game, against all odds and against the cream of the country's female squash players, Heather won the Australian Championships. 'That was a bloody shock to everybody,' Heather puts it succinctly. 'No one had ever heard of me, and there I was winning the whole thing.' From that win, Heather went into a perpetual orbit of victory. Once launched, she couldn't be stopped. With the exception of the loss in the 1962 Scottish

Championship during her first trip outside of Australia, she simply kept on winning. She won at home and she won abroad. She won with her extraordinary physical fitness and her impeccable racket finesse. She won on instinct and she won with intelligence. She was the best in the world.

McKay, *Heather McKay's Complete Book of Squash* (1978), pp. 12–13.

A MOST UNLIKELY HERO

Ken Mackay was an unfashionable and dour cricketer but Australians took him to their hearts.

I grew to love Mackay mainly because of what he wasn't: he wasn't handsome, he wasn't tall, he wasn't well built, he was neither eloquent nor elegant. He seemed to limp on both legs and, when he batted, he stabbed and leapt and jabbed as if to prove that it was not coached strokes that kept him at the crease ... so much so that a sports columnist once wrote when Mackay batted particularly well: 'The man who pulls the strings on the puppet that is Ken Mackay batted particularly well today.' As he waited for the ball, Mackay's jaw traced large circles as he chewed his gum, his body wriggled the opposite way, his right hand constantly adjusted protective devices. And, when he finally did face up, there was no flourish of the willow: just a poke, with no backlift at all, to leave not the slightest chance that he might get out. Admittedly it didn't look the best. And Peter May's comment about Mackay 'squirting' the ball instead of hitting, wasn't too unkind in the circumstances. But that stroke was surely the reason why Mackay—before any Australian cricketing Adonis— was the man to bat for your life.

He didn't come from the right background either—not a Melbourne public school, not even a Queensland private school. Just Virginia State in a poorer part of Brisbane. Perhaps that is why he didn't get in a test team until the end of his twenties, even though he had been among the top couple of scorers in the country for several years. But Those In The Know in the

Adelaide and Melbourne cricket clubs said his technique was poor, and, besides, he wasn't a good advertisement for the sunbronzed Aussie. He looked untidy. Of course no one ever actually said that, but that's what they thought.

Anyway Mackay kept proving them wrong. Although he batted first wicket down for Queensland it was suddenly noticed that he held the state record for the number of times not-out: an unheard of record—and all because he refused to see his weak state side beaten. How hard this man would fight not to lose.

Lunn, *Queenslanders* (1984), p. 7.

SIX JUDGES DEADLOCKED

John Devitt won a sensational Olympic Gold Medal in 1960, even though two of the second-place judges believed that American Lance Larson was the winner.

Winning the 100 m freestyle, the glamour event of Olympic swimming, meant that after all the years of playing second fiddle to swimmers like Jon Henricks, Murray Rose and John Konrads, he was finally the top 100 m freestyle swimmer in the world. His triumph, though, was tempered by the most sensational controversy of the Games.

In the final of the 100 metres, with about 10 m to go, Devitt was in the lead, but American Lance Larson put in an incredible rally for an extremely close finish. Two of the three first-place judges had Devitt as the winner, but two of the three second-place judges had him second. The six judges were deadlocked!

Among the timekeepers there was no doubt. All three timers on lane 3, Devitt's lane, gave him 55.2 sec, while the timers on Larson's lane had him at 55.0, 55.1 and 55.1 sec—all faster than Devitt's. Larson's time, 55.1 sec, was thus a new Olympic record. On the basis of the first-place judges' decision, however, the chief judge awarded the race to Devitt and ruled that the official time for both would be 55.2 sec.

The Americans immediately put in a protest, but the ruling

was upheld by the jury and the International Swimming Federation (FINA). Max Ritter, the US representative on FINA's executive committee, then lodged a protest directly with IOC President, Avery Brundage, an American, on the grounds that:

> the FINA rule called for the use of the timing machines ... in the event the judges were unable to decide ... the chief judge was in no position to judge the finish and that FINA rules do not provide him with a vote ... most observers at the finish line believed that the tall blond Larson had capped a rally by touching first by inches.

But Roger Pegram, the Australian Manager-Coach, stated unequivocally:

> John won ... My personal opinion confirmed the decision as I had taken up a position in line with the finish and I would give a winning margin of 4 to 6 inches.

Further controversy ensued when the Americans claimed that the CBS television film demonstrated clearly that Larson won. Norman May concluded in his book *Gold! Gold! Gold!* that, after closely watching the film in slow motion, frame by frame, 'there was no way of reaching a decision. All it showed was the flurry and splash of an extremely close finish.'

Howell, *Aussie Gold* (1984), p. 202.

WHEN A 'SECRET' MARRIAGE BURST LIKE A BOMBSHELL

Swimmer Lorraine Crapp was taken aback by the hostile reaction of officials to her marriage prior to the 1960 Olympics.

> When I was in Italy in 1957, I fell in love with the place. I could not afford to go back on my own, so when I realised that I could make the team for the Rome Olympics, I was determined to do it. My motivation for the 1960 Games was primarily to get back to Italy.

No longer at her competitive peak, but still a world-class swimmer, Lorraine found a place on the 4 x 100 m freestyle relay team. During training in Sydney early in 1960, she met and fell in love with Dr Bill Thurlow, who had been attached to the team to advise on weight training. Shortly before she left Sydney for the Olympic training camp in Townsville, she and Dr Thurlow announced their engagement.

In Sydney, on 17 August, the evening before she was due to fly out for Rome, Lorraine married Bill Thurlow in a small, private church ceremony in Parramatta. She was 21; he was 38. No public announcement was made about the wedding. When news of the marriage finally hit the newspapers on 28 and 29 August, shortly after Olympic competition had begun, Australian swimming officials in Rome cracked down on Lorraine. She was slapped with 'strict curfews and surveillance of all her moves around the Village'. By contrast, athletics officials encouraged Herb Elliott to spend as much time as possible with his wife in Rome and Murray Rose was allowed to live outside the village with his parents. To make matters worse for Lorraine, reporters tried to hunt her down, seeking a statement on the 'secret' marriage that had 'burst like a bombshell' over the Australian Olympic team. As Dawn Fraser later described it, Lorraine found herself 'enclosed inside a solid wall of disapproval'.

Surprised and hurt by this turn of events, Lorraine shied from the media and asked privately, 'Why should I make a statement to the press just because I got married?' Her morale plummeted. To this day, she has difficulty comprehending the ferocity of the reaction against her.

Phillips, *Australian Women at the Olympic Games* (1992), pp. 79–80.

THE MOTORISED MISCALL

There is little margin for error for a racecaller. ABC and Victoria Park announcer, Alf Gard, made a spectacular 'blooper' in Adelaide.

Victoria Park racecourse in Adelaide is well placed on the edge of the city proper, surrounded by access roads and with plentiful public transport. The back straight of the course, in particular, has only a fence and a line of gum trees between it and a busy highway. This led former ABC and Victoria Park course announcer Alf Gard into an historic, and hilarious, blooper.

Calling a race, Gard became excited by what he took to be a fabulous run down the back straight by a horse ridden by a jockey wearing red silks and a black skull cap. 'It's an incredible run', Gard enthused. 'I have never seen anything like it. He's absolutely storming past the field on the outside, absolutely mowing them down ...'

Gard was searching his memory for the horse carrying red and black colours, when he was given the bad news. 'That's not a horse and jockey, you twit. It's a bloke in a red jumper and black helmet on a motorbike on the road outside!'

Higgins and Prior, *The Jockey Who Laughed* (1982), pp. 37–8.

A NINE-YEAR-OLD KID WITH A BIT OF TALENT

Vic Edwards recorded in his diary his first impressions of the future star Evonne Goolagong (later Evonne Cawley).

Mixture of annoyance and curiosity when Col Swan phones me from Barellan ... Long trip, had to fly, just to look at a 9-year-old kid ... but Col and Faith Martin are good judges of talent, can't dampen their interest by disregarding their call, like to see what gets them that excited ... the girl is named Evonne Goolagong, Aboriginal, and I'd say the trip was worth it, in a way ... She has athletic ability, no doubt of that, moves beautifully, fast ... Bill Kurtzman's a good man and apparently she's his protégée, like to help him and her, but how? Strokes aren't much, but ability's there ... no such thing as a natural tennis-player because of the racket work involved, but this girl's a natural athlete and ability can be developed ... Her father's a wanderer, a shearer, knew plenty like him when I worked in the scrub ... no money, no idea what it would take for their daughter to get on in tennis ...

probably don't care ... big family, can't centre attention on her just because she's fair tennis-player. Aboriginal aspect might not sit well in tennis circles ... but a challenge ... interesting to see how far first Aboriginal could go in tennis if properly handled ... maybe an inspiration to her people ... I'll talk more to Kurtzman ... must talk to Eva, too, maybe we could bring the girl to Sydney for holidays, see what she's like, if she'd fit in ... maybe by then her family will have moved on and that's that ... interesting challenge to think about ...

Goolagong, *Evonne* (1975), p. 46.

THE LEGENDARY CRICKET DRAW

Ken Mackay was a national hero when he and Lindsay Kline helped achieve an improbable draw holding out against the West Indies at Adelaide in 1961.

But the thing for which Mackay should be remembered as a hero happened in the fourth test against the West Indies in the 1960/61 series. Australia had only a few wickets to fall on the last day to level the series. The match seemed all over, except that Mackay was still there. Wickets fell consistently as the day wore on until Mackay stood alone with spin bowler and non-batsmen, Lindsay Kline, with two hours to go against a West Indian attack boasting Wes Hall and Garfield Sobers. People kept leaving their wirelesses and TVs for an hour or two and coming back to find Australia, inexplicably, still there. 'He can't do it,' people kept saying, to keep themselves from hoping for the glorious impossible.

But with half an hour to go Mackay was no longer the only person who thought he could do it. Taking just a single off the last ball of almost every over (eight ball overs in those days) he faced almost every ball instead of Kline. No attempt to score other than this.

With fifteen minutes to go Mackay is surrounded by fieldsmen.

The announcer says gravely: 'Every man on the field except the bowler could pick Mackay's pocket'.

The last ball of the second last over: Mackay scores a single to face the last over against the fastest man in the world, giant Wes Hall.

'Mackay needs a snorkel tube to breathe,' says the announcer, 'the fieldsmen are so close.'

Twice he is hit, but seven balls have gone. Hall runs in for the eighth, loses his run-up, and the crowd, who thought it was all over, have to be cleared from the field. The match has run ten minutes over time but the over must be finished. Mackay chews on nonchalantly.

Hall puts his country into the last ball, it rears up at Mackay's rib cage, the fieldsmen rise from their crouches expecting some sort of deflection as the left-hander defends himself from the ninety-mile-an-hour red projectile.

Mackay, seeing the ball cannot possibly hit the wicket, pulls the bat away with his left hand at the last second and the ball crunches into his exposed right side. As he doubled up, the crowd rose. For, like Horatius, such a gallant feat of arms had not been seen before.

The match was saved. The series saved. Australia saved. Pictures of the bruise left by that last ball made all the front pages.

Mackay was a hero.

Lunn, *Queenslanders* (1984), pp. 5–8.

A MATTER OF PRIORITIES

Mr J. Smith of Hawthorn was a cricket zealot.

A balmy afternoon during a Test match at the Melbourne Cricket Ground was rudely interrupted by a between-overs announcement through the public address system.

'Would Mr J. Smith of Hawthorn please go home,' the voice announced, 'your wife is having her baby and must be taken to hospital.'

Laughter flowed around the ground as the spectators pictured a harrassed father-to-be hurrying off home to his wife. Not so, however, because about half an hour later the voice again boomed across the ground, this time with some urgency:

'Repeating our earlier message to Mr J. Smith of Hawthorn ... would he please go home immediately, because his wife is in labour and must be taken to hospital straight away.'

Much more mirth from the crowd, this time picturing a man reluctant to leave the cricket—but surely by now bidding farewell to his mates to dash to his vehicle and tear off home. How wrong were 20 000 spectators! Much to their delight, the now pleading message was repeated with grim urgency some 20 minutes later. After a further 30 minutes passed there was a bland announcement:

'Would Mr J. Smith of Hawthorn please go to the Mercy Hospital, where his wife has now given birth to a baby son!'

Brayshaw, *The Wit of Cricket* (1981), p. 18.

THE BEST-LAID PLANS ...

The relationship between a coach and his players is often a strained one. Journalist Hugh Lunn recalls his playing days in the Deep North during the 1960s.

One of the great things about Rugby though is that it has a position for every physical type: if you are too slow for the backs and too small for the forwards you can always become a fullback. And it was from back there that I saw enough Rugby to make me the expert I am today.

For example, it was in Toowoomba playing Downlands College that I learned the importance of kicking the ball when in your own twenty-five. Because this wasn't a competition fixture I tried to run the ball a few times and, unluckily, got caught with it when their eight forwards managed to close the gap.

At half time the coach said: 'if you're not going to kick the ball, son, get on the bus and go home.'

I also learned the power of the press and the need to stick to the pre-match plan.

The coach was a bit upset when the *Sunday Mail* named me as 'the best tackler on the ground'. 'How come, Lunn, our fullback's the best tackler on the ground and we lost by thirty points?' he asked.

At training before that match against Nudgee College the coach seemed obsessed by what one of their players might do to us, a chap called Dallas O'Neill (who later played for Australia). So obsessed, that he told a big forward in our pack—I'll call him Jones to save a reputation—that his sole role in the match would be to watch O'Neill.

'Jones, I want you to follow him wherever he goes. Hound him. If he brushes you off—even if he passes the ball—stay with him.'

The coach was right to have worried.

By halftime O'Neill had run riot. I saw him down with me so often I began to think he wanted to play in our team. They led 19–3 and an angry coach turned on Jones: 'And you, Jones, you haven't tackled O'Neill all day.'

'Which one is O'Neill, Sir?' Jones asked, and I saw the coach look to the sky in despair.

Lunn, *Queenslanders* (1984), p. 67.

IN THE LAND OF THE CUCKOO'S NEST

The international tennis circuit is not without its hazards, as champion tennis player Margaret Smith (later Margaret Court) discovered.

Our team split up after Wimbledon, with John Newcombe and Tony Roche flying off to Mexico to join up with the Davis Cup team under Harry Hopman. By now Roy Emerson and Fred Stolle had been wooed back by the LTAA and I could not help thinking that the two boys, who had left Australia expecting to play Davis Cup matches, would now be employed in a secondary role.

Our next target was the Federation Cup in Philadelphia. Robyn Ebbern had been added to our team and we were all hopeful that we could win the trophy this year. We had gone so close the year before when America had beaten us in the final and success in Philadelphia would have been a nice reward for manager Brian Tobin. We were again given the top seed for the tournament, ahead of America, Great Britain and Germany, but before playing our Federation Cup matches Lesley and I competed in the US national doubles title in Boston. We were staying at the home of Mrs Hazel Wightman for the tournament, and one morning, midway through the championships, I was called to the phone and a male voice on the other end introduced himself as a newspaper reporter. 'I would like to ask you a few questions,' he said. He sounded quite rational and his questions were harmless enough, but towards the end of the conversation I was staggered to hear him say: 'If you win the doubles title you will be beaten up and your head smashed in.'

I froze on my end of the phone and quickly put down the receiver. I called Lesley and told her what had happened. A short time afterwards the phone rang again and it was for me, but I refused to answer it.

It was the same person and Mrs Wightman, who took the call, ticked him off for his 'rudeness to a visitor to our country'.

He repeated the threats to me and not long afterwards a doctor member of the Longwood Cricket Club hurried into the house and saw me talking to Mrs Wightman. 'Thank goodness,' he said. 'We have just been told at the club that you had been seriously injured in a fall and that your face had been badly gashed and you were suffering from concussion.'

This extraordinary chain of events was starting to scare me, although it was obviously the work of someone irresponsible.

An hour later I hard that the *New York Times* had telephoned the tennis club for confirmation of a report that I had been shot dead. What next?

I believe the calls were eventually traced to a mental asylum in the area and the poor man who had made them was put away where he did not have access to a telephone any more.

Smith, *The Margaret Smith Story*, (1965) pp. 174–5.

THE MECKIFF INCIDENT

Ian Meckiff's resurrected Test cricket career came to an abrupt end at the Gabba in 1963 when umpire Col Egar no-balled him three times in his first and final over.

Was Meckiff set-up for the guillotine in Brisbane? I suppose this is one of cricket's top secrets that will never be divulged. Did Richie Benaud, the Australian captain of the day, have the slightest inkling of what was about to happen? If he did, he gave not the slightest indication. He remained throughout the crisis as inscrutable as the sphinx, itself. He walked up dutifully to Meckiff and spoke some words of encouragement during the prolonged over. But, as though resigned to it all, he did not bother to bowl Ian from the other end at all to test the feelings of umpire Lou Rowan, nor did he bowl him again in the match.

Some experts criticised Benaud strongly for that and Meckiff's supporters argued strenuously that one umpire should not have such complete authority to banish Meckiff from Test cricket. But I would have done exactly what Richie Benaud did that day. After all, Col Egar was our No. 1 Test umpire. He had declared three of Meckiff's deliveries 'throws' (though they all looked very much the same to me, and, no different to what he had served up over the years for Victoria, even in front of umpire Egar). That was sufficient and it would have been unfair to prolong the agony of Meckiff by asking him to bowl another over. So, in the unhappiest of circumstances, one of the great personalities of Australian cricket moved into the shadows.

Lawry, Run-Digger (1966), pp. 58–9.

Australian captain Richie Benaud later recorded his own feelings on the incident.

There really was no choice, in the light of the statements I had made to the other captains and to the chairman of selectors that, as soon as anyone was no-balled, I would instantly remove him from the attack, which is exactly what I did with Ian Meckiff.

It was very sad because it had a most detrimental effect on one of the nicest men ever to step on to a cricket field. Ian never played first-class cricket again. It had an effect on his family because it put enormous pressure not only on him but also on his wife and his children and it left a hollow feeling with everyone who had taken part in that game—it was an awful day and it all seemed sightly unreal.

It was also, I can tell you, a very strange way to captain your last Test match.

Benaud, On Reflection (1984), p. 56.

Weighed down by his decision not to bowl Meckiff, Benaud was a sucker for a practical joke.

There is nothing worse in the cricket world than not being able to get out on the field, particularly if there is some sort of pressure weighing you down. I was sitting in the luncheon room next to the dressing-room, musing on life in general and wondering if it were all worth it, when suddenly a strangely-garbed figure appeared in front of me. It was Jock, the team masseur. He had on his masseur's clothes but over the top he had a plastic raincoat and he was wearing a hat, something I had never seen him sport previously. He was also carrying a copy of a pink newspaper, the Melbourne *Sporting Globe*, which in banner headlines asked why I hadn't bowled Meckiff from the other end, with a secondary story of police protection being provided for the captain.

Jock looked a bit strange. The whites of his eyes were showing and he said, 'Why didn't you bowl him from the other end?' 'Jock,' I said, 'please go away, I've got enough problems at the moment.' All of a sudden he whipped away the pink *Sporting Globe* from . . . the gun he had in his right hand . . . and said, 'You should have bowled him from the other end.' The story of my life went before me as he pulled the trigger of the gun producing a bright flash from the barrel.

It took me a couple of seconds to realise nothing had penetrated the area adjacent to my heart and, as I slumped in a wave of relief, I caught sight of the figure rolling around on the floor outside the luncheon room. It was Bill Lawry. He had pulled off one of the greatest practical jokes of a cricket lifetime, although at that particular instance I didn't really feel like chuckling too much. It took me a few seconds to pull myself together and then I could see the humour of it.

Benaud, On Reflection (1984), pp. 56–7.

THE WORLD IS YOUR OYSTER —
IF YOU WIN

A football coach has many duties, including the pre-game and half-time oration to inspire his charges. Alan Killigrew, coach of North Melbourne Football Club in 1963, attempted to lift his team to greater effort.

This is it. THIS IS IT. You're in the BIG TIME after today. Now I want you to go out on that ground in a body all tight together. I want you to look like a VFL SIDE—the cream of Australian football. Let the whole WORLD know—it's US—against THEM.

You're going to fight now for North Melbourne and believe me, there's no better cause. North Melbourne always has been noted for GUTS. Don't you forget that ever. There's never been a North Melbourne team that didn't have GUTS. North Melbourne teams have been beaten, yes, they have been annihilated, but they have never been frightened. NEVER.

And if someone does something good, takes a good mark, give him a rap. Tell him. You're a team, remember. You got to LOVE each other. Yes, LOVE EACH OTHER.

The silk is here to see you today. Great names. The world is your oyster—if you win. But this is a ruthless business, the jungle. DOG eat DOG. If you go down, you're finished. NOBODY'S INTERESTED IN YOU. Already they're saying North Melbourne for the four. You can do it IF YOU BELIEVE IT. Well, I believe you can … It's the truth.

All right, I can't tell you how to win. I can't put blood in your heart. I can't push the blood through to work your muscles.

HEART IS SOMETHING YOU GOTTA HAVE ON YOUR OWN. Now North has won only five times here in thirty-eight years. Well, what are you going to do?

(Very soft now) Are you going to be one of those teams who COULDN'T or one of those who CAN?

(Applause and shouts of enthusiasm as the team runs out on to the ground).

Dunstan, Sports (1973), p. 229.

'GO FOR YOUR LIFE ... THE DEMONS ARE COMING'

Dawn Fraser obviously enjoyed a devilish escapade in Tokyo in 1964, even though it ended her Olympic career.

Around 2.30 a.m., while the party was still very much alive, an official (whose name I don't intend to reveal) took me aside, and muttered conspiratorially, 'Listen girl ... I know where we can pick up some good flags. Are you with me?'

I told him I was, all the way. 'Just stay here a while,' he whispered with a wink and a devilish leer. 'I'll spy out the land for us.'

He was gone from the party maybe half an hour, and when he got back, people were starting to wander off home. 'It's a beauty,' he said. 'Wide open. Flags everywhere. Not a cop about for miles.'

While we were preparing to leave, a third member joined the expedition, a hockey player who'll have to remain anonymous also. 'Where are we heading?' I asked the official.

'To the Palace,' he said. I thought he meant the Palace Theatre, or maybe the Palace Hotel. After we'd gone about a mile, I found that he meant the Emperor's Palace. The Palace with a moat.

We followed the moat for a while, and suddenly we were in the middle of a large flutter of flags. The flag poles were sprouting like exclamation marks all round us. We chose a fine big

Olympic banner, with the five circles on it; and one of my companions bunked himself up on the shoulders of the other. They swayed around a little, and they swore once or twice; but finally they pulled the flag loose.

'Quick,' said one of them. 'Cop this.' I took the flag.

'Go for your life,' said the other. 'The demons are coming.'

What happened next is a little confusing. The demons were certainly coming. Whistles were blowing, and a bunch of little men in uniforms were moving in on us. I hopped into the foliage of a very large shrub, clutching the flag, and bunched my body up tight and still. Unfortunately, my feet stuck out a bit, and the policemen had torches. Somebody whacked me on the foot with a baton, so I tossed the flag away, and started to run like mad. I was wearing blue jeans with a green tracksuit jacket and it seemed they thought I was a boy. They clobbered me with their batons around the legs and bottom, but I pushed them off and kept sprinting.

I jumped from the grass into a street, and saw a pushbike leaning against a wall. I ran to it, grabbed it, and started pedalling ... right through the gardens of the Imperial Palace. I hadn't ridden a bicycle since the old days in Balmain, but I was handling it fairly well, swerving round the shrubs and trees with a policeman after me. What I didn't realise at the time was that the bicycle belonged to that policeman. He was yelping and whistling, and I knew that a fairly large posse was travelling behind him. Then I saw the moat again ... on a level about five feet below the gardens through which I was cutting. I decided to abandon the bike and jump down to that moat. I'd seen it by day ... it was murky, it housed a lot of fat carp, and it was about forty or fifty yards wide. It was a beautiful moat. I figured that no policeman would ever catch me once I hit that moat.

That was when I ran into a brick wall. I'd been so busy studying escape routes that I hadn't seen the damned thing; and suddenly I'd hit it hard. I picked myself up, and decided that the only thing to do was dive into the moat. I climbed on the wall and jumped to the lower level, which was maybe eight feet down. I landed badly, on one foot, and I jarred and twisted my left ankle. It hurt a lot, and for a moment I lay there ... then I started to hobble towards the moat. Before I'd got more than a few yards, a policeman had dived at my ankles, and was flailing me around the back with his baton. A couple of his pals arrived, and they whacked me, too. I gave in.

Gordon and Fraser, *Gold Medal Girl* (1965), pp. 189–91.

HIT FOR SIX BY HOLLAND

Norman O'Neill recalls how, having defeated England in 1964 the Australian cricket team was acknowledged as the best in the world — until it met Holland.

No more surprising result has occurred in the long history of international cricket than Holland's three-wicket defeat of Australia on 29 August 1964. I was a member of the losing side that momentous day and I can assure you we tried our hardest to win against a side in which enthusiasm dwarfed technique.

We had arrived at The Hague from England acknowledged as the best team in the world, having just defeated England for the Ashes. We were the second Australian side to visit Holland, Lindsay Hassett having led his 1953 team to 157-run victory in the first-ever appearance by an Australian team on the European continent.

To our surprise a capacity crowd of more than 15 000 people watched the match, played on a coir mat stretched over concrete, similar to the surfaces many of us had begun on in Australia. The game looked a pushover despite the hospitality lavished on us throughout the day.

Australia scored 197 for the loss of nine wickets after Jack Potter took a nasty blow on the side of the head and had to be carried away to hospital. Potter thought the ball was a lot shorter than it was and when the ball kicked up he sustained a skull fracture. I managed to top-score with 87 but nobody else got more than 20, but with McKenzie, Connolly, Veivers and Martin in our attack 197 looked enough to win.

Holland started splendidly with a 99-run stand for the first wicket between Marseille (77) and Vandervegt (33) but playing cricket without understanding a word of Dutch was quite eerie. From 3 for 160, Holland moved into the last two overs with 20 runs still needed to win and they got them without the slightest trouble, through some spirited hitting by a tailtender named Onstein, who hit two sixes and a four in a knock of 24 not out. I remember looking round at the disbelief of my team-mates as Onstein clubbed the last ball from Bob Cowper right out of the ground and over the fence.

O'Neill in Pollard, *Middle & Leg* (1988), pp. 49–50.

'MY OATH WE'VE WON IT'

A last-minute goal by Melbourne footballer Neil Crompton capped a celebrated Melbourne Grand Final win in 1964. Coach Norm Smith recalls the euphoria.

'Umpire Ron Brophy waved the ball aloft and then bounced and my first strange thought was a slightly washed-out one: "In two hours it will be all over. Thank goodness." That attitude lasted one split second and then the tension mounted with every second of play. I saw Bluey Adams streak away with the ball and was furious to see it called back. I did not see what Tassie Johnson did, but I was annoyed he should infringe when Bluey had the ball in the clear.

'Then Waters marked, but I couldn't see him kicking the goal from the boundary against that tricky wind. The kick was on its way, and my heart sank as the Collingwood fans roared their delight. The Magpies were away to a flying start and the agony was on. Would they get a break?

'I never really believe we will be beaten, but it is agonising when it looks as though you can be. Play flashed to the Melbourne end and John Lord kicked poorly and out of bounds—an opportunity wasted, and you cannot waste opportunities in Grand Finals. John Townsend made amends with a beautiful snap and scores were level. My hopes soared when we swung into attack in the second quarter and slammed on three goals.

'Tassie Johnson was hit hard. I knew he would get up and go

on with the game. He knows football is a game for hard knocks. Soon I was in the depths of despair as Collingwood came back tenaciously. They scored three goals easily and I was praying for the half-time siren before they could widen the gap. It blared with Collingwood in front by two points.

'I will not repeat the things I said to the players at half-time. During the first half I was worried about Barassi's inability to lift his game. I kept sending the runner out to needle him and urge him to lift himself. I know Ron could react violently. He might abuse the runner, but he would also take it out on the opposition. All to no avail, he could not fire and seemed leg-weary. I said some harsh things because we had a fight on our hands and I was worried. I was most caustic with the players and tried to sting their pride. But I was disturbed. I did not think I was getting through to them. It is hard to tell, when players set their faces to conceal their feelings.

'In a match of soaring hopes and despair, my hopes again sky-rocketed in the third term. We had the play but could not put the score on the board. I was starting to get fearful again and felt Collingwood would have the scoring end in the final term. The Magpies were playing hard and tenaciously. They were not slowing up and I was very worried at the orange-time break.

'I told the players that guts alone would decide the premiership. Eleven points was a handy lead in a slogging low scoring game. But it might not be enough.

'That last quarter was the most agonising I have experienced in football. What a fantastic quarter it was! I was disturbed when the goal umpire ruled Townsend's shot for goal as a point. John and many others believed it was a goal. Still the umpire's decision is final. But it was a vital decision.

'We held on and held on and my heart was in my mouth. Then Gabelich, with great strength, kicked a goal and the difference was only three points. I had expected Gabelich to blow out. Instead he was playing on strongly.

'I was horrified a little later at the lack of discipline in the Melbourne side, when Gabelich again got the ball on his own and there was not a Melbourne defender between the goals and the half-back line. As Roet closed in, Gabbo bounced. It was awkward and I prayed the ball would run away. He recovered it and bounced again, again awkward, but again he gathered. I was praying he would have a shot, but he closed the gap between the goals with another bounce, which he again almost lost.

'I could see Roet could not make the grade and I was hoping Gabbo's final bounce would run away and through for a point. Another bounce and it flew out at a tangent, but his long arms scooped it back and from the goal square he slammed it through. That must have been the most stirring and thrilling individual effort in all football history. It was a great captain's effort, but I was in no mood for praise.

'Collingwood were in front and our premiership was gone— or so I thought. Melbourne showing plenty of guts, struck back and Hassa Mann took a great mark. My hopes rose again, I knew he would score and put us in front. He missed and our final hope was gone as the time keepers searched for the siren button.

'I couldn't believe my eyes as the ball came back into play and I saw Neil Crompton dash into the forward line, pick up the ball and slam through a goal. He should have been in the back pocket. I didn't know whether to abuse him for his lack of discipline or cry on his shoulder. He had no right to have kicked the goal to regain the lead. I was glad he used his initiative. There are times when a player has to, and without him we would not have won. As the siren was about to blast I noticed the photographers moving in on me. I steeled myself and resolved no matter which way the game went I would not put on a show. Yet the siren sounded and I found myself leaping in the air and yelling to Checker Hughes: "We won it! We HAVE won it!" Checker replied: "My oath we've won it".'

Dyer and Hansen, *Wild Men of Football* (1968), pp. 176–8.

Tony Lock's 'Nude Nut'

Bald English cricketer Tony Lock, who represented Western Australia in the 1960s, was a popular target for barrackers.

No one, however, attracted more comment than Tony Lock who had the double 'misfortune' of being both English and bald. In addition to 'nude nut' and the more banal 'Pommy bastard',

Lock was the object of a classic comment at the SCG. With a great sense of the dramatic a barracker repeated the comment, 'Lock, I'm awake to you', a number of times in the space of a few overs. Then, with the audience in his hands, he delivered the punch-line, 'You're not actually bald, your head's grown through your hair.'

Cashman, 'Ave a Go, Yer Mug! (1984), p. 125.

QUEUEING FRENZY

Fans queued for eight days in Melbourne in the mid-1960s to secure precious Australian Rules Grand Final tickets.

For the true picture of the behaviour of the football fan it is interesting to study how they behave at finals time. All the seats for finals at the Melbourne Cricket Ground are pre-sold during the second week of August. The peak years of the queueing frenzy were probably 1964 and 1965. The devotees started to queue immediately after football matches finished on the Saturday afternoon and then remained in line until ticket selling started eight days later on the Monday morning. In 1965 the main build-up began four days before selling day, and it reached its peak with ten thousand queuers. On selling eve there was a marvellous atmosphere, perhaps like 'canvas town' in the days of the gold rush of 1852. Melburnian queuers did it in style. They moved in with rugs, storm lanterns, sausages and crates of beer. Many, as soon as they established a permanent spot in the queue, put up a tent.

They brought along furniture, tables, chairs, kitchen dressers, camp stoves. One family, I remember, had a lounge suite—a sofa and two armchairs of quite charming contemporary design. During the night there was all sorts of entertainment to be had from record players, guitars, community singing, to the occasional portable television set.

It rained, frequently it was miserably cold, yet the queuers were undaunted. Altogether there were five thousand cars, many of them bogged in the mud. Some brought caravans or furniture trucks fitted out with beds. Experienced, well-trained queuers ran a shift system of queueing, four hours in the furniture trucks, four hours in the queue. In the early hours of the morning it was a remarkable scene—thousands of little fires—and as dawn came there was the smell everywhere of sausages and eggs.

This was the peak. The queue frenzy never happened again to quite the same degree, and all sorts of methods were devised to improve the distribution of tickets. There was an angry debate in Parliament. Sir Herbert Hyland, a former Country Party Leader, thought the scene outside the Melbourne Cricket Ground was akin to 'Oriental squalor' and he called for a full inquiry before a judge. The Deputy Premier, Mr Rylah (later Sir Arthur), said it must never happen again.

The following year the order went out; no camping equipment, no stoves or fires, no lounge suites and queueing was restricted. Queuers were forbidden to start lining up until twenty hours before the windows opened. Selling started on Tuesday so that queuers had to restrain themselves until noon on the Monday. Many defied the order and the Essendon cheer squad admitted that it was in the vicinity as early as the previous Wednesday. One would hesitate to say that there was any tunnelling, but queuers acted with the stealth of guerillas. They lurked behind trees and at the approach of City Council officers disappeared into the jungles of Richmond Park.

Dunstan, *Sports* (1973), pp. 215–6.

THE IMMORTAL PERCY SLEDGE-ING

The term 'sledging', first used by Australian cricketers in the 1960s, had an unusual origin.

Grahame 'Ilbe' Corling was a fast bowler for NSW and Australia in the early sixties. Ilbe (a shortening of the Frank Ifield song title 'I'll be calling you') is a likeable character who was a bit ahead of his time. Grahame used to swear in mixed company before it became fashionable.

On this occasion, the NSW team had a party in Grahame's hotel room in Adelaide. The room had quickly taken on the appearance of a London nightclub, but one of the players had to leave to attend a company function. On his return, he knocked on the door of Ilbe's room, at the same time as a waitress arrived with a tray of drinks for the party.

Corling opened the door and it became immediately obvious that what was a swinging gathering had been reduced to a drink and a discussion amongst a few teammates. 'What happened to the party?' enquired the latecomer.

'It's all f...ed up,' came Ilbe's straight-to-the-point reply.

Taken aback, the NSW player cast an embarrassed glance in the direction of the waitress and admonished the quickie. 'Ilbe, you're as subtle as a sledgehammer.'

The players who were left in the room burst out laughing and Grahame, who acquired nicknames like an autograph hunter gathers signatures, quickly became 'Percy' for the next few weeks.

Percy? Well one of the big hits at the time was 'When a Man Loves a Woman', sung by Percy Sledge. Hence the nickname, Percy. From that moment on, any cricketer in Australia who made a faux pas in front of a lady was said to be a 'sledge', or guilty of 'sledging'.

It was quite an appropriate term and was the cause of both mirth and embarrassment in its embryonic stages, but I'm afraid it has been spoilt for me by misuse.

Chappell, *Chappelli* (1992), pp. 154–5.

THE BATTLE OF MATARANKA

A match between four visitors and eight or nine men of Mataranka was the only game of Rugby League ever played in the town.

I myself have a small claim to notoriety in Mataranka as a participant in the only game of rugby league football ever played in the township. The field was an open, dusty area across the road from the hotel, and the match was not arranged—it just happened, in 1966. Frank Geddes and I, former team-mates in the Brothers rugby league club of Darwin, had called in with a couple of other fellows on our way to Borroloola. We were talking football in the pub and drinking beer. The barman joined in with a story of what a wonderful rugby player he had been some years before.

'By God, if you blokes only had a team we'd play you right now,' Frank Geddes said. 'A bit of a workout would do us all a power of good.'

'You're on!' the barman said at once.

The young men of Mataranka must have been waiting years for a chance like this, because within seconds somebody had produced a football. The big barman, who doubled on weekdays as the local schoolteacher, pulled on a tattered football guernsey he had grabbed from somewhere and leapt the bar, ready for battle.

The game was played in bare feet on the stony ground opposite the hotel, no doubt to the amazement of passing travellers. There were four men on our side. The Mataranka team had eight or nine players—the number varied as one or other would duck into the pub and serve himself a beer.

As we lined out before the match a wag on the sideline had a look at the expanding waistlines of some of the fellows and shouted 'Well, you mightn't *look* much like bloody footballers, but you've certainly got a *ton of guts!*'

We played for an hour or so, with several breaks for refreshment, and the Mataranka boys won by scoring the only try. Even so, we very nearly levelled the score when Frank Geddes darted around the side of the three-man scrum, swarmed over the top of the big schoolteacher, and raced for the line. With only ten yards to go, he unfortunately became entangled with a dog which had chosen that moment to wander on to the field.

We had a rousing celebration before resuming our journey and we had turned east from Daly Waters and were well on our way to Borroloola before we took stock of our skinned knees and hips and other ailments. Every one of us had holes gouged out of him by stones.

We were out bush in and around Borroloola for some days with nothing but a little spirits to put on our wounds. Of course many of the cuts became poisoned and on the return journey to Darwin we all had to troop in to the Katherine hospital for repairs and injections.

It had been a bloody good game of football, just the same. I have noticed on later visits to Darwin how the facts have expanded gradually over the years until our friendly match has become known in some circles as the Battle of Mataranka.

Willey, *Ghosts of the Big Country* (1975), pp. 54–5.

GATTELLARI'S BIG HEART

When boxer Rocky Gattellari fell to the canvas, Lionel Rose knew that his first defence of the Australian title would be successful. But Gattellari refused to lie down and the fight went on.

My first defence of the Australian title against Gattellari ranked among the biggest fights ever in Australia. The pre-fight publicity was enormous and apparently created as much interest as the Vic Patrick–Tommy Burns bout in 1946. And that was a big fight. The seat prices were the biggest asked for any of my fights to date: $10 ringside. The gate was over $50 000, a record for an indoor fight in Australia.

Despite the high prices, the Stadium was packed an hour before the fight. It was the first time since Jimmy Carruther's comeback fight against Aldo Pravisani in September of 1961 that the stadium had been filled to its capacity of 10 500 people. And it was directly televised to Melbourne and many other parts of Australia, and a relay started on Sydney television before the actual fight was finished. We had the biggest viewing audience for any fight yet held in Australia.

I was confident without being over-confident. Jack felt Gattellari might be worried by the big occasion and told me to try to unnerve him early in the fight. Our usual plan was to throw in a hard one to the chin in the second or third round to sap confidence, but this night the chance came much earlier, and I hit Gattellari with a double left hook to the head in the first

212

round. They were two of my best punches, and I felt Rocky's feet almost lift off the floor. The plan worked perfectly, and I was in command from the word go. Gattellari never had a chance to settle down and build confidence. I was the boss.

Gattellari's style suited me down to the ground. He kept moving up slowly with his head open to a left hook nearly all the time. Having been upset early, Gattellari was spraying his punches off target, and they carried little power. At one stage, after missing with a right-hand punch, he dropped his hands and shook his head in sheer frustration. I used body rips as often as I could, because it is the best way to slow a man.

I knew I was right on top and wanted to go all out for a knockout in the tenth round. But Jack felt Gattellari still had some fight left in him and told me to delay the attempt. In the tenth, eleventh, and twelfth rounds Gattellari slipped even more. Coming up for the thirteenth I said to Jack, 'I could go twenty rounds tonight.' 'Well, see if you can do it this round,' he replied.

I banged my gloves together and when the bell rang made straight for Gattellari. I hit him with a left hook to the side of the head, and he was hurt. Instinct forced him to fight back twice as hard; it amazed me for a few seconds that he still had the strength. I caught him with another left hook, but this time there wasn't the same retaliation. Then I remember landing about five more left-hand punches in a row—jabs and hooks— and Rocky slowed right up. The plan was to let the left hook do all the lead-up work in softening Gattellari, but we knew the right hand would be the danger punch. I let my right go—it was only a short punch—and Gattellari fell to the floor with his head and upper part of his body under the ropes. I thought it was the end, as I couldn't see him beating referee Vic Patrick's count. But he did.

Rocky had taken a lot of punishment, and nobody would have blamed him if he had stayed down. I had him beaten—I knew it and he knew it. It took tremendous courage—probably more than most people will ever realize—for Gattellari to lift himself off the floor. Rocky was never at the top of the popularity polls with the Australian boxing public, but I think he won himself more friends that night in defeat than he ever did in success. His gameness and courage were really something.

Patrick looked right into Gattellari's eyes to see if he was all right. I don't know whether Patrick spoke to him, but Gattellari nodded as if to say, 'I'll be OK'. Patrick let the fight continue because he felt Gattellari was in complete control of his senses. And he definitely was when the fight restarted. Many people have attacked Patrick over letting the fight continue. But he and I were in the best position to know how Gattellari was. Gattellari definitely knew everything he was doing and was capable of boxing on. When I cornered him on the ropes he cunningly slipped away to the centre ring. Even though I was on the verge of winning, Gattellari was still throwing punches in a bid to keep me at bay.

An opening came, and with another short right-hand to the head Gattellari was down again. On falling, Gattellari hit his head hard on the canvas. I don't know whether it was that last punch or the fact his head hit the floor, but Rocky was out cold. Patrick started to count, but only reached five when he realized that Gattellari had no chance of getting up. There was a funny feeling in my stomach when Patrick turned and yelled for the Stadium doctor and the ambulancemen at ringside. The doctor pulled out his stethoscope and I said to myself, 'He couldn't be badly hurt.' The fact I had won the contest and finally proved myself to Sydney fight fans and to millions of others on live television throughout Australia meant little at that moment.

My right hand was throbbing from the last punch, which put Gattellari down. But that was by the way. Gattellari's face was cut and bruised, and blood trickled from the corner of his mouth. It was a terrible sight. A radio announcer, whose hand was shaking, kept talking to me and turning me away from the scene on the other side of the ring.

Gattellari became conscious again while lying on the ring floor and started yelling and screaming, 'Let me up! Let me up! I want to get up!' But he was delirious, because he couldn't answer the doctor who kept frantically saying to him, 'Who am I? Who am I? What's two and two—two and two?' Then he lapsed back into unconsciousness.

Rose, *Lionel Rose* (1969), pp. 90–2.

THE INFAMOUS BOWLER HAT

The story about the man in the bowler hat—the Rugby League player who walked down a street in Leeds with nothing but a bowler hat on—has become a little confused in the telling.

The best Raper story is that he was *not* the man in the bowler hat. For years Raper has traded on the fact that he was the mysterious player who walked down the main street of an English town during the 1966–67 Kangaroo tour, wearing nothing but a bowler hat. He even did the Jax the Ripper tyre advertisements with a bowler hat and cane and at his 50th party the guests were all given plastic bowler hats to wear (Incidentally, the 80-year-old Christian brother, Brother Lawrence Wilkes, who had taught Raper football as a 10-year-old and who was flown over from New Zealand as a surprise guest asked all the guests to remove the hats while he said grace). Raper will admit he was not the man with the bowler hat and while he has made money from the commercial, he is slightly chagrined by the fact that today's adolescents remember him for the vaudeville act he did on TV and not for his football ability. 'I was at the SCG one day with Singo (John Singleton) and a father told his son to go and get my autograph,' Raper remembers. 'The kid asked why and the father told him I was a great player and then I overheard the kid say, "I thought he was Jax the Ripper".'

For years 'insiders' said the real man in the bowler hat was Parramatta second rower and lock Ron Lynch but Raper confessed it was Queenslander Dennis Manteit who later played with Canterbury and Balmain. 'We were staying at the Ilkley Moore hotel out of Leeds which has since burnt down and should have been condemned. It was a dreadful place and some of the guys would have a sin-bin every Saturday night in the lounge bar. Saturday was party night and there was an old bowler hat on the hat stand. Some of the boys would wander around wearing it and a jockstrap and braces and do acrobatics with a cane. But Manteit went a step further and actually walked down the street in the middle of the night with nothing on but the hat. The story went straight back to Australia and a photographer caught me wearing the hat one day as a joke. Then I started to wear it everywhere. Singo later got the idea to use it in an ad and it went from there. Dennis Manteit rang me up and said, "You bastard, you're making a fortune out of me".'

Masters, *Inside League* (1990), pp. 170–1.

'MY SISTER'

Evonne Goolagong inevitably encountered racism in the first years of her tennis career.

Trisha and I played for White City in the Linton Cup, a women's inter-club league. This was on grass, a surface I took to right away when I came to Sydney. There's nothing as delightful underfoot as a good grass court. Grass suits my attacking game, and I suppose it's my best surface, although by this time I feel at home on anything.

We were playing these two 'old women'—I suppose they were in their thirties—and beating them, and they didn't like it. And maybe we weren't on our best behaviour either. In matches we were certain to win, Trisha and I tended not to pay too much attention. We'd forget the score and dawdle about. It isn't polite to your opponents. Finally we won, and came to the net to shake hands.

Nobody was smiling. The woman I'll always remember glared at me, her eyes fierce beneath those plucked eyebrows. 'That's the first time I ever lost to a little nigger,' she growled.

Trisha began to cry.

'What are you crying about?' The woman was startled.

'You hurt my sister,' Trisha somehow said between sobs.

'She's not your sister!'

'She is my sister, and when you hurt her you hurt me—'

I hadn't been hurt because I'd never heard 'nigger' before, but I could tell by the way she said it that the woman was trying to be hateful.

Goolagong, *Evonne* (1975), p. 91.

Bifocal Or By Todman

Horse-racing has fostered many yarns.

A battling horse trainer's eyes faded until he could hardly see.

At last he went to be tested for glasses. On the appointed date he called to pick them up and was told the price was $75.

'What!' he replied. 'I could buy about 30 bales of oaten hay for that money. It seems a lot to pay for a pair of glasses.'

'Bear in mind,' the eye specialist said. 'These glasses are bifocal.'

'I don't care if they are by Todman,' the battling trainer replied, 'Seventy-five bucks is too dear.'

Hardy and Mulley, The Needy and the Greedy (1975), p. 17.

England 'Snowed Under'

The Australian Rugby League team overcame Great Britain, blizzard-like conditions and a snow-covered field with a treacherous flint-hard surface to win a Test match at Swinton on 9 December 1967.

While most of England was at a standstill because of the snow and extreme cold, at Swinton on December 9, 1967 Australian Rugby League had one of its finest moments.

It was the 'Ashes' deciding Third Test. Snow had been falling for a week and to make the ground anywhere near playable, officials had 21 tons of straw laid. The straw was removed on the Thursday, two days before the match started. But it had the right effect. It at least gave groundsmen the chance to make the ground ready for play.

Snow fell on the Friday and on Saturday morning. There were hurried conferences on the state of the pitch. Officials decided to go ahead, although there was little sport throughout England this day. The weather was bitterly cold and the field started to freeze when play began. The Australians claimed after the match they had never played on a harder surface. Not even some of the flint hard grounds back in Australia could match the Swinton pitch. But it didn't deter the Australians. They were the winners, 11–3 scoring three tries to England's one.

The English had no answer to the tough tackling of the Australians. They were given orders before they went out. 'Tackle as if your life depends on it'. The English didn't appear to enjoy the 'tactics' of the Australians. They had won the first Test 16–11, but lost the second 17–11. The Australians because of injuries never used the same combination in successive tests. Johnny Raper and Billy Smith missed the Second Test, but were back for the Third. Ron Coote, given Raper's lock spot, in the Second Test couldn't be left out of the decider and played second row when Raper returned. The move proved a master stroke and Coote's speed and determination brought Australia its first try and the halftime lead, 3–0 . . .

Australia's lead stretched to 8–0 when replacement Tony Branson scored a fine individual try . . . Branson was one of the stars of the second half and he was the player who set up Johnny King's touchdown to lift Australia's tally to eleven points.

Great Britain's only try came 15 minutes from the end when centre Malcolm Price crossed. By then Australia had the Test wrapped up. They were clearly on top with Raper in outstanding form. Coote's speed, in defence as well as attack, was another dominant feature.

The one sour note came three minutes from the end when Noel Kelly was sent off after he had flattened Great Britain half Tommy Bishop. Bishop made a quick dash and kicked the ball ahead. Kelly hit the little Englishman after he had kicked the ball and referee Fred Lindop immediately sent Kelly off . . .

But the result of the match was not in doubt at this stage. The Australians led 11–3 and at the final whistle the Australians chaired Raper from the field. They then gave coach Reg Gasnier, who had been badly injured on tour, similar treatment. The match was an unhappy one for Johnny Gleeson, who the following day left for Australia with his badly broken jaw wired. Doctors told him he might never play again, although he was later to prove them wrong.

But all this was forgotten in the midst of the great victory. For the second successive tour Australia had beaten Great Britain for the 'Ashes' on their own soil.

Greenwood, *Australian Rugby League's Greatest Games* (1978), pp. 56–8.

A RED WEAL ON THE THIGH

Commentating from the back of a truck during country cricket games can be hazardous.

Cricket commentators can get themselves into some pretty precarious positions—especially at grounds not designed for cricket. And that's just what happened when India played the West Australian Country XI at the rural town of Harvey during their 1967–68 tour of Australia. The ground at Harvey was laid out for Australian Rules football and trotting. So the temporary broadcast position for the ABC's commentator, George Grljusich, was on the back of truck parked at the boundary edge on the trotting track at one end of the ground. George's technical assistant that day, an English-born cricket fanatic called Eric Hill, was also acting as the scorer for the broadcast. The pair were reasonably happy carrying out their duties from this position when the Indian captain, the Nawab of Pataudi, let fly and lofted the ball straight back over the bowler's head and right on target for the truck top. Grljusich tried to catch the ball but missed and it flew through to hit Hill, who was wearing a pair of shorts, a very painful flow on the inside of his right thigh. Immediately a bright red weal showed up on his leg and the game stopped while the players jogged down to check on his well-being. Somewhat fortified by their presence, Hill reached for his pen, muttered with a forced grin:

'I suppose I'd better mark it down as a six'—and, using the outline of the ball as a circle, marked the remainder of the figure '6' on his leg!

Brayshaw, *Wit of Cricket* (1981), pp. 41–3.

THE VITAL VISUAL

Medical examinations for Australian Olympic athletes in 1968 were stringent, even humiliating. Female athletes, including Raelene Boyle, had to undergo a sex test to prove their gender.

All Australian teams chosen for the Olympic Games must undergo stringent medical examinations before departure, and 1968 was no exception. Victorian representatives were tested at the Melbourne University's veterinary clinic, and it was there that I concluded that the trip to Mexico was not going to be the fun excursion I had imagined.

I had not trained for two months after the Adelaide championships and was far short of acceptable physical shape when Dad dropped me off at the university at 9 o'clock one morning. I was still there at 5.30 p.m.

A squadron of doctors prodded, poked, quizzed and studied me for those eight-and-a-half hours. It was an ordeal that I was totally unprepared for, and one which planted the seeds of doubt in my mind about my responsibilities to the Games. I was required to reveal written and oral information about myself that I had not even disclosed to my mother. At one stage, the medical men suspected that I was suffering from a goitre. There were sections of the examination that I failed outright.

The humiliation was dreadful, and reached a depressing point when the female members of the team were ordered to subject themselves to a sex test to prove their femininity. There were three parts to this trauma. The first involved pricking a finger with a needle to obtain a blood sample. Then followed scraping of the inside of the mouth for a saliva specimen. It was the third step which really stirred up my indignation. Each competitor's pubic region was visually examined by a male doctor to ensure that it was, in fact, a woman's hair formation. It was frightfully disconcerting, at 16, to walk into a room with a much older guy and be told: 'Pull your pants down.'

I was indeed grateful that my allies for the sex test segment were swimmers Sue McKenzie and Sue Eddy. They helped infuse some humour into the situation. The three of us were examined as a group for the first two parts, then required individually for the visual inspection. Somehow, Sue Eddy, who was just 14, misunderstood the instructions and wandered off before the third section. When the doctor discovered that she was missing, he asked Sue McKenzie and I to locate her. This gave us the opportunity to engage in some sinister merriment.

'Sue, we're sorry but you've failed the sex test,' we announced, upon finding her.

Sue Eddy produced a reaction which we had not bargained for and, for a few moments, we thought our conspiracy had gone astray. But she, too, joined in the laughter after she had hastened back to the doctor to submit herself to that vital visual.

Boyle and Craven, Rage Raelene, Run (1983), pp. 33–4.

NONCONFORMIST AND WINNER

Humour helped some Olympians cope with the regimentation that is part of international touring. Maureen Caird had the last laugh when she won the Olympic gold medal in the 80 metres hurdles at the Mexico Games in 1968.

Shirly Strickland may have been a champion hurdler and sprinter, but she was a stern and systematic manageress. She demanded that rooms be kept clean and tidy, and made inspections each Sunday about 7.30 a.m. For somebody as experienced as Jean Roberts, this regimented scrutiny was unacceptable, particularly when my Coburg club-mate was still in bed. Arguments followed.

It was Maureen who injected some unintentional humour into those otherwise drab meetings of Shirley's. She arrived belatedly, as usual, one evening and casually bowled into the assembly in a long dressing gown, with tooth brush dangling from her mouth, an assortment of cream decorating her face, and her hair drawn back.

'Maureen, you're late again,' Shirley barked.

Without flicking an eyelid, my room-mate replied: 'The door handle's loose.'

To this day, I do not know what Maureen meant by that weird explanation. I doubt that anybody else does, either. But nearly everybody in the room rollicked with laughter.

Maureen, however, had the last chuckle on us all. She scored an unexpected victory in the 80 metres hurdles and equalled the recognised world record of 10.3 s. with her outstanding run.

Boyle and Craven, *Rage Raelene, Run* (1983), pp. 40–1.

PAST THE LIMITS OF ENDURANCE

Champion athlete, Ron Clarke, established seventeen world records in distances up to 10 000 metres, but an Olympic medal eluded him. The Mexico Games of 1968 represented Clarke's last opportunity for Olympic success but he ended the race in agony.

Australia's Ron Clarke collapsed after finishing a heart-breaking sixth behind Kenya's Naftali Temu in the Olympic 10 000 metres today. Clarke lay like a broken doll on the grass under a blanket for 10 minutes, his arms and legs writhing.

Australian team doctor Brian Corrigan wept as he knelt to massage Clarke's chest and stroke his head. Mexican doctors gave Clarke oxygen.

All around Australian athletes stood in stunned silence. Their faces showed their disappointment at the failure of Australia's greatest hope for a gold medal. It was a tragic end to Clarke's hopes of gaining at last the Olympic gold that has always eluded him. And it bore out Clarke's fears that mountain men runners from high altitude countries would dominate the distance events at Mexico's 7400 feet.

After 10 minutes of the treatment Clarke sat up, wiped his brow with his left hand and held on to a wire to help himself to his feet. Then he walked slowly off the track, his arms around Dr Corrigan and Australian track coach Ray Weinberg.

World marathon record holder, Derek Clayton, said: 'This is a sad day for all of us and most of the Australians, including me, could not stop crying when we saw Ronnie fighting to keep his legs going. Ronnie ran past the limits of endurance. It's as simple as that.'

Dunstan, *Sports* (1973), p. 304.

'A SECRET ABORIGINAL FORMULA'

When Lionel Rose fought for a world title in 1968 against Japanese boxer, 'Fighting' Harada, one Japanese reporter scurried to a library and read all he could about Aborigines. He developed a startling theory on how to beat Rose.

The next day Fighting Harada and I had separate two-round sparring bouts for live television. Jack made me strip off to actual fighting gear and a head-guard. I am big around the shoulders and arms for a little man—particularly for a bantamweight. One of the reasons I can make the 8.6 limit is that I carry very little weight in my legs. Harada was a couple of inches shorter than me, and although compact he didn't look anywhere near my size. Jack felt that if I paraded around and showed off my shoulders and arms it might just worry the Japanese a little more.

We will never know what Harada and his manager thought about my size. But it certainly had the local press intrigued. An Aboriginal was something new to the Japanese. They kept pumping Jack about how I was so big yet still a bantamweight. We found them quite gullible and played on it. I told them I burned gum leaves and inhaled the smoke as a weight reducer. It was a secret Aboriginal formula. One particular Japanese reporter hung around our room to catch a glimpse of me taking a special brew.

One other reporter went to the library and read all he could find about Aborigines. His report in the sporting newspaper *Nikka Shimbun* gave Harada a clue, through anthropology, on how to beat me. The report said: 'It seems Harada's best bet is to hit Rose on the leg. Australian Aborigines have notoriously hard heads. When the first European settlers went to Australia and fought with the natives, like the American settlers with the Red Indians, they found that even if they hit an Aboriginal on the head with a big stick several times it had no effect. They were vulnerable in the legs and fell down immediately if hit there. This is a tactic familiar to all white men when fighting Aborigines.' I couldn't stop laughing—it was priceless.

Rose, *Lionel Rose* (1969), pp. 105–6.

A STRANGE PREPARATION FOR THE 200 METRES

Five female athletes, including Raelene Boyle, had a novel preparation for a meeting in Hamilton, New Zealand, in 1969. Boyle routinely triumphed.

I was one of five Victorians selected to participate at women's meetings in Hamilton and Christchurch against teams from New South Wales and New Zealand for the R.H. North Trans Tasman Cup. The others were Jean Roberts, Pam Kilborn, Lauris Oakley and heavyweight thrower Ann Karner.

On January 22, the day of the twilight meeting at Hamilton in the rich Waikato district of the North Island, the five of us piled into a borrowed Hillman Imp car and headed off to the famous Waitomo glow-worm caves, 74 kilometres away. With Jean driving and the rest of us contributing in graduating forms to the substantial weight in the chugging vehicle, it wasn't long before a mysterious smell began to emanate from the vicinity of the engine. But we shrugged off this trivial inconvenience, cracked a few jokes, and continued on merrily. For the first time in my life I was a tourist, and I was loving it.

The return journey was not so pleasant. Just a few kilometres from Waitomo, the strength of the odour increased and a burnt-out clutch resulted. We were stranded. Jean insisted that she continue to steer while the rest of us hopped out and pushed, hoping that the car would re-start. This arrangement was abandoned after 3 km, however, when the work-horses at the rear of the Hillman rebelled on Jean after breathless fatigue had set in. We promptly made a panicky phone call to the meeting organisers, advising that we may be late. Then we spread out at 30-metre intervals along the road, raised our thumbs in the air, and prayed that some kind soul would pick up five desperate hitchhikers. We were lucky. A most courteous gentleman came to our rescue, drove us to Hamilton, delivered us to our respective lodgings, and we arrived at the track in the nick of time. I won the 200 metres.

Boyle and Craven, Rage Raelene, Run (1983), p. 56.

BILL LAWRY'S STRAIGHT BAT

Australian cricket captain Bill Lawry was not greatly concerned with a riot that interrupted a Test between Australia and India at Brabourne Stadium in 1969.

One of my most frightening experiences came on the field at the Brabourne Stadium in Bombay. It stemmed from an altercation in the crowd after the umpire had given India's Venkataraghavan out caught behind. The umpire took a while to raise his finger and in that time a local broadcaster made the unfortunate statement that Venkat. wasn't out, and should be recalled by Australian captain Bill Lawry. The incident started when Alan Connolly, Australia's opening bowler, induced Venkat. to cut at a ball well outside the off stump. There was a clear noise of ball hitting bat and Australia's wicketkeeper Brian Taber completed the 'catch'. From my position at first slip I thought it was out and went up in an appeal. Halfway through the appeal, I became aware that 'Tabs' wasn't appealing at all, so I stopped. But Keith Stackpole at second slip was giving it the full Indian war-cry treatment. Eventually Venkat. left the wicket and as he did a tremendous ruckus began in the crowd. It wasn't long before one of the canvas sun canopies in front of a grandstand was set alight and half the stands were in flames. People began to break up chairs and pile them into a corner of the stands to be set alight. The entire ground was soon shrouded in a huge pall of smoke and the official scorers asked the umpires to stop play because they couldn't see what was happening. The scoreboard stopped operating for the half hour before stumps and the situation was chaotic. Although Australia was well poised for victory it looked for a while as if the game would be abandoned. Bottles were thrown on to the playing area and the riot squad stationed itself between the crowd and the players. Just as fast as the crowd was dispatching bottles, the riot squad fired them back into the crowd. There was broken glass everywhere and some of the crowd began to jump from the stands on to the ground. As the crowd started pushing against the fence around the playing area, the fence threatened to give way. At this stage I went to Bill Lawry and suggested we group together at the end of play and leave the ground *en masse*. I don't think Bill even heard me. He just turned and said, 'Hell, we need a wicket badly'.

Chappell, Cricket in Our Blood (1976), pp. 66–7.

THE SOUND OF A SNICK

It took an eternity for an Indian umpire to give a decision in favour of the visiting Australians during the 1969 tour of India. He later explained why.

An Indian umpire gave the Australians one of our funniest moments during the 1969 tour. It was in a game against one of the zone sides and Johnny Gleeson, the Australian spinner who bowled with one finger folded underneath the ball, was giving one of the local batsmen a torrid time. The batsman couldn't pick which way the ball was turning and he repeatedly played and missed. Our wicket-keeper Brian Taber took about seven deliveries as they just missed the edge of the bat or the stumps, and we were becoming exasperated by this performance. Eventually the batsman played, got an edge and Taber completed the catch. We appealed loudly, very pleased to see the end of this particular fellow, but the umpire just looked and, for what seemed like an age, continued to look. Thinking he was going to deny us the wicket, a couple of us repeated the appeal. After what must have been thirty seconds, the umpire raised his finger and gave the batsman out. Relieved at his decision, we gathered around, patting Gleeson on the back and congratulating Taber, when suddenly the umpire appeared in the middle of our group. Pulling Johnny aside, he said, 'Mr Gleeson, I must apologize for taking so long over that decision. But there is a very strong wind blowing in the wrong direction and it took such a long time for the nick to carry to my end!'

Chappell, Cricket in Our Blood (1976), p. 175.

'YOU'VE KILLED THE BIRD, YOU ROTTEN SWINE'

Cricketer John Inverarity was completely baffled when a wild delivery, short and wide, mysteriously deviated to scatter his stumps. It took him some moments to realise the source of this freakish delivery.

Conditions were ideal for batting that afternoon. The second-day wicket was flat and true and the light so clear one could almost distinguish each stitch on the ball. Greg Chappell was bowling tidily but unthreateningly to me at medium pace. He had prevented me from scoring for the first 10 minutes of my innings and then, quite unexpectedly, bowled a wild delivery, short and wide of the off stump, which looked certain to provide me with a gift boundary to open my account. I prepared to give it the full swing of the bat as it went past at about waist high.

An instant later my stumps were scattered. I could not believe it. The ball looked so inviting before it vanished. Now I was out for a duck, clean bowled without even offering a shot, utterly baffled by the Chappell delivery. All the confidence and faith I had in my ability to bat drained from me. My eyesight and my judgement had deserted me. My cricket world was in tatters; it flashed through my mind that if I could make such an awful misjudgement and fail so badly I had best try no more. It would be impossible to continue if one shaped to square cut such an easy offering, lost it and simply stood by ineffectually and allowed it to crash into the stumps. It was an intolerable humiliation; I felt finished as a cricketer.

As these thoughts rushed through my mind I was unaware that anything extraordinary had occurred; only that my judgement had been terribly astray. Within moments, however, the truth of what had happened to that freakish delivery became apparent.

I had taken but a step or two towards the pavilion when I heard Greg Chappell say he had killed two birds with one stone. Simultaneously Rex Blundell, the South Australian 'keeper, held up a dead swallow. 'You've killed the bird, you rotten swine,' he said, jokingly.

Inverarity in Pollard, Middle & Leg (1988), p. 143.

'IMPROVED BY THE RUN'

Some punters never learn.

There were these two punters, strangers to each other, sitting in a Newsreel Cinema. A film of the two horse race between Rain Lover and Big Philou came on.

As the horses turned into the straight, one punter said to the other: 'I'll bet you ten dollars that Rain Lover wins.'

'That's a bet!' said the other.

Of course, Rain Lover did win.

Afterwards, the loser handed over his ten bucks.

The winner said: 'I can't take your money, I saw the film yesterday.'

'So did I,' was the reply, 'but I thought Big Philou would be improved by the run.'

Hardy and Mulley, The Needy and the Greedy (1975), p. 71.

SEX BEFORE SPORT

Is sex detrimental to sporting achievement?

Until recently sporting coaches believed sex was a fearful danger. The Lawn Tennis Association of Australia was horrified when Lew Hoad married during Wimbledon week. Football coaches have ordered their players not to have sex on the nights before matches. Bill Barrot, when playing as centreman for Richmond, believed that players needed even greater dedication. He wrote: 'I don't think footballers should be married while they are playing football. I regard both football and marriage as full-time jobs. That is why, for me, the two do not mix.'

Then, of course, there was the awful fear, the involuntary wet dream, or as it is sweetly known the 'nocturnal emission'. Johnny Famechon has told in his book 'Fammo' of his dangerous error in not taking 'the usual precaution' while having a doze before his world title fight against Jose Legra. The precaution was to tie a piece of string around the base of the penis. Then if an erection came during sleep, the tightening effect of the string was enough to wake him up. Then upon urinating the danger passed.

This view now is a little old-fashioned. Some athletes believe sexual intercourse even improves performance. Dr Tony Miller, director of research at the Institute of Sports Medicine at Lewisham Hospital in Sydney, says it depends very much on the athlete. Some are relaxed by it, but others are wrecked—they become very excited. Even so he did not think it wise for an athlete to slide between the sheets if, say, he was running in an event the next morning. But even this is disputed. The *Daily Telegraph* in Sydney had this quote from a 10 000-metre specialist: 'I don't know how you're going to put this into print but I had one of my best races when I'd had sex immediately before.'

Dunstan, *Sports* (1973) p. 18.

Six Bottles Of Beer Before A Match

Champion cricketer Doug Walters had a most relaxed approach to the game.

In the public mind Walters was an archetypal 'ocker'. Consciously or unconsciously Walters conformed to this image, as demonstrated by an incident recounted in his autobiography, *The Doug Walters Story*. During the 1969–70 tour of South Africa Walters and room-mate, Brian Taber, had enjoyed a surprise breakfast of six bottles of beer prior to the match against Western Province. As they were about to leave for the ground the bar opened on the first floor and Taber went straight in and ordered two beers. Walters wrote, 'I was trying to rush him to the ground, but I couldn't leave him to drink on his own, could I?' Walters and Taber finally arrived at the ground just five minutes before the match—they were supposed to be there one hour before—and he went out and made his only century in South Africa.

Cashman, *'Ave a Go, Yer Mug!* (1984), p. 141.

Dancing With The Opposition

Rugby Union players found new ways to socialise on a 1970 tour of Japan, as Steve Finnane relates.

The music was good, the lighting soft and it was our first opportunity to dance on the entire eight-match Australian Colts tour of Japan. So it might not have seemed unnatural to think of whispering a few sweet nothings. But my partner was a problem. His ears were so cauliflowered that nothing less than a full-throated shout had any hope of penetrating their leathery folds and to shout my thoughts might have been embarrassing. Yes, I did say HIS ears. It was one of those improbable situations you tended to drop into on a tour of Japan—the language barrier was almost absolute and the social patterns were a recurring mystery to a group of young Australians. Still, we did not imagine before that evening that we would end up dancing with opposing rugby players. We were at a club after our biggest win, 62–12, over All Hiroshima and as usual there was hardly a girl to be seen. If you want casual female company in Japan you generally have to pay for it and this situation has led to the practice of young men dancing with each other. There are no homosexual overtones in most of these encounters, or so we were assured, but when those Hiroshima players first asked us to dance we were sure they were joking. They convinced us of their sincerity and somebody said: 'What the hell, we might as well have a bit of a laugh.'

It was fine while the music was fast and we were all jazzing around, but there was a switch to slow, sentimental tunes and as most of the 'couples' went back to their tables, my partner, a squat, balding fellow with terrible ears and scar tissue over both eyes, grabbed me and held me tight. I thought: 'Blimey, I've got to put a stop to this.'

Finnane, *The Game They Play in Heaven* (1979), p. 32.

THE AUSSIE RULES DAWN SERVICE

Phillip Adams describes a suitable commemoration of Australian Rules Football.

I can see it now, a Dawn Service by a vast scoreboard which begins with a melancholy blast from a footy siren, a tribute to the Unknown Ruckman and a moment's silence in honour of those who've gone to the Grand Final in the sky. Then off they'd march, the rovers of yesteryear, the superannuated umpires and the old trainers stinking of Wintergreen. And instead of wearing those little red poppies on their lapels, the supporters who line the street to throw beer cans in their hero's path could wear small meat pies, with sauce.

Perhaps to give the ceremony real significance, a blood sacrifice could be considered. We really could kill an umpire!

Adams, *Australian*, 27 June 1970.

'THE LITTLE BLOKE IN THE FUNNY HAT'

When Pope Paul came to Randwick in 1970, he was upstaged by 'Percy the Punter'.

There was a Randwick identity called Percy, the punter. Everyone knew Percy.

When the Pope came to Randwick, Percy decided to make himself known to the Pontiff. He decided to front the Pope on the rostrum just before the Mass.

Two Randwick trainers were watching the Mass from a vantage point on the roof of an old stable outside the course.

One of them had binoculars.

The other asked: 'What can you see?'

'There's two blokes up on the rostrum.'

'Who are they?'

'Well,' replied the trainer with the binoculars. 'I can't place the little bloke in the funny hat—but the other bloke is definitely Percy, the popular punter.'

Hardy and Mulley, *The Needy and the Greedy* (1975), p. 49.

THE COLLIWOBBLES

Collingwood's inability to win a VFL premiership after 1958 was legendary until 1990. The myth of the Colliwobbles was born in 1970 when Carlton, eight goals behind at half-time, outplayed Collingwood in the second half to win the Grand Final.

The Magpies defeated Carlton three times that year and each win was noteworthy. Though behind all day at Waverley, including by twenty points at the last change, Collingwood roared back to beat Carlton by 23 points on 23 May. The rematch at Victoria Park in August was sheer annihilation, 13.23 to 2.12. Carlton put up a struggle when the two teams met in the second semifinal but succumbed by ten points. Naturally, the Magpies were hot favourites to end the run of bad luck under Bob Rose and beat Carlton when the two teams met again in the Grand Final.

An all-time record crowd of 121 696 went to the MCG on 26 September 1970. Some were thrilled; some were dumbfounded. All were shocked. The game proceeded as anticipated in the first half. Collingwood had a ten-goal lead until time-on in the second quarter, and entered the dressing rooms at half-time with a 44-point lead (10.3 to 4.5). What happened next has been retold too often. With nothing to lose, Carlton coach, Ron Barassi, issued his famous dictum: 'Handball. Handball. Handball'. An unsung player, Ted Hopkins, came onto the ground to kick four goals, much as he had done in the second semifinal and Carlton won by ten points. The myth of the Colliwobbles was born.

Stremski, *Kill for Collingwood* (1986), p. 224.

FINE-TUNING

Evonne Goolagong had a novel way of concentrating on the court.

So we were all at Wimbledon, and everything was apples, as we'd say in Australia. Actually it was strawberries and cream, in terms of the most publicized item on the Wimbledon menu. I had my music with me, a transistor radio-tape recorder that I'd taken to carrying round, and I hoped it wouldn't bother anybody in the changing room. Billie Jean King, the 'Old Lady' to many of her colleagues and the ringleader of the women's movement in tennis, gave her approval: 'About time we had some music in here to liven the place up.'

Otis Redding was my favourite that summer and I heard a lot of '... sittin' on the dock of the bay ...' Mr Edwards can't understand my passion for this kind of music, but concedes, 'It has something to do with keeping her relaxed and happy, no doubt of it.'

He likes to tell about a time in Dusseldorf when I was playing horribly against the German Heidi Orth. Lost the first set and was losing the second, whereupon I did a complete turnabout and won rather easily.

233

'For God's sake, sweet, what was going on out there?' He was a little cross with me. 'For the longest time you're playing absolute rubbish, as though you'd forgotten everything you ever learned. Then—like turning on a light switch—everything changes and you become a bloody dream, hitting winners all over the place. Do you mind helping me try to understand?'

'Well, uh, I was trying to think of this tune—it just wouldn't come to me. But there, in the second set, I got it, and started humming it, and everything was all right. Ah yes, I guess I was in a bit of a fog until then.'

He gave me one of those 'she's round the bend' looks and headed for the bar.

The song was 'Ain't No Sunshine When She's Gone' on a tape I liked by Bill Withers. Billie Jean may have liked my music, but there was no sunshine for her when she was gone from the semifinals, 6–4, 6–4, on one of my best performances.

Goolagong, Evonne (1975), pp. 136–7.

THE EVONNE PHENOMENON

Evonne Goolagong's coach Vic Edwards was surprised by the amount of 'junk' that fans lavished lovingly on his tennis protégée.

Unbelievable the amount of gifts Evonne has accumulated ... I call it her 'junk' but actually it's quite valuable, don't know how valuable ... most of it in trunks in storage ... wouldn't have room in the house for all of it ... we'd have to live in the garden if her junk was in the house ... this is part of the phenomenon of Evonne—that everywhere she goes she's greeted like an empress ... they give her jewels, clothing, silver, furnishings of all kinds ... it's her nature, different to any other athlete before her ... the freshness, the unassuming attitude ... she looks at these things, then puts them in a trunk ... how much jewellery can one person wear ... a few things she treasures, a gold watch, some china ... she gets enough clothing to keep a women's college well dressed, all gratis, but Evonne is essentially a person most at home in jeans and bare feet ... how can you turn people down ... this giving is an expression of people's love for her and the way she affects the public ... it's a very touching thing ... I'll hold the storage checks and maybe someday she'll look at it all and decide what to do with it ... thank God people don't give me things ... sometimes they buy me a beer—that's fair enough ...

Goolagong, Evonne (1975), pp. 71–2.

GETTING THE FIELD RIGHT FOR SOBERS

When Garry Sobers scored 251 against the Rest of the World XI at the MCG in 1971–72, Ian Chappell had a ready response for those offering advice on how to set the field.

The best batsman I've ever seen was Garry (now Sir Garfield) Sobers. I'm not including all his other assets as a cricketer, this is as a batsman pure and simple. His technique was simple and his batting a pure joy to watch.

He had every shot in the book and he had the technique to bat anywhere in the order. In his first Test, Garry played as an orthodox spinner and batted number nine. In his fourth Test he opened the batting against Ray Lindwall and Keith Miller, and made 43 before he was dismissed by off-spinner Ian Johnson.

As an eighteen-year-old twelfth man for SA, I watched open-mouthed as he demolished a NSW attack including Alan Davidson and Richie Benaud, while making 251. When Benaud recalled Davidson to put the brakes on his progress, he promptly hit him for four, six, four. The six scattered the delirious patrons at the Adelaide Oval scoreboard bar.

I had the part pleasure, part painful experience of captaining an Australian team that fetched and carried while he amassed 254 for the Rest of the World XI at the MCG in 1971–72.

Lillee had got Garry for a duck in the first innings and he was keen to make amends. By stumps on the third day he was 132 not out, and over a drink in the Australian dressing-room he confided, 'Ian, Prue [his wife] has left me.'

'Garry,' I said, mindful of the thrashing we were receiving, 'if that's what is making you angry, give me her phone number. I'll talk her into returning home immediately.'

After Garry had completed his demolition job (and Prue had returned home), I got a call from a mate of mine, Ray Hogan, who had played against Garry in the Leagues in Lancashire.

'Ian,' he started, 'you've got your field in the wrong place for Sobers.'

I didn't let him get any further. 'Yes, you're right Ray,' I answered. 'They were at the MCG. If I'd had any sense we'd have been at the SCG.'

Chappell, *Chappelli* (1992), pp. 126–7.

HOLY WATER

All sections of Australian society follow sport.

It is doubtful whether the gambling passion will ever decline. It is important to keep a number of sports, like horse-racing, dog-racing, football and even professional foot-running, healthy, in order to give gambling respectability. We are said to be the world's champion gamblers, $160 a head a year, compared with $90 for the Americans, $50 for New Zealanders and $30 for the British.

As an illustration of the passion this surely was the most revealing story of 1972. Igloo, the racehorse of the day, was in Perth for the Cup carnival; this almost priceless creature had an injured leg and was in danger of being destroyed. A Perth nun sent holy water from the Shrine at Lourdes to rub on that injured leg.

Dunstan, *Sports* (1973), p. 30.

FOR EVER IN THE GOAL SQUARE

For some Australian Rules fans the team is everything.

In April 1972 the *Herald* reported the case of a gentleman, who, just before he died the previous October, expressed the wish that his ashes be buried on the Richmond football ground. The club secretary, Mr Alan Schwab, made this possible; the ashes were buried right in the goal square. There are other cases of similar devotion. In June 1969 a Perth man had a similar last request. He had himself buried in the number 18 guernsey of South Fremantle, plus South Fremantle football socks.

Dunstan, Sports (1973), p. 214.

NO PUSHY PARENT

Lorna Boyd, mother of Rugby League international Les, had very limited interest in the game in which her son starred in the 1970s.

Les's mother only saw him play two games. Lorna says, 'One was a game when Les was playing for Wests. The other occasion was when the chap next door at Nyngan took me. I saw this young fellow running down the field and I said, "Isn't *he* good?" The chap said, "Don't you know who that is?" When I said "no", he said, "That's Les. That's your son." Rugby league's too fast for me. I can't understand it. I like to hear it on the radio where they explain it to you.' Les says, 'Mum never showed any interest. She never said I couldn't play football. She didn't show any interest in watching football. Sure, she asked if we won and all that kind of stuff.' Bill and Lorna Boyd certainly don't appear to be the textbook examples of psychologist Bay's pushy parents.

Masters, Inside League (1990), p. 39.

THE JOY OF SIMPLY PLAYING

*Evonne Goolagong wanted spectators 'to take home a good memory'
from her matches.*

Some of my best friends are white.

Without them there'd have been no tennis, no Wimbledon,
no discovering and refining this talent I have for pursuing and
pummeling a ball. It isn't a talent that necessarily enriches
mankind, but entertainment does have value. It enhances life.
Neither winning nor losing means as much to me as knowing the
crowd has enjoyed my match. Some players feel that winning is
everything, and losing a disaster. Not me. I want the spectators to
take home a good memory. If I'd lost my 1972 Wimbledon
semi-final to Chris Evert in three sets instead of winning in three,
I'd have been disappointed. But not displeased or angry. Because
of the occasion, the tension, the fight we both displayed, and our
shot-making, it will rank as one of the memorable matches. I was
told that it was an emotionally draining experience for the
viewers. Above all: An Experience. Playing a part in a gripping
sporting drama is all I can ask.

Goolagong, *Evonne* (1975), p. 33.

LIFE AFTER GOLD

*Shane Gould would have been at her peak in 1976, and still only
nineteen, but she chose to retire from competitive swimming after the
1972 Munich Olympics.*

The Australian swimming establishment was, of course, eager for
Shane to go back. Here was a gold medal machine like Dawn
Fraser but without Dawn's rebelliousness. In 1972 many 'experts'
confidently predicted that Shane's third placing in the 100 m

freestyle at Munich would be sufficient to assure her presence at the Montreal Games in 1976. By then, she would still be only 19 years old and, presumably, eager to avenge her 'defeat' in one of her favourite events. But the experts did not know Shane Gould as well as they thought. Still very young, she was on a quest to find a spiritual meaning that went far deeper than the glitter of Olympic gold or even the satisfaction she had once derived from swimming.

In 1973 she became involved with Alan Walker's Wesley Central Mission. There she discovered in Christianity the spiritual dimension she had been seeking. At the age of 16, she announced her retirement from swimming. She met West Australian Neil Innes at a Christian youth camp and the two were married in 1975. Contrary to what experts had predicted, the next year Shane was not at the Montreal Olympics. Instead, she was helping Neil set up their modest 30-hectare property in the Margaret River district of Western Australia. There they have reared four energetic children far from the intrusions of the media. When awarded an MBE for her services to swimming in 1981, she said that she felt she deserved it more for being a mother than for winning races.

Phillips, *Australian Women at the Olympic Games* (1992), p. 100.

SAVED BY A WEE DROP

Raelene Boyle was beaten in the 100 metres at the 1972 Munich Olympics by the East German, Renate Stecher. Stecher also outclassed Boyle off the track in the compulsory dope test. Boyle was rescued by Munich ale.

Not only did Stecher eclipse me on the track, but she later gave me an embarrassing thrashing when we submitted ourselves for compulsory dope tests after the medal presentation. We were required to enter cubicles about the size of paraplegic toilets, and urinate into small plastic containers in the presence of a female medical supervisor. For Stecher, this procedure did not present the remotest problem. For self-conscious and fluid-drained me, the exercise was a complicated marathon.

At a conservative estimate, I reckon my nerves forced me to visit the toilet a dozen times in the few hours surrounding the semifinals and final of the 100 metres. I hadn't saved a drop. Stecher amazed me. She produced her urine sample in five minutes and vanished to celebrate her victory.

During the next two hours, I consumed several litres of soft drink in a bid to manufacture the necessary specimen. I stood by running taps, and the ever-watchful overseer flushed the toilet many times. But it was to no avail. I was beginning to think that I would never urinate again. Australian officials occasionally popped into the dope-testing area to see how I was progressing. My predicament was becoming a joke.

The section manager of the Australian track and field team, Alex McIvor, eventually suggested that he accompany me to the Press Bar at the stadium for a couple of beers. I was willing to try anything at that stage. Amid much back-slapping and encouragement from amused journalists, I downed a moderate quantity of excellent Munich ale before returning, under the obligatory escort of the supervisor, to the place of urine production.

The overseer resumed her presence in front of me, to check that it was my sample being deposited in the container, but still there was lack of activity.

'Look, there's no way I can have a wee with you peering at me,' I complained, finally and frustratedly.

I added: 'It may be all right for Europeans and Asians, but it's not the sort of thing we do in Australia.'

As a compromise, the supervisor agreed to vacate the cubicle provided I stripped off my clothes, exposed myself to a search, and remained alone until the bladder performed. With me wearing nothing but an innocent blush, the beer did what it was supposed to do and the specimen arrived after about 10 minutes.

Boyle and Craven, *Rage Raelene, Run* (1983), pp. 94–5.

'LET DE TIGER LOOSE'

The Australian cricket team received generous support from one particular West Indian spectator.

Stories about those good-humoured West Indian spectators abound. In 1972 when Australia beat England at The Oval to square the series, Dennis Lillee bowled magnificently. In the crowd that day there was one big West Indian who kept up a continual stream of advice and humour. He was very much a Lillee supporter and whenever I took Dennis off for a rest he started up a chant that echoed around the ground, 'Chappell, let de tiger loose, man, let de tiger loose'. The longer Lillee was away from the bowling the louder and more frenzied our friend's chant became. At the end of the game, the West Indian and some of his friends stood in front of our dressing-rooms, chanting and telling us we would find the going much harder in the West Indies. Eventually, we passed down a bottle of champagne to them, because they had wanted so much for an Australian victory. But the story doesn't end there. It continues when the Australians arrived in the West Indies early in February the next year, five or six months after The Oval Test. We played our first match against a university side in Kingston and at lunch-time we had to leave the dressing-room and walk right across the ground into a basketball stadium to eat. As I was climbing the fence around the ground I heard a raucous voice behind me, 'Hey, man, let de tiger loose'. That's right, it was our friend from The Oval. He had come 'home' to watch the series.

Chappell, *Cricket in Our Blood* (1976), p. 96.

241

WATCHING CRICKET 200 FEET UP

Ian Chappell was intrigued by some of the vantage points of spectators at Sabina Park, Jamaica, in 1973.

The authorities at West Indian grounds never worry about capacity crowds or shutting the gates when the crowds get bigger than the ground can hold. I remember talking to the secretary of Sabina Park, in Kingston, Jamaica, the day before we started the First Test. I asked him what sort of a crowd he anticipated, and he said on Friday, the first day, we could expect about 11 000 people. I asked him what was the capacity of the ground, and he replied, 'Oh, about 14 000. But there will be 15 000 or 16 000 here on Saturday and anything up to 17 000 on Sunday'. Arithmetic wasn't my best subject at school, but it didn't take me long to figure out that the Sunday crowd would be well above the capacity. So when I asked where they would all fit, the secretary pointed out the roof of the grandstand and said there would be a couple of hundred there. He admitted the grandstand had collapsed a few years earlier and several people had been killed, but said that didn't make much difference. He also pointed to the trees surrounding the ground and said several hundred spectators would be perched in the over-hanging branches. 'There will also be a big crowd perched on top of the sightboard', he said. The sightboard at Sabina Park is a big brick wall about twenty or thirty feet high and it's certainly not my idea of a good viewing spot for a day's cricket. Then the secretary added, 'The biggest asset we have at this ground is the four light-pylons'. I looked out over the ground at the four pylons, each about 200 feet high, which were used to light the oval for night soccer. When the secretary said the capacity of each pylon was about 500 people, I laughed, thinking he was having me on. Anyhow, on the Saturday, a big crowd turned up, as the secretary had forecast. When we went out for practice before the start of play there were people everywhere, on top of the stand and hanging from the branches. As I looked up at one of the pylons, there, about 200 feet up, was a man standing on a metal ledge about three or four inches wide, clinging for dear life to the pylon with one hand and clutching the ever-present bottle of West Indian rum with the other. That chap intrigued me, and I kept watching him even after play started. Every now and then I noticed he took a swig from the bottle. As the day went on I became more fascinated as to why he didn't fall and break his neck. Eventually, about 2 p.m. after he had been up there about three or four hours, he finished the bottle. But to my surprise he kept hanging on to it. My curiosity aroused, I asked one of the West Indian batsmen why the man didn't throw the bottle away and hang on to the pylon with two hands. 'Keep watching' was the advice. I did, and soon enough I had my answer. I think I can say on behalf of the couple of hundred people on the pylon below him—and especially Alan McGilvray if he was one of them—that they were eternally grateful he kept the bottle for the reason he did.

Chappell, *Cricket in Our Blood* (1976), pp. 98–9.

MY BOY ROY

Celebrated Australian fiction writer Olga Masters had her own style of reporting on the sport of her son, Rugby League coach Roy Masters.

All the male reporters were down with 'flu on Thursday and there was a threat that no one would be available to report the Manly–Penrith match at Brookvale Oval.

Late in the afternoon the editor suggested I go along.

This came as a great surprise, because I did not know anyone in the office was aware of my affiliation with big rugby league through my boy Roy.

Wisely I keep my personal life to myself, and had never mentioned that my boy Roy took the triumphant Australian schoolboy rugby league team to England in 1972 and his brilliant coaching resulted in their line being crossed only once in the thirteen-match tour.

He came back to take a national coaching examination with a distinction, and joined the Penrith club as a coach for the premiership 1974 season.

When told of my assignment I flew to the phone to make another illegal call to Penrith.

Roy told me not to worry; he would fill me in on the game and explain such quaint phrases like scrum going down, finding touch, and so on.

In fact he said he could tell me the score then.

'With Ashurst kicking, Stephenson getting most of the ball, Glen West running like a deer, Walton taking every goal, we should be jake.'

'We should be level at halftime,' said my boy Roy.

'The last two points in the last five minutes of play could go either way. Probably ours.'

I went home and baked a batch of rock cakes for him to share with the team on their ride home to Penrith after the match.

I took the tin to him in the coach's box at the start of the game.

This was a disappointment. I thought he would be in his blue coach's gear—a perfect match for his eyes—but he was in an orange-coloured shirt, tweed sports coat and brown pants, and looked like an ordinary person.

I went and sat close to the oval and my thoughts went back over the years to the days when he was in the six-stone team at Mummulgum.

Then a thought hit me.

Oranges! Where were the oranges?

At Mummulgum we mothers used to go on after the game with oranges cut into quarters and hand them out for the players to suck to ease their parched throats.

I left the ground and ran a mile along Pittwater Road, to find a fruit shop.

There were people inside with glazed eyes, and foolish grins on their faces, and the one with a radio going full blast.

One moved forward to serve me, like he was in a trance.

'Hamilton is back in form ... Eadie is brilliant ... there's no holding them now ... we'll make it to the finals.'

These names were unfamiliar to me, so they must have been following another code of football—perhaps the World Cup Soccer series —as they were New Australians.

I ran back to the ground with my oranges.

An interested bystander looked at me counting them out on the seat.

'You won't need one for Ashurst, lady,' he said. 'He's been sent off!'

I wheeled round and looked for Big Bill, who only a couple of weeks ago had cooked a steak for me at a Penrith barbecue.

I could not see his amiable lumbering figure and his darling black head.

'Why, oh why?' I cried.

'Rough play, luv.'

He wouldn't have meant it.

Out there on that cold, bleak field he would have been homesick for the chaffinch singing in the orchard bough in England now and, in passion of loneliness, he must have flayed the air with his great arms and accidentally hit someone.

I turned back dumbly to the oranges.

I had no knife to cut them into quarters, like we did in Mummulgum.

But my boy Roy, as well as everything also, was a Queen's Scout in his youth and he always carried his six-bladed knife, adding in recent years a corkscrew—through association with some of the rougher types—inevitable unfortunately, in the process of reaching adulthood.

I raced to the coach's box.

I asked for the loan of his knife.

'Don't Mum, don't!' he cried.

'Don't cut your throat until the game is over . . . the final score on the board. I'm hanging on to hope. You can too.'

I went back to my place and naturally had to have my back to the field to cut up the oranges.

But I kept my ear on the game, as it were, through the spectators around me.

I knew we must have been winning because they were all Manly supporters and were yelling, 'Kill the bastards.'

These are the kind of things said at the height of a passionate desire to see Manly win—an understandable attitude, with opposition like Penrith.

I put the cut-up oranges back into the bag to take them to Roy.

I raced after him into the dressing shed because it appeared that, as the players were coming off, the game was over.

Somebody rudely tried to shut the door in my face.

'Get out lady,' said this large burly man. 'They're changing.'

This was ridiculous.

My boy Roy was in there and I had seen him without his clothes hundreds of times.

Besides, I had to ask him which side took the last two points.

Masters, *Manly Daily*, 22 June 1974.

THE RARE SIGHT OF DOUG WALTERS AT PRACTICE

To see cricketer Doug Walters at practice was a rare event.

At the start of the 1974–75 season, the Australian cricket team was set to launch into an era in which it would dominate the international scene. Jeff Thomson was about to join Dennis Lillee to give the side its most potent attacking force since Lindwall and Miller in the 1950s and there was a look of depth to the batting. Going up to Brisbane for the First Test against England, there was only one batsman in the Australian line-up whose form was worrying—Doug Walters. The New South Wales dasher hadn't had the best of series against England in 1970–71 (in Australia) and 1972 (in England) and he was coming into this game with an average for the season that was down in the 'teens.

Walters himself must have been a bit concerned. Well, just a tiny bit, because he shocked his team-mates by arriving at the nets on the morning of the first day of the Test. It was such a rare sight, Walters *practising*, that he was immediately the centre of attention. He had brought along a bat and ball and he proceeded to 'practise'. First he tossed the ball in the air with the obvious intention of hitting it into the side of the nets, just to 'feel' the ball on the bat. But the ball wasn't there—it landed on his shoulder. Now *everybody* was watching! The second throw produced the desired result and Doug hit it right in the middle. 'I'm seeing them much better now,' he declared, and without even stopping to pick up the ball, he headed back to the dressing-room.

Brayshaw, *Wit of Cricket* (1981), pp. 26–7.

THE MACHO MUSTACHIOED NEANDERTHAL OF AUSTRALIAN CRICKET

Roy Slaven (alias John Doyle) has his say on the 'underhand, underarmed, money-grubbing narcissistic Age of Chappell'.

Brian James, the English cricket commentator, said in 1975, 'The progress of the Australian cricket team around England last summer was marked by the sound of slammed pavilion doors, four-letter greetings, and high-decibel descriptions of the previous night's spewing.' These were lads, hardly in the tradition of great ambassadors of the past, who seemed not to care for the green baggy cap. I worry. But I know from whence it stems. It was the Chappell era that heralded this trend of the macho mustachioed neanderthal Australian cricketer, who could wink at the Queen and call the Governor-General 'mate', or drop his daks un-ashamedly on the hallowed turf of the MCG—to be, in short, a contrived lovable larrikin, the sort of rogue we should have come to love. But this was not to be: it was far more insidious than this. Yep, it was almost solely that self-professed greatest of all modern Australians, I. M. Chappell, who lowered the tenor of cricket to that of its ugly sister from over the Pacific—baseball. It has created the mentality that would have us bringing 'lucked out' and 'taking a raincheck' into our everyday usage, and refusing to use adverbs, and dropping the 'and' in the quoting of numbers over three figures, like 'Jones scored one hundred eighty-four'. The mentality that welcomes Bryant Gumbel as an acceptable face in news telecasting and hopes the Americans really care about the Cup, and is keen that it be mandatory that our tennis players pump themselves up and get fined for racquet abuse. It's giving the two fingers with the horn at traffic lights, and going to the Demolition Derby. It's having an apple pie on the fourth of July and knowing that Marino is having form problems with the Miami Dolphins. It's the mentality that encourages us to buy a four-wheel drive pick-up, and destroy the environment at one hundred Ks with the windows down and the air on full, and to get teary listening to Charley Pride through its graphic equaliser, and accept Botham spitting and Zoehrer bad-mouthing Qasim Omar, and elevates sporting hoons to superstar status like Dennis the Despicable.

Thanks heaps, Chappelli. Oh, please let us have the Peter Taylors and the Bruce Reids and the Allan Borders who are taking cricket in its rightful direction back to its traditional roots, where the most important thing is the game and the way one plays it. Let us kill forever the last vestiges of the underhand, underarmed, money-grubbing narcissistic Age of Chappell. The house of Chappell has become synonymous with the New Professionalism, which translates as the New Ugliness, in Australian culture. Bring back the old values: cricket without the commercials. A plague forever on both your houses, Chappell.

Doyle in Buzo, *The Longest Game* (1990), pp. 362–3.

'I JUST SHUFFLE UP AND GO WANG'

Jeff Thomson had a simple recipe for fast bowling.

Until he busted his shoulder at the Adelaide Oval in a collision with Alan 'Fitter'n' Turner, as they both attempted to catch a skied pull shot from Zaheer Abbas, Thommo was the most lethal fast bowler I'd seen.

He made the ball climb off a good length and go past about Adam's apple height. I saw a few batsmen who faced Thommo come away with a look on their face that suggested they wished Adam and Eve had never met.

Thommo was the only fast bowler that I felt was unhookable. His bouncer usually passed by a few feet overhead and the 'climber' was never short enough to hook.

He was never quite the same after that collision in 1976. And I think Thommo had an inkling of what was to come at the time. As he lay on the ground a few feet away from Turner, he muttered, 'I'll knock this bloke's [Zaheer] head off.' Then he added as he grimaced in pain, 'That's if I ever fuckin' bowl again.'

Thommo was unique. He was a genuine speed merchant who

liked nothing better than bowling fast. In Trinidad in 1979 he took five wickets in the first innings, but in the second dig on a wicket that had flattened right out it was virtually impossible to bowl him after his opening spell.

After we'd won the game by about twenty runs, I had a quiet chat with Jeff. 'Why,' I suggested, 'don't you have a yarn with Dennis about how to cut the ball and bowl on slower tracks?'

'I know what you're saying,' replied Thommo, 'but if you don't mind, I'd like to do it my way.'

I also understod. He was a fast bowler, and he was going to live or die on speed. When asked to describe his action, Thommo once said, 'Ahh, I just shuffle up and go wang.'

When I told this to former NSW opener Warren 'Wacky' Saunders, who'd been hit in the head by Thommo whilst batting for St George, he replied, 'Yeah. But he went wang pretty bloody quick.'

Chappell, *Chappelli* (1992), pp. 124–5.

GOD AT HAWTHORN

Champion full-forward Peter Hudson had almost divine status in Hawthorn, as historian Ian Turner noted in his 1978 Ron Barassi Memorial Lecture.

Mobility also has a spill off into politics. Traditionally ex-footballers became policemen. Today they tend to become publicists, publicans or politicians. Thus, three weeks ago I was scrutineering for my local, friendly councillor in Richmond and the opponent's scrutineer was sitting beside me. Kevin Sheedy came in, and I opened the electoral roll and ruled off his name. My opponent's scrutineer said, 'Who's that?' and I said, 'Kevin Sheedy.' And he said, 'Who's Kevin Sheedy?' At that moment, I knew we had taken Richmond.

Beyond this there is a consequence of professionalism in the growing involvement of the game and the players with the mass communications media. The players become pop stars. John

Gould designs gear and Don Scott used to model it. Royce Hart and Neil Balme look more and more like [the international soccer players] Charlie George and Georgie Best, who in turn look more and more like the Beatles and the Stones.

The players themselves become charismatic heroes. A couple of years ago, outside a church in Hawthorn, the vicar had posted a notice saying: 'What would you do if God came to Hawthorn today?' A graffitist had written underneath it: 'Move Peter Hudson to centre half-forward.'

The colleague who reported that to me said: 'When I tell the story outside Hawthorn, they say, "Who's Peter Hudson?" but when I tell the story in Hawthorn they say, "Who's God?"'

Hutchinson, *The Great Australian Book of Football Stories* (1983), p. 297.

BEATEN TO THE CHOP BY THE BASQUES

Australia has produced many world champion axemen but they were beaten by the Basques at the 1977 Royal Easter Show in Sydney.

... the damned Basques [continued to claim] that they were world champions. In the early seventies the Australians got around that awkwardness by declaring Sydney's chops as the world *hardwood* championships and leaving it at that.

In the end the confrontation had to come, and it occurred in 1977 at the Royal Easter Show. A gentleman by the name of Jose Ignatio Orbegozo, who cut under the name of Arriya II, arrived. He was the Spanish champion and his father was champion before him. To meet him the brotherhood chose Martin O'Toole, son of Victorian policeman and former world champion, Jack O'Toole. But the Spaniards had the brotherhood boxed in even before the competition started. Because it wasn't going to be an Australian racing event, it was to be conducted by Spanish rules—in other words a test of endurance.

Well, the inevitable happened in the five hundred dollar match. Martin O'Toole got off to a good start on the first of his five 15 inch logs and knocked it off in a mere 44.4 seconds. But he started to weaken about log number three and Arriya II finished the fifth half a log ahead of O'Toole. He left Australia with his three hundred and fifty dollars share of the purse, another two hundred and fifty dollars in a whip around conducted by Australian axemen, and 20 Australian axes as souvenirs. The brotherhood was crestfallen and a few officials said they thought things might have to change.

Since then things haven't changed much, although there have been several endurance chops between Australians and New Zealanders but Australian woodchopping rules still stand. Perhaps because of the Basque experience and perhaps for other reasons, Australians and New Zealanders have not shown any interest in Finnish competitions where the winner is the man who can chop his way through the largest tonnage in a two hour period—an event that, from the spectator's view at least, must be extraordinarily boring to watch.

Beckett, *Axemen Stand By Your Logs* (1983), pp. 18–20.

A STAGGERING FORM REVERSAL

Everyone had virtually written off Tracey Wickham in the 400 metres at the World Swimming Championships, following the Edmonton Commonwealth Games, but she produced the goods when it counted, as Norman May relates.

After the Commonwealth Games in Edmonton in 1978, I travelled to Berlin to cover the World Swimming Championships and edited videotapes were transmitted by satellite back to Australia.

Most of the Australians had arrived in Berlin feeling a little jaded after the Games. Our main hope was Tracey Wickham who set a world record for 800 metres in Edmonton in 8 minutes 24.62 seconds (in that race, Michelle Ford, who finished second, also clipped five seconds off the old world record). But the day before the Championships started there were disturbing rumours about Tracey's fitness and she withdrew from the 200 metres. An injured arm was given as the reason.

Then in the 400 metres Tracey drew the final heat and she looked a dejected figure as she walked out in an overcoat and scarf in the near freezing conditions at that open air pool. (The air temperature was 2° celsius but the water was heated.) She recorded a mediocre 4 minutes 18 seconds and she made the final in lane one in the second slowest time.

I think most people had written her off but I wasn't so sure. I'd seen her in action before and she's what's known in racing parlance as a 'dudder'; she never let the opposition know what was going on.

In the final it was an entirely different story. Tracey had drawn beside the champion East German sprinter, Barbara Krause and she had a good pacemaker for the first 200 metres. At the half way point, she was about 0.5 second behind the leaders.

While most of the crowd were watching the American Cynthia Woodhead in one of the middle lanes, Tracey steadily made up ground and she was only 0.01 of a second behind at the 300 metre turn.

In the seventh lap she really took off and she was clearly in front with fifty metres to go. During her career, nobody swam past Tracey Wickham once she hit the front and she stunned the experts by winning the race in world record time 4 minutes 6.28 seconds, an improvement of twelve seconds on her time in the morning heats.

It was a staggering reversal of form and if the event had been held at Randwick Racecourse she might have incurred a twelve months suspension. Her performance as a swimmer was great and her performance as an actress was just as good.

Later that night, I ran into her coach, Bill Sweetenham, and a group of Australians and they were still laughing about the whole affair. I said to Bill, 'Next time, why don't you bring her out in a wheelchair?' He grinned and said, 'Gee, that's a good idea!'

May, Sporting Laughs (1985), pp. 106–7.

'ABOUT TIME YOUR BLOODY ARSE RAN OUT'

Australian cricketers have often been guilty of harsh and even mindless comments directed against the opposition.

Apart from finding out valuable information, the dressing-room is the place where any disputes that occur on the field can be watered down. If harsh words have been spoken on the field, it's amazing how it can be joked about later, even by the protagonists, when they're amongst team-mates in the more relaxed atmosphere of the dressing-room.

And it doesn't have to be in the dressing-room. During a WSC match in Mildura I'd become extremely frustrated as the World XI made a great recovery, thanks to some aggressive batting by Imran Khan and Alan Knott. We eventually clinched victory by just a few runs when Imran was out for 98.

I was still hot under the collar over dropped catches, and as Imran walked past me I made some mindless comment that it was 'about time your bloody arse ran out'. A couple of hours later, I turned up at the dining room of the motel where the teams were staying to find the restaurant full. As I stood there waiting for a table, South African Eddie Barlow got up and paid his bill, leaving one empty seat in the room.

Without any hesitation I walked over and sat down. Right next to Imran. As if on cue, the other World XI players got up and left the table to pay their bill, leaving Imran with a half eaten fish meal and me as his sole dinner companion.

I said, 'Good evening Imran. Great knock of yours today.'

He looked at me amazed. 'Thank you Ian,' he replied, 'but I didn't expect you to be talking to me.'

'Why not?' I asked, a little surprised.

'In Pakistan,' Imran explained, 'if two players exchange words on the field, that's it. They don't talk again.'

I laughed and said, 'It's different in Australia, that's accepted as part of the game. Afterwards,' I added, 'it's all forgotten.'

With that sorted out we had a friendly chat over dinner, but on the field continued to have a very competitive outlook. We have remained friends ever since.

Chappell, *Chappelli* (1992), pp. 32–3.

EVEN SEAGULLS WATCH CRICKET

Seagulls on cricket grounds are an Australian icon.

Just about every cricket broadcaster has fiddled away time during a quiet period of play discussing the hordes of seagulls which invariably congregate at Australian cricket grounds. When a stroke carries the ball into a nestling gaggle of gulls, sending them soaring angrily into the air, it provides the commentators with a little embellishment for their talk. What can really get them talking is when a particularly fiercely struck ball hits a gull before it can move—as happened during the Adelaide Test between Australia and the West Indies in the 1979–80 season. The dazed bird was carried to the boundary by Dennis Lillee and placed in the care of a gentleman in the outer. This saga was strung out by the commentators until the bird had regained enough strength to fly off.

But have you ever wandered what induces hundreds of seagulls to fly in to cricket grounds during matches, when they're rarely sighted on other days? If it is the scavenging seagull's eternal hope of an easy meal, then why do they always settle so close to the wicket (and thus far from the crumbs of the crowd)? The great seagull question has been the subject of endless idle contemplation over many a cricket season, without substantial conclusions ever having been reached. That is, until a gentleman telephoned his local radio station in Western Australia with the following:

'Seagulls are attracted to cricket matches by the tension generated by the players. Hence on days when there is no cricket, there are no seagulls either.'

Well, er . . .? But then to reinforce his self-possessed erudition on the subject, the gentleman became more expansive.

'What's more,' he said, 'the birds can anticipate bowling changes and move to safer positions prior to a new over.'

Well, I never ...

Brayshaw, *Wit of Cricket* (1981), pp. 89–90.

DAY OF SHAME

There were calls for the sacking of Greg Chappell as Australian cricket captain after the infamous underarm bowling incident in 1981.

One of the dark happenings of the 1980–81 Australian summer was the 'underarm incident' during the third World Series Cup final between Australia and New Zealand at the Melbourne Cricket Ground. With just one ball remaining and with the Kiwis needing six runs to tie the match, Greg Chappell instructed his younger brother Trevor to bowl a play-safe underarm delivery. The umpires were informed. They in turn told the incoming batsman, rank tailender Brian McKechnie, who merely blocked the ensuing delivery and threw away his bat in disgust. There began a controversy that brought to an angry boil Australian and international feeling. It wasn't that Greg Chappell had gone outside the laws of cricket ... more that he had acted outside the spirit of a game that had long been recognised as a standard-setter in sportsmanship.

Perhaps the degree of feeling was exacerbated by the fact that earlier in the same day Greg Chappell himself had stood his ground after apparently having been brilliantly caught in the outfield by Martin Snedden off Lance Cairns. The New Zealander had run some 25 metres in the deep at mid-wicket and dived headlong to apparently snap up the ball millimetres off the grass in what was a memorable effort. Chappell was uncertain as to whether the catch had been made cleanly and declined to walk off, despite the fact that Snedden had held the ball up and that a nearby fieldsman had also signified a clean catch. The Australian captain was within his rights to remain if he had any doubts about the catch and the matter went to the umpires, who gave the batsman the benefit of the doubt that existed. Much heated debate raged between the New Zealanders and the umpires — but the decision stood and Chappell, who was on 58 at the time, continued. He had moved to 90 when he was caught in exactly the same circumstances, this time by Bruce Edgar off the bowling of Snedden. This time Chappell walked on the indication of the fieldsman that the catch had been taken.

But back to that underarm delivery. The hue and cry that followed must have stirred memories of the days of bodyline bowling when feeling also ran high right across the nation. Greg Chappell was the almost unanimous target for a tirade of abuse from critics and the public. There were calls for his sacking or resignation from the captaincy. Even the Prime Ministers of Australia and New Zealand were brought into the matter.

Finally Chappell emerged from hiding to issue a statement deploring his action, explaining that it was the act of a tired man who was fearful that one almighty swipe by McKechnie could have forced his weary team to play another game in the finals series. He'd had enough — so had his players — Chappell reasoned.

Brayshaw, *The Wit of Cricket* (1981), pp. 41–3.

THE 'BRUTAL' AUSTRALIANS

Socceroo coach Frank Arok cleverly engineered a psychological advantage before a critical match against Israel in 1981.

Arok travelled to Tel Aviv, with a brief acclimatisation stopover in Athens which also served to lessen the impact of jet lag. He hoped that what he had heard about the objectivity of European referees was wrong.

Meanwhile, Arok had orchestrated quite a surprise for the Israelis. Knowing that his hosts were, fallaciously, of the opinion that the Socceroos were basically thugs in studs, and knowing the Israeli need to prove manhood with machismo, he concocted a clever ploy. The day before the match, he ordered the Australians to mock viciousness in a training game at practice. With Israeli journalists standing agape, and their Australian counterparts briefed to not give the game away, the Socceroos proceeded to kick the living daylights out of each other. They played their roles so convincingly that one Israeli reporter approached Arok, his bottom jaw dropped in disbelief, and asked whether his team always trains with such indifference to safety.

'Of course not,' said Arok, 'it's usually much worse than this but as you know we have to play an important game tomorrow.'

Arok had just sold his biggest dummy yet. Screaming headlines of how brutal the Australians were greeted the party on the morning of the match. Arok hoped the Israeli players also read the papers, for without their crucial supporting roles, it would have all been for nothing.

Lusetich, *Frank Arok* (1992), pp. 108–9.

MAD DOGS

Press conferences can have unfortunate consequences, as Frank Arok discovered in 1981.

It was a routine enough news conference, with Arok and Kosmina predicting the Israelis would come at Australia with all guns blazing in the return game and both appealing to the public, for once, to get behind the team, *their* team. From it, came the controversy which never was. Using his colourful vocabulary to describe the triumph of Tel Aviv, Arok had said: 'You know, they used to call us mad dogs, but we were more than that against Israel'.

Arok's penchant for using the term 'mad dogs' landed him square in the pound. An experienced reporter, who should have known better, grossly misquoted Arok as saying: 'We used to call them mad dogs, but they are also vicious and dirty and I think they lost their temper'. The reporter's story went around the world, sparking a diplomatic incident. The Israeli embassy in Canberra demanded an immediate apology and the Israeli FA complained to FIFA about anti-Semitism. It seemed Hitler had once referred to Jews as mad dogs. When the Department of Foreign Affairs contacted Arok asking for an explanation, he referred them to a tape of the news conference, which clearly showed he had not said what he was alleged to have said. Nevertheless, the stench of that incident hung in the air for some time.

Lusetich, Frank Arok (1992), p. 115.

THE MCG — A SACRED SITE

There is nothing like the football Finals atmosphere in Melbourne. Garrie Hutchinson describes the 1981 Grand Final between Carlton and Collingwood.

Apprehension. It's an emotion that seems to lie around the MCG like a fog, engulfing everyone as they walk through the carpark. It's a quiet reverential feeling, as if we're outside a church, or at Gallipoli, or on a sacred site.

There are clowns, and jazz bands and a place to get your face painted ... But there is hardly a sense of carnival there, just the nervous jokiness of an army before hitting the beach, going over the top.

I reached into my back pocket for my ticket at about 12 o'clock, up before the game. It wasn't in the back pocket. It must be in the coat pocket. 'Hello,' I say to someone. Not in the coat pocket. Entrance 12 is around that way. Have a look in the wallet. 'Two *Records*, thanks.' It dawns on me. I have lost it. Carlton are playing Collingwood in a Grand Final and I've lost the ticket! ...

There's only one thing to do. I sidle up to a scalper, you know he's a scalper because he's unshaven and looks nonchalant, confident.

'How many you want, mate?' he asks. 'Just the one, mate. How much?' 'Sixty.' To be perfectly truthful I didn't know whether that was a rip off, or not. I didn't know there was no bargaining to be done. 'Take it or leave it.'

'Beaut ticket,' he says, 'under cover, Southern stand, fair dinkum ticket'. I stand there looking at it. It's a sorry sight. Stained, with something, coffee perhaps, and stuck together with grubby tape. It looked dodgy, but I thought if it was dodgy it would doubtless look really spruce. I bought it. I went in. I sat down. Two hours to go.

The time passes ... and I find myself standing, singing Waltzing Matilda with Jon English, every footballer's favourite male singer.

Suddenly it comes home to me. It's about to begin and that strange pre-match indifference gives way to total fear. But with the fear is a sense, singing that song, that it's just about the only moment in the life of our city where everyone is together, where you feel this is ours. That this is a moment which transcends football and becomes pure emotional patriotism. Then they play the English national anthem and the grim siege of the game begins.

Time passes. Half a game of silent struggle. Half a quarter of Collingwood supporters coming out of their shells, luxuriating in hope, crossing themselves at three-quarter time, going sour in the last quarter, of Carlton fans having a victory spread over them like a glass of old cognac, like the sun creeping out from behind a cloud.

Suddenly it's over. I hop over the fence in front of the Southern stand, flashing a pink pass at a startled policeman, and run straight at the writhing, jubilant mass of players and officials in the middle. They're slapping each other like well-fed, solid sides of beef. Whack! Whack! They're leering at each other through their mouthguards. Hug! Crunch! They're making strange noises. 'Errrrrgh! Ay! Grrrrrrng!' Blokes are coming up to them. 'Goodonyer ... geez ohhh geez ...' helplessly expressing an emotion that has no words.

And all in a strange, silent, private hole in the middle of 116 000 voices. I mean they're making a hell of a noise, and in the centre it's just like the far away roar of the surf. And the Carlton team is dancing around to the sound of no music, completely oblivious to anything. Glassy-eyed, white-faced, open-mouthed, stoned ...

There are two blokes up on the dais. We can't hear what they're saying, but the Collingwood team is collecting losers' medals. And then Carlton lines up, still punching and slapping each other. A few are wearing the scalps of fallen opponents. Ashman's wearing Tony Shaw's, Glascott Irwin's, Maylin Brewer's, Hunter Daicos's, Harmes Kink's.

But the last man up, the mighty Fitzpatrick wears his own. He calls up the coach to join him. Parkin nearly falls off the rostrum. They hold up the shining cup. Bosustow shakes a bottle of Bodega and the foam spurts all over the coach. He doesn't mind. No one minds. They can't feel a thing. They herb off around the ground, and wave after wave of the distant surf breaks over them as they pass. They disappear into a hole in the ground, up the race. It's all over bar the shouting.

Hutchinson, *From the Outer* (1984), pp. 220–3.

'DON'T LET YOUR EMOTIONS RUN FREE YET'

Raelene Boyle describes the strange lead-up to her victory in the 400 metres at the 1982 Commonwealth Games in Brisbane.

Athletes do some strange things in the few hours before crucial challenges as they fight to contain nerves, but I was firmly in control of my faculties when I awoke about 7.30 a.m. on the morning of the final. I chose to stay at the village overnight to avoid the 50 km drive to Brisbane, and even the noise of banging doors and chattering competitors did not upset me.

My only oddity, I guess, was that I requested Mrs Margaret Mahony, assistant manageress of the women's track and field team, to sit with me at the breakfast table while I chewed on a piece of toast and sipped tea. I didn't want her to say anything. Her pleasant presence was sufficient. Perhaps I needed some form of security blanket.

It was 2.40 p.m. when that blanket was no longer of any use to me. Just a month earlier, I was on the verge of chucking the whole thing in when I hurled my blocks at Ronnie. Thank God for his commonsense. An excruciating hush had descended over the 40 000 spectators. I surveyed my seven rivals. At 31, I was older than all of them. My credentials were far superior.

'This race is mine,' I muttered. 'I'm going to win this bloody gold.'

The crowd had roared encouragement when I was introduced: 'You've got to control that noise, Raelene,' I thought. 'Don't let your emotions run free yet.'

The race was 100 metres old and I hadn't heard anything: 'You've got to get up there and establish a smooth pattern,' I grimaced.

The race was 200 metres old and my hearing was still blocked: 'Where's Hoyte-Smith?' I wondered. 'She should have caught me from lane 1 by now.'

The race was 250 metres old and I was singing 'Eye of the Tiger', the theme from Rocky III, as I steamed along in lane 4. 'Are you hungry enough?' I asked.

The race was 300 metres old and I stammered: 'This is good. This is the way you've always wanted to run the 400 metres.'

The race was 310 metres old and I opened my ears to the thunderous boom of human sound: 'Carry me home now,' I pleaded. 'Thanks for the help.'

It was 51.26 secs. after the starter fired his gun and the race was over. Triumph! The biggest thrill of my life. No question about it. Rick Mitchell had told me the night before that I should run a lap of honor if I conquered.

'Don't be stupid,' I had retorted. 'I've got to win first.'

I trotted off on my lap, but stopped dead after 50 metres. The race did hurt, and my aching thighs were telling me all about it. I pushed on and the hugs and kisses followed. First Geoff Martin, then Jim Barry, then Malcolm Fraser, then Ronnie. Then it was all blurred.

Boyle and Craven, *Rage Raelene, Run* (1983), pp. 195–6.

THE WINGED KEEL

On the fifth leg of the seventh and deciding race in the 1983 America's Cup, Australia II *did what a twelve-metre boat wasn't supposed to do. The Americans were dumbfounded.*

As soon as the Aussies rounded the mark and hoisted their spinnaker for the 4.5-mile run down the fifth leg, they started gaining, though no one outside of the boats knew it at first. Both began the run on starboard tack at a slight angle to the wind. *Liberty* was about seven boat lengths in front. As they sailed away from the mark and each other, their only reference points, it became impossible for spectators to tell who was gaining or by how much.

Realization came slowly and by different signs. The men in the boats knew it first. Aboard *Liberty*, Herreshoff took ranges on their opponent and Conner, the human computer, digested the results: The Aussies were gaining at a rate that would put them ahead at the next mark. Halfway down the leg the boats were spread well apart in light and shifty winds. Many spectators believed the Americans were still comfortably ahead. But Conner knew otherwise; the Aussies were only 15 seconds behind, and gaining fast.

On the press boat, the alarm was given by Gary Jobson, who had signed on as a commentator after his losing effort as tactician aboard *Defender*. He saw *Liberty* jibe over suddenly, back toward *Australia II*. He grabbed a microphone from an Australian commentator, who was beginning an explanation of the Aussies' impending defeat. 'He must be behind,' Jobson said urgently. 'Conner must think he's falling behind or he would never have jibed over like that.'

Indeed, the Aussies had caught two isolated wind shifts that boosted their speed. Conner was trying desperately to sail back across the course in time to cover *Australia II* while he still could. Meanwhile, aboard *Black Swan*, Lexcen and Schnackenberg were still below, still unable to watch. They were staring glumly through a porthole at the New York Yacht Club's committee boat. Suddenly, their attention was riveted. 'We could tell by the expressions on their faces that we were catching up,' Lexcen said later. They scrambled for the deck in time to see the boats converge.

Conner managed to get in front of the Aussies, but Bertrand simply bore off, sailed right through *Liberty's* cover and crossed in front of her by 10 or 15 feet.

For several seconds no one spoke aboard *Liberty*. 'Does anyone here have any ideas?' Conner finally asked, breaking the silence. No one did. A 12-metre boat simply isn't supposed to be able to do what *Australia II* did—sail both lower (more directly in front of the wind) and faster, and pass another boat to leeward despite its wind shadow. 'It was very frustrating for us, of course, but there wasn't much we could do at that point,' Conner said later.

Riggs, *Keelhauled* (1986), pp. 275–6.

THE VALUE OF THE AUSTRALIAN KANGAROO PIN

Dawn Fraser's generosity was rewarded in kind by some Los Angelenos during her visit there for the Olympic Games in 1984.

That great swimmer, Dawn Fraser, has a special spot in my store of memories because her history making win at the Tokyo Olympics in 1964 was my first Olympic Gold as a broadcaster. Dawn won the 100 metres freestyle three times; in 1956, 1960 and 1964, a feat not equalled by any swimmer in any event. I was more than pleased that she was able to visit Los Angeles for the Games in 1984 and she stayed in the same hotel as the ABC radio team.

It was the Ambassador, a former luxury hotel which has seen better days. It was a comfortable place and one of the entertainment areas was the Coconut Grove, the nightclub which featured in many a Hollywood film in the 1930s and 40s. The hotel also achieved notoriety because it was here that Bobby Kennedy was shot and killed.

The Ambassador is no longer in the ritzy part of town as the character of the city has changed quite a lot. Now the rich and famous are seen around Beverly Hills which was about fifteen minutes away by car to the north west. Now, the Ambassador is right on the fringe of the black area which has a very high crime rate and we were warned not to walk in the streets at night.

During her stay, Dawn Fraser drove about in a hire car, and one evening she returned from one of the competition venues and was lucky enough to find a parking spot in the street behind the hotel where there was space for only four cars.

Three black youths were lounging nearby and Dawn struck up a conversation. Like all Australians she was carrying a supply of Kangaroo Pins and before she left, she gave one to each of the Los Angelenos.

The next morning, she returned to the parking spot. The other three cars had been stripped clean, Dawn's was left alone.

Such is the value of the Australian Kangaroo Pin.

May, Sporting Laughs (1985), pp. 128–29.

'PISTOL PACKING MUM'

Fifty-two-year old Pattie Dench, who was the first Australian to win an Olympic medal in shooting, faced a lengthy ordeal to secure the bronze medal in 1984.

The first medal won by an Australian at the '84 Games was also the first Olympic shooting medal ever won by an Australian male or female. On 29 July at the Prado shooting range in Chino, just outside Los Angeles, 52-year-old Pattie Dench—described by the Australian press as a 'pistol packing Mum' because she was the mother of two sets of twins—won the bronze medal in the women's sport pistol event.

The oldest competitor on the 1984 Australian Olympic team, Dench took up shooting in 1975 after serious injuries in a car smash 'ruined [her] golf game'. Her competition in Los Angeles was so close that her score of 583 placed her only two points behind the Canadian gold medallist. While the final scores were still being calculated, an American friend who meant well enthusiastically informed her that she had won the bronze medal. Half an hour later, with a celebration already in progress in the Australian camp, news came that Pattie had actually tied for third. A shoot-out was required to decide the medal (the competition was so close that a shoot-out was also required to decide the gold and silver medallist). As the Australian Olympic Federation's *Official Report* for the 1984 Olympics makes clear, Pattie displayed remarkable coolness in the final test; 'It showed the quality of the Sydney mother when she walked back onto the range and calmly won the shoot-out for a bronze medal.'

Pattie Dench was now ready to celebrate in style. 'I'll have champagne,' she declared, 'as long as it's Australian.'

Phillips, *Australian Women at the Olympic Games* (1992), p. 123.

AN INCREDIBLE RIDE

Winter surf in Hawaii can be hazardous to your health, as champion surfer Mark Richards is aware.

Mark Richards thought he was about to drown. He was at Waimea Bay, a picturesque cove on the north shore of the main Hawaiian island of Oahu. It was 7 December 1986.

He watched a giant wave fold neatly before him about 20 metres away. 'This is it,' he thought. 'I'm going to die.' The circumstances of his impending demise didn't surprise him. After all, he had been surfing for more than twenty years and was on his sixteenth trip to Hawaii. The irony that he would drown in the Billabong contest in front of peers, friends, admirers and anonymous spectators struck him momentarily. But the overriding emotion was the fear, the bowel-loosening terror that goes with confronting huge waves at Waimea Bay. To be caught in such a situation where the ocean has taken over and you have lost control of your destiny, haunts every surfer with its inevitability.

Most days of the year Waimea Bay is a tranquil, sandy inlet with a beach that is less than 100 metres wide. A Catholic church overlooks the bay, which is at the end of a lush, green valley, home of the beautiful Waimea Falls. As the northern winter swells get bigger, Waimea Bay loses its attraction to the casual swimmer. Waves begin to dump very heavily on the shore while further out, waves begin to fringe the rocks on the northern side and slam into the menacing outcrop on the southern side.

Adventurous body boarders and body surfers come to tackle the pounding shorebreak and surfers ride the fat, relatively unexciting waves next to the northern point. When the swells reach a certain size, the shorebreak becomes far too dangerous to ride and the main break shifts out to a submerged rock plateau off the northern point. Huge swells travel unimpeded for thousands of kilometres before hitting this submarine shelf, where they steepen dramatically and break ferociously.

The middle of Waimea Bay is so deep that it is rare for a wave to break right across it. On this day, however, the swell was so big, not even the depth of the canyon next to the impact zone could prevent the bigger waves from breaking.

Mark Richards saw a set coming and 'when a set comes at Waimea the horizon goes dark. In Australia you just see a bump out to sea, but at Waimea the whole ocean goes dark at the horizon and you are confronted with this colossus of water. It's like getting a Manhattan-sized skyscraper, dropping it on its side, painting it black and sending it charging toward the beach.' He saw the caddies (surfers with spare boards for competitors) paddling frantically and 'then I realised the set was so big it was going to close out the Bay. The first wave reared up and it was probably about 25 ft and I was paddling like there was no tomorrow, as were the others behind me, and then the wave broke right in front of me, top to bottom, 20 or 30 yards away, this giant wall of white water ... I was so mesmerised and so terrified by the wave I didn't really dive. I just slid off the side of my board. I got rumbled around but the worst part was being dragged along by my board. I was wearing a 12 ft and a 6 ft leg rope tied together and it was like skiing underwater. I thought my leg was going to get ripped off.'

Miraculously, Mark Richards finally got to the surface and reeled his board in. Eighteen feet of leg rope had been stretched to almost twice its length. 'From that moment I felt I was invincible at Waimea because nothing worse could happen.' He became selective, choosing only the bigger waves which he surfed with stylish expertise in what was tantamount to an exhibition heat in giant Waimea.

In that heat and the next, which he also won, the judges awarded Mark perfect 10 scores for two of his waves. Randy Rarick, one of the north shore's most experienced surfers and observers, believes that Mark rode a 25 ft wave that day—a feat very seldom accomplished even in that arena. James Jones, one of the great big-wave riders in Hawaiian history, isn't renowned for his quickness to praise. But when Jones, twice winner of the Duke Kahanamoku Classic, bumped into Mark a few days later he said, 'That ride was incredible'. Jack Shipley, Hawaii's most experienced contest judge, said that if the Eddie Aikau Memorial big-wave event, open only to invited big-surf specialists, had been held at Waimea on 7 December 1986, Mark Richards would have won. Shipley said it was arguably the best Waimea had been ever ridden.

'Forget the finals. Just stop the contest and give it to the guy' was the succinct observation of a spectator. He summed up the feelings of many who had witnessed the world's finest surfer enjoying one of his finest hours.

Knox, *Mark Richards, A Surfing Legend* (1992), pp. xi–xiii.

ANOTHER SIDE OF 'THE KING'

Wally Lewis, when captaining the Queensland State-of-Origin Rugby League teams in the late 1980s, went to great lengths to make training more enjoyable and even fun.

Despite the newly-found professionalism, Lewis has the showman's ability to sense those occasions when the team needs to lapse into childish relaxation. Riding the team bus has always been a rite of passage, a form of dues-paying as well as an inspiration to play better. But Wally, like Muhammad Ali who always insisted on driving the bus which accommodated his entourage, takes it beyond this. He drives so outrageously, steering seems to be an afterthought. Beetson says, 'I don't know how he keeps a licence' and Bennett (a former policeman) refused to travel with him when he was State coach. Ask Wally why he drives so recklessly and he says, 'I don't know why. I suppose it is because I have seen so many boring bus drivers. The players sit there (at the motel) not wanting to train ... It [the bizarre bus riding] was a bit of light-hearted entertainment, distraction ... to get their minds off training. They wouldn't think about not wanting to train until they got there and then they'd say 'Thank Christ we're here. We didn't think we were going to make it.' They'd just get straight out of the bus and train. I don't know why I do it. It was always fun to get in the bus, have the blokes giggling and laughing and carrying on. There was probably only one time I wish I wasn't driving the bus and that was when I put Jacko through the windscreen. I thought I'd killed him.

Roy Masters, *Inside League* (1990), p. 130–1.

ONE DAY, TWO LOSSES

Coaches don't always successfully separate their personal and sporting lives, as Rugby's Peter Fenton discovered.

Sometimes it is difficult being a coach and a father on the same day. In 1987, Eastwood fielded a very strong side and at the end of the season were playing extremely well. We beat Randwick in the second last game and only had to win our last game against St George, who were running last, to make the play-offs. While I rested the skipper Scott Johnson, who had a recurring ankle problem, we still had a marvellous back line with Adrian MacDonald, Brett Papworth, Matt Parish, Ian Williams, Dennis Facer and Marty Roebuck, all representative players, behind a pack that had more than held their own the previous week against the premiers.

There is probably no need to tell you we 'blew' the game, missed the final four by a point, and I drove home in some sort of daze on a wet and miserable night. It was the evening of the club ball and I drove down to the bottle shop with my younger daughter, Amy who went to the video shop next door. I was having a shower some half-hour later when there was a knock on the shower door.

'Who is it?' I asked.

'It's Amy, I made it.'

'Made what?'

'I made it home, you left me down there!'

Fenton, Sport the Way I Speak It (1992), p. 98.

IMMORTALISED BECAUSE OF ONE KICK

A spectacular goal kicked by Charlie Yankos was a critical turning point when the Socceroos humbled the Argentinian world champions, 4 goals to 1, in 1988.

Almost everything was going Argentina's way until the 43rd minute. The Socceroos were awarded a free kick about 35 metres from goal. Yankos tried to play a quick pass but alert defenders covered his options. How he would make them rue their swiftness. It took almost a minute for the defensive wall to get back the required ten metres. During that time, the always apprehensive Arok suddenly became quiet. He had been, albeit briefly, into the future. He saw the ball travel into the top corner taking what seemed an eternity to cover the enormous distance. The vision momentarily frightened him, but the fear quickly subsided and he was overcome with joy. Arok blinked his eyes and saw Yankos march back almost ten metres from the ball.

Arok rose to his feet, stretching his arms to the starry night sky, as the right foot of Yankos connected, ever so sweetly, with the ball. The last man on the Argentine defensive wall turned his back, his face wincing, as he realised the immense power with which the ball was heading towards him. Yankos pays particular attention to working his leg muscles; there are few legs with more muscle than his. But all those years of hard work in the gym seemed a pittance to pay, a penny for a pearl, for that moment. The ball sliced and dipped, always away from the outstretched Islas. His dive was futile. He had more chance of stopping a meteorite from crashing into the earth.

From the dozens of thousands of times he has kicked a soccer ball, Charlie Yankos will be immortalised because of this one kick. If this goal of goals, this treasure cut from the roughest of diamonds, needed further acknowledgement, then it could only be that given to it by the British commentator, Martin Tyler, who was calling the game for the ABC. Tyler is effervescent, intelligent, articulate, emotive, knowledgeable and able to bring to the viewer a tingling sensation, a confirmation of the greatness of the moment. He only said 'Charlie Yankos ... my word!' But what force those four words conveyed. He uttered those words as we would all wish we could. Perfect inflection, dictated by the genuine surprise of the quality of what he had just seen. He needed not his sizeable vocabulary to convey that what he had just seen was worthy of any of his usual ports-of-call—London's Wembley Stadium, the San Siro in Milan, the Bernabeu in Madrid, Glasgow's Hampden Park, the Olympiastadion in Munich, Lisbon's Estadio de Luz or, in Paris, the Stade du Parc de Princes.

Lusetich, *Frank Arok* (1992), pp. 190–1.

A GOLD MEDALLIST (FOR 11 MINUTES)

Kayaker Grant Davies gained a silver medal at the 1988 Seoul Olympics but went closer than most to the elusive gold.

In the kayak singles Queenslander Grant Davies missed out on a gold medal by 0.005 of a second. As he paddled ashore after the race, the scoreboard flashed his name as winner of the gold medal. Grant's father, confined to a wheelchair after a near fatal automobile accident, made the trip to Seoul and told his son that he would stand and applaud if Grant won a medal. True to his word, he gripped the rail of the wire fence and pulled himself to his feet, applauding wildly. For 11 glorious minutes Grant was the gold medallist. Then the judges reported that a computer-enhanced photo of the finish indicated Greg Barton of the United States had won the race. Even though Davies had signed the official document recognising him as the gold medallist, he emerged from the presentation ceremony with the silver. In a remarkable display of sportsmanship that brought him more respect than the gold medal would have done, he smiled and told waiting reporters, 'That's the way it goes. If that's my biggest disappointment in life, then I have no problems.'

Phillips, Australian Women at the Olympic Games (1992), p. 129.

A PECK ON THE CHEEK

Cricketer Merv Hughes' tongue is as much celebrated as his moustache.

Today's cricket is much more of a team game. When a team-mate does well, it is only natural that I want to congratulate him. If I give him a peck on the cheek it is a show of friendship, my way of saying 'Well done'. Kissing is supposed to increase the heart rate, tighten the muscles and release sugar into the blood stream, so I'm sure it must give him a tremendous lift.

Early in 1989 I was accused by a magistrate in Alice Springs of setting a bad example for the public of Australia. My 'homo-sexual-type behaviour' and 'unmanly activities' on the field were encouraging indecency off it. He also referred to conduct by the Australian cricket team 'such as kissing, which is otherwise not normal and certainly objectionable to the community'. The magistrate made his comments while sentencing a man who had admitted to 'unzipping his trousers and revealing his buttocks' in the eatery of the Alice Springs Truck Stop.

I gave the magistrate's comments the deep consideration they deserved. I certainly have a responsibility to the public when representing my country and there are limits to what is seen as proper on the cricket field. I have therefore made a solemn oath: if truckies begin dropping their pants in truck stops all over Australia, I shall never kiss another soul.

Along with kissing, my moustache has also created a good deal of comment in the press (most of it unkind). Moustaches have a long and detailed history. They first became fashionable in the early 19th century when the waxing of moustaches was common, and the German Kaiser tied two small helium balloons to the ends of his moustache, so that they would point skyward. I am told that my moustache is similar to that of Lord Kitchener, who was pictured on recruiting posters during World War I pointing and saying, 'Your Country Needs You'. From the position of his finger, I wouldn't be surprised if Lord Kitchener had been an umpire in his spare time.

There is a scientific theory that suggests that men who wear hair on their faces are able to 'scare off sexual competitors and attract and mate with more females'. When you consider the success of Clark Gable, David Niven and Tom Selleck, this theory is not without merit. But there is one exception to this rule. Me. Perhaps my lack of success with the ladies is because, as Honor Blackman once said, a moustache is 'the thing that makes a girl feel like she's kissing her toothbrush good night'.

Perhaps I should shave mine off. Maybe I should stop kissing other players. I have never done either to seek publicity. My problem is that I am as attached to my moustache as it is to me, and if I shave it off people will have to look at my face. And that is not a pretty sight. Most importantly, though, my team-mates might enjoy a whiskerless kiss, and we can't have that. What would the truck drivers say?

Hughes, *Merv—My Life and Other Funny Stories* (1990), pp. 126–7.

BREAKING THE ICE WITH
SUPERSTAR TEAM-MATES

Australian basketballer Andrew Gaze was the last player cut from the roster of the Seattle SuperSonics in 1989.

Andrew spent 12 days in Seattle's training camp in San Diego before going on the road with the Supersonics for a series of pre-season exhibition games. Andrew recalls breaking the ice with his superstar team-mates: 'When I arrived I was petrified by all these hero figures and phenomenal athletes around me. I kept to myself and didn't say boo to anyone. After the first four or five nights of training camp they had rookie night. After dinner the rookies had to get up and perform for the veterans. Sing a song, tell a joke—you've got to get up there for about 15 minutes. If they don't like you, they've got the right to throw food at you. I told a couple of standard jokes, but I incorporated the players in the team into the jokes. I was taking the mickey out of the senior players and I had them rolling. From then on I didn't have any problems.'

Harris, *Boom* (1992), p. 39.

ONE BROKEN JAW AND THREE
BROKEN ARMS

Fast bowlers, such as Craig McDermott and Mike Whitney, have long memories.

Although I bowl bouncers only occasionally, I guess I must have bowled a thousand or more of them in first-class cricket over the years, so by the law of averages it was unavoidable that I would cause a few injuries along the way. In fact, I have caused four fairly serious injuries in the whole of my career, one broken jaw and three broken arms. Needless to say, I deeply regretted each one of them. The most recent of these victims was Mike Whitney. I was bowling to him at the Sheffield Shield match at Newcastle in 1989. He turned his head away from a rising delivery and it crashed into his arm, just below the elbow. There was a loud crack, and I knew the arm was broken. When we next played against New South Wales, this time at the Sydney Cricket Ground, Whitney was back in the team. He was fielding when I walked out to bat, and he called out to me, 'Right. I want you, I'm going to break your—arm today.' As it happened, I was out before Whitney had a chance to bowl at me, and as I walked off I heard him berating the bowler who took my wicket for depriving him of his revenge. As recently as 1991–92, Whitney bowled me a few bouncers in yet another Queensland–New South Wales match. One of them, I am proud to say, I managed to hook for four. Another struck me on the arm. Seeing me rubbing it, Whitney called down the pitch: 'That makes us even.' I replied, 'No it doesn't. I'm still one break up.' Naturally, I copped a few more bouncers after that.

McDermott, *Strike Bowler* (1992), p. 91.

UMPIRE CAUGHT OUT

Had a West Indian umpire known all the rules of cricket, Dean Jones would not have been run out at Georgetown in March 1991.

Jones, perturbed by a sudden loss of form after a productive and thrilling limited-over series, had faced six balls in 10 minutes when he was bowled by Walsh for three. A frenetic soul, in one abrupt movement he left his crease, tucked the bat under his arm and, crestfallen, headed for the pavilion. He had not heard Clyde Duncan's call of 'no-ball' nor seen the umpire's arm held wide to signal the illegal delivery. By the time he had responded to Border's anguished cries to regain his ground Carl Hooper had emerged with the ball from the gully region, ceremoniously uprooted the stump and led a robust appeal. At square leg,

Cumberbatch, standing in his eleventh Test in as many seasons, either was unaware of the relevant laws or suffered a blackout for he unhesitatingly agreed to the demand. Duncan, whose first verdict in Test cricket five days earlier had been palpably wrong, made no move to intercede.

Law 38 (2) states: 'If a no-ball has been called, the striker shall not be given out unless he attempts to run.' At no stage did Jones attempt to run. He was also entitled to the protection of law 27 (5): 'The umpires shall intervene if satisfied that a batsman, not having been given out, has left his wicket under a misapprehension that he has been dismissed.'

As the West Indies players huddled together and tried to reach consensus on the legitimacy of the decision, Border turned away from the retreating figure of Jones and swore vehemently. His hissing and cussing was born of frustration and not of perceived injustice and he made no move to speak with Jones, Richards or Cumberbatch. It was not until he reached the pavilion for the tea adjournment and examined the laws of the game in a *Wisden Cricketers' Almanack* hurriedly borrowed from the press enclosure, that Border realised Cumberbatch had made a grave error. With cap and *Wisden* in hand, Australian team-manager Lawrie Sawle approached the acutely embarrassed officials, but in their hearts the Australians realised the decision could not be rescinded.

Coward, *Caribbean Odyssey* (1991), p. 96.

THAT WORLD CUP TRY

Michael Lynagh's composure was a critical factor in a last-minute match-winning World Cup try in 1991.

Then came the Irish try five minutes before full-time. It was very well executed. We drifted across and had the right number of defenders, but Ireland put a grubber kick through and capitalised on it. The try showed up a lack of cover defence. In this Test we played the back row which we hoped to take into the semifinals and final—Simon Poidevin and Jeff Miller as flankers and Willie Ofahengaue as number-eight, which is where he plays for his club. This was the most mobile back row we had available, yet the cover defence was not there. In fact, it was Rob Egerton from the other wing who tackled the Irish try-scorer, Gordon Hamilton, as he went over the line.

Suddenly, with only a few minutes of play left, Ireland had hit the front. The Irish crowd screamed with joy. Like other Australians in the grandstand I was momentarily stunned. I remember thinking to myself, 'Surely, we aren't going to lose. Surely it's not all going to end here.' When we collected our thoughts, we realised not all was lost. The feeling on the bench was that we had enough time to do something about it, and I later learned that this was also the attitude of our captain, Michael Lynagh, on the field. The Irish players assumed they had won, and who could blame them? I have been told that while they waited for the conversion attempt the Irish players spoke among themselves about their prospects against New Zealand in the semifinal a week later, although I very much doubt the truth of this.

Lynagh's composure at this point was critical. It may well have been the finest moment of his career. He told the Australian forwards he would kick off deep and that it was up to them to keep the Irish down at that end and win possession. If they won possession, he said, the backs would score. This is what they did. Lynagh himself scored two minutes before full time and Australia won the match.

The try was a fairly standard move but it happened to be one of the moves we had practised endlessly during the previous week. The ball went from Slattery the half-back to Lynagh the five-eighth and then on to Horan the inside-centre. Horan passed to Roebuck the fullback, cutting out the outside-centre Little, who looped around to take the ball from Roebuck and pass it on to Campese the winger. Campese was tackled but as he was going down he managed to toss up the ball to Lynagh, who went over for the try. The move almost came unstuck because Little was held back without the ball by an Irish defender, Brendan Mullin, and it was only Lynagh's brilliant intervention at the end which made the try possible. If Little had not been held back, I have no doubt that Campese would have scored himself. Australia had scored a try with exactly the same move, in exactly the same position on the field, earlier in the same half, and on this occasion Campese scored the try as planned. In fact, the same Irish defender tried to hold Little back without the ball then, too, but Little was able to shrug him off.

Having had their spirits raised to the heavens six minutes before full time, the Irish had now had them dashed. This dramatic reversal must have been awfully disappointing for them, but they bore it with remarkably good grace. Immediately after the match, an Irish official came up to me and said, 'Congratulations, Bob. You were far the better team.' I turned to Bob Templeton a moment later and said, 'Did you hear what he said? I couldn't have said that. Even if I thought it, I wouldn't have been able to get the words out.'

Dwyer, *The Winning Way* (1992), p. 138.

CAMPO MAGIC

An unconventional tactic set up a brilliant World Cup try by David Campese in 1991.

Campese was brilliant. He scored the try running across the face of the defence. There were plenty of defenders in front of him, but because of the angle at which Campese was running they were all afraid to chase him, lest he gave a scissors pass to one of the Australians running outside him, or cut back inside himself. So each of the defenders played safe by making sure he had his own zone of defence covered, but Campese kept running out of their zones, one after another. Finally, only John Kirwan was left, and he allowed Campese to turn him around. I suppose this was a mistake by Kirwan, but it did not matter anyway, because Campese had Phil Kearns and Rob Egerton in support, each of whom would otherwise have scored. Nevertheless, the fact Campese ended up scoring *outside* Kirwan was remarkable.

There is a small story behind this try. Against Argentina three weeks earlier, Campese had set up a try after running at a similar angle quite unintentionally. John Eales had thrown an awful pass, which Campese gathered only with difficulty. At this point, he found that the only direction left for him to run was across the face of the Argentinian defence. A hole appeared in the defence, Campese went through it and Tim Horan scored under the posts. This gave me the idea of using this method of attack again if an opportunity presented itself. So at training afterwards I tried to get Campese to practise running at the slanting angle, but he found it difficult to do. All his instincts were to close the angle and run straight. Eventually, I decided to show him myself how easy it was. So, with ball in hand, I ran across the field while Campese watched. He applauded derisively when I had finished, but he had obviously not missed the point.

Dwyer, *The Winning Way* (1992), pp. 142–3.

SOURCES AND ACKNOWLEDGEMENTS

The following list contains the sources used in this book. The editors and publisher thank copyright holders for granting permission to reproduce copyright material.

Adams, Phillip, *Australian*, 27 June 1970.
Agnew, Max, *Australia's Trotting Heritage*, Standard Bred Publications, Mitcham, 1977.
Ahern, B., *A Century of Winners: The Saga of 121 Melbourne Cups*, Boolarong Publications, Brisbane, 1982.
Andrews, Malcolm, *Great Aussie Sports Heroes*, Lilyfield Publishers, Sydney, 1986.
Argus, 27 July 1896.
Beckett, Richard, *Axemen Stand By Your Logs*, Lansdowne Press, Sydney, 1983.
Benaud, Ritchie, *On Reflection*, Fontana/Collins, Sydney, 1984. Reprinted by permission of Angus & Robertson.
Bennett, Scott, *Clarence Comet: The Career of Henry Searle 1866–89*, Sydney University Press, Melbourne, 1973.
Blades, Genevieve, Australian Aborigines, Cricket and Pedestrianism: Culture and Conflict, 1880–1910, BHMS thesis, University of Queensland, 1985.
Blainey, Geoffrey, *A Game of Our Own*, Information Australia, Melbourne, 1990.
Boyle, Raelene & Craven, John, *Rage Raelene, Run*, Caribou Publications, Melbourne, 1983.
Brayshaw, Ian, *The Wit of Cricket*, Currawong Press, Sydney, 1981.
Bulletin, 3 and 10 April 1897.
Buzo, Alexander, *The Longest Game: A Collection of the Best Cricket Writing from Alexander to Zaros, from the Gabba to the Yabba*, Heinemann, Melbourne, 1990.
Cadigan, Neil et al., *Blood, Sweat and Tears*, Lothian, Melbourne,1989.
Cashman, Richard, *'Ave a Go, Yer Mug!' Australian Cricket Crowds from Larrikin to Ocker*, Collins, Sydney, 1984.
Cashman, Richard, *The 'Demon' Spofforth*, NSW University Press, Sydney, 1990.
Cashman, Richard, *The Rise of Organised Sport in Australia*, Oxford University Press, Melbourne, in press.
Cashman, Richard & Meader, C., *A History of Marrickville*, vol. 2, Hale & Iremonger, Sydney, in press.
Cashman, Richard & Weaver, Amanda, *Wicket Women: Cricket and Women in Australia*, NSW University Press, Sydney, 1991.
Chappell, Ian, *Chappelli: The Cutting Edge*, Swan Publishing, Nedlands, 1992.
Chappell, Ian, *Cricket in Our Blood*, Stanley Paul, London, 1976.
Clarkson, A., *Lanes of Gold: 100 Years of the NSW Amateur Swimming Association*, Lester Townsend, Sydney, 1989.

Corris, Peter, *Lords of the Ring*, Cassell, Melbourne, 1980.

Coward, Mike, *Carribean Odyssey*, Simon & Schuster, Sydney, 1991.

Cox, D. & Hagon, W., *Australian Motorcycle Heroes 1949–1989*, Angus & Robertson, Sydney, 1989.

Cumes, J.W.C., *Their Chastity was not too Rigid: Leisure Times in Early Australia*, Longman Cheshire, Melbourne, 1979.

Cuthbert, Betty & Webster, Jim, *Golden Girl*, Pelham, London, 1961. Reproduced by permission of Michael Joseph Ltd.

Dunstan, Keith, *The Paddock that Grew: The Story of the Melbourne Cricket Club*, Cassell & Co., Melbourne, 1962.

Dunstan, Keith, *Sports*, Sun Books, Melbourne, 1981.

Dwyer, Bob, *The Winning Way*, Rugby Press, Auckland, 1992.

Dyer, Jack & Hansen, Brian, *Wild Men of Football*, Southdown Press, Melbourne, 1968.

Empire, 29 March 1871.

Farrelly, Midget, *This Surfing Life*, Rigby, Adelaide, 1965.

Fearn-Wannan, William, *Australian Folklore: A Dictionary of Lore, Legends and Popular Allusions*, Lansdowne Press, Melbourne, 1970.

Fenton, Peter, *Sport the Way I Speak it*, Little Hills Press, Sydney, 1992.

Ferry, Francis, *The Life Story of Les Darcy*, Goodman & Little, Sydney, 1937.

Finnane, S., *The Game They Play in Heaven*, McGraw-Hill, Sydney, 1979.

Fitzpatrick, Jim, *The Bicycle and the Bush*, Oxford University Press, Melbourne, 1980.

Galton, Barry, *Gladiators of the Surf*, Reed, Sydney, 1984.

Geelong Advertiser, 6 March 1920, 31 December 1953.

Goolagong, Evonne, Collins, Bud & Edwards, Victor, *Evonne*, Hart-Davis, McGibbon, London, 1975.

Gordon, Harry & Fraser, Dawn, *Gold Medal Girl: Confessions of an Olympic Champion*, Circus, Melbourne, 1965.

Greenwood, Geoff, *Australian Rugby League's Greatest Games*, Murray, Sydney, 1978.

Griffiths, Samuel, *Turf and Heath: Australian Racing Reminiscences*, A.H. Massina & Co., Melbourne, 1906.

Guiney, David, *The Dunlop Book of the Olympics*, Eastland Press, Suffolk, 1957.

Gwynn-Jones, Terry, *The Air Racers: Aviation's Golden Era*, Lansdowne, Sydney, 1983.

Hardy, Frank, & Mulley, George, *The Needy and the Greedy*, Libra Books, Tasmania, 1975.

Harris, Brett, *Boom: Inside the NBL*, Sun Books/Pan Macmillan, Sydney, 1992. Extracts from *Boom: Inside the NBL* by Brett Harris reprinted by permission of Pan Macmillan Publishers Australia. Copyright Brett Harris 1992.

Harris, Brett, *The Proud Champions: Australia's Aboriginal Sporting Heroes*, Little Hills Press, Sydney, 1989.

Harrison, H.C.A., *The Story of an Athlete*, Alexander McCubbin, Melbourne, 1923.

Harte, *SACA: A History of the South Australian Cricket Association*, Sports Marketing, Adelaide, 1990.

Heads, Ian, *The Story of the Kangaroos*, Lester Townsend, Sydney, 1990.

Heads, Ian & Lester, Gary, *200 Years of Australian Sport*, Lester Townsend, Sydney, 1988.

Herald, Melbourne, 9 June 1979.

Higgins, Roy & Prior, Tom, *The Jockey Who Laughed*, Hutchinson, Melbourne, 1982.

Hoad, Lew, *The Lew Hoad Story*, Horwitz, London, 1958.

Hordern, H.V., *Googlies: Coals from a Test Cricketer's Fireplace*, RNB Sports Series, Sydney, 1932.

Howell, Max & Reet, *Aussie Gold*, Brooks Waterloo, Brisbane, 1984. Reprinted by permission of Jacaranda Wiley.

Hughes, Merv, *Merv—My Life and Other Funny Stories*, Pan Macmillan, Sydney, 1990. Extracts from *Merv—My Life and Other Funny Stories* by Merv Hughes reprinted by permission of Pan Macmillan Publishers Australia. Copyright Merv Hughes 1990.

Hutchinson, Garrie, *From the Outer: Watching Football in the 80s*, Penguin, Ringwood, 1984.

Hutchinson, Garrie, *The Great Australian Book of Football Stories*, Currey O'Neil, Melbourne, 1983.

Johnson, Joseph, *Amazing Grace: The Story of the Grace Park Lawn Tennis Club 1889–1989*, Grace Park LTC, Hawthorn, 1989.

Kellermann, Annette, *Physical Beauty: How to Keep It*, George H. Doran Co., New York, 1918.

Kinross-Smith, Graeme, *The Sweet Spot*, Hyland House, Melbourne, 1982.

Knox, *Mark Richards, a Surfing Legend*, Angus & Robertson, Sydney, 1992.

Lawry, Bill, *Run-Digger*, Souvenir Press, London, 1966.

Lester, Gary, *The Story of Australian Rugby League*, Lester Townsend, Sydney, 1988.

Lillye, Bert, *Backstage of Racing*, John Fairfax, Sydney, 1985.

Lowe, A.M., *Surfing, Surf-shooting and Surf-lifesaving Pioneering*, Manly, 1958.

Lunn, Hugh, *Queenslanders*, University of Queensland Press, St Lucia, 1984.

Lusetich, Robert, *Frank Arok: My Beloved Socceroos*, ABC Books, Sydney, 1992.

Maclaren, *ANZ Golfer's Handbook*, 5th edn, A.H. & A.W. Reed, Sydney, 1975.

Mailey, Arthur, *10 for 66 and All That*, Shakespeare Head, London, 1958.

Mancini, A. & Hibbins, G.M., *Running with the Ball*, Lynedoch, Melbourne, 1987.

Mason, Percy, *Professional Athletics in Australia*, Adelaide, Rigby, 1985.

Masters, Olga, *Manly Daily*, 22 June 1974.

Masters, Roy, *Inside League: The Main Players*, Pan Books, Sydney, 1990. Extracts from *Inside League: The Main Players* by Roy Masters reprinted by permission of Pan Macmillan Publishers Australia. Copyright Roy Masters 1990.

Matthews, Bruce, *Game, Set and Glory: A History of Australian Tennis Championships*, Five Mile Press, Melbourne, 1985.

May, Norman, *Gold! Gold! Gold!*, Horwitz Grahame, Sydney, 1984.

May, Norman, *Sporting Laughs*, Horwitz Grahame, Sydney, 1985.

McDermott, Craig, *Strike Bowler*, ABC Books, Sydney, 1992.

McKay, Heather with Jack Batten, *Heather McKay's Complete Book of Squash*, Angus & Robertson, London & Sydney, 1978.

Messenger, Dally R., *The Master*, Angus & Robertson, Sydney, 1982.

Mickle, Alan D., *After the Ball: A Book of Sporting Memories*, F.W. Cheshire, Melbourne, 1959.

Mills, Frederick J. 'The Twinkler', *Square Dinkum*, Melbourne, 1917.

Mullins, Pat & Derriman, Philip, *Bat and Pad: Writings of Australian Cricket 1804–1984*, Oxford University Press, Melbourne, 1984.

Mulvaney, D. & Harcourt, R., *Cricket Walkabout*, Macmillan, Melbourne, 1988.

Noble, M.A., *The Game's the Thing*, Cassell & Co., London, 1926.

Opperman, Hubert F., *Pedals, Politics and People*, Haldane Pub. Co., Sydney, 1977.

Paterson, A.B., *Songs of the Pen*, Lansdowne, Sydney, 1983.

Phillips, D., *Australian Women at the Olympic Games*, Kangaroo Press, Sydney, 1992.

Philpott, Peter, *A Spinner's Yarn*, ABC Books, Sydney, 1990.

Piesse, Ken (ed.), *The Great Australian Book of Cricket Stories*, Currey O'Neil, Melbourne, 1982.

Pollard, Jack, *Australian Cricket: The Game and the Players*, Hodder & Stoughton, Sydney, 1982, revised edn Angus & Robertson, Sydney, 1988.

Pollard, Jack, *Australian Golf: The Game and the Players*, Angus & Robertson/Harper Collins, Sydney, 1990.

Pollard, Jack, *Middle & Leg*, Macmillan, Melbourne, 1988.

Ramsay, Tom, *Golf: It's a Funny Game*, Rigby, Melbourne, 1985.

Ricketts, Andrew, *Walter Lindrum's Billiards Phenomenon*, Brian Clawson, Canberra, 1982.

Riggs, Doug, *Keelhauled: Unsportsmanlike Conduct and the America's Cup*, Angus & Robertson, Sydney, 1986.

Robb, Frank Maldon, *Poems of Adam Lindsay Gordon*, Humphrey Milford/Oxford University Press, London, 1913.

Rose, Lionel, *Lionel Rose: The Life Story of a Champion*, Angus & Robertson, Sydney, 1969.

Sladen, Douglas, *Adam Lindsay Gordon: The Life and Best Poems of the Poet of Australia*, Hutchinson & Co., London, 1934.

Smith, Margaret, *The Margaret Smith Story*, Stanley Paul, London, 1965.

Smith, Terry, *Australian Golf: The First 100 Years*, Lester Townsend, Sydney, 1982.

Smith's Weekly, 11 June 1932.

Spofforth, F.R., 'Australian Cricket and Cricketers: A Retrospect', *New Review*, vol. 10, 1894.

Sporting Globe, 16 July 1938.

Stephenson, Harry, *Skiing in the High Plains: A History of the Ski Exploration of the Victorian Alpine Area*, Harry Stephenson, Armadale, 1982.

Stivens, Dal, *The Demon Bowler and Other Cricket Stories*, Outback Press, Melbourne, 1979.

Stremski, Richard, *Kill for Collingwood*, Allen & Unwin, Sydney, 1986.

Sun, Melbourne, 11 August 1959.

Taylor, E.C.H., *100 Years of Football: The Story of the Melbourne Football Club 1858–1958*, Wilke & Co., Melbourne, 1957.

Telegraph Mirror, 6 February 1993.

Tip & Tony, *The Life, Adventures, and Sporting Career of Joe Thompson: The King of the Ring*, American Publishing, Melbourne, 1877.

Trueman, Fred & Hardy, Frank, *'You Nearly Had Him That Time...' and Other Cricket Stories*, Stanley Paul, 1978.

Twain, Mark, *Following the Equator: A Journey Around the World*, Hartford, Conneticut, American Publishing Co., 1897.

Whimpress, Bernard, *The South Australian Football Story*, SA National Football League, Adelaide, 1983.

Whitington, R.S., *Great Moments in Australian Sport*, Sun Books, Melbourne, 1975.

Whitington, R.S., *An Illustrated History of Cricket*, Viking O'Neil, Ringwood, 1987.

Willey, Keith, *Ghosts of the Big Country*, Rigby, Adelaide, 1975.

Wilson, Jack, *Australian Surfing and Surf Life Saving*, Rigby, Melbourne, 1975.

Worrall, John, *Argus*, 3 October 1936.

INDEX

Rosewall, Ken   150–2, 164–6

Sabina Park, Jamaica   242–3
Samuels, Charles   37–8
Saqui, Austin   24–6
Scotch College   8
Searle, Henry   45
Seattle Supersonics   273
Seoul Olympic Games (1988) 270–1
Slaven, Roy (John Doyle)   247–8
Slessor, Kenneth   135–7
Smith, Margaret   197–8
Sobers, Sir Garfield   235–6
South Melbourne Football
    Club   110
Spofforth, F.R. 'Demon'   38–9
State of Origin, Rugby
    League   267–8
Sydney Cricket Ground   31–3, 38,
    66, 93–5, 127, 173–6, 274

Tallon, Bill   142–3
Tallon, Don   142–3
'Terrible Trio', the   110
Thompson, Joe   9–10
Thomson, Jeff   248–9
Tokyo Olympic Games (1964)
    202–4
Trickett, Edward   35

Trumper, Victor   69, 69–74, 78–9,
    91–3
Turner, Alan   248–9
Turner, Ian   249–50
Twain, Mark   50–1

Victorian Alps   11
Victorian Amateur Athletics
    Association   162
Von Nida, Norman   143, 149,
    170–1

Wagstaff, Harold   93–5
Walla Walla   125–6
Walters, Doug   230, 246
Warrior   25–6
Waterman, L.W.   127
West Indies cricket team   194–5
Whitney, Mike   273–4
Wickham, Tracey   251–2
Williams, Harry   128–9, 143
Wimbledon tournament
    (1952)   164–6
    (1971)   233–4
Woodcock, Tommy   133
World Swimming Championships,
    Berlin (1978)   251–2

Yankos, Charlie   269–70